THE

S

/alk,

Please return on or before the latest date above.
You can renew online at www.kent.gov.uk/libs
or by phone 08458 247 200

Libraries & Archives

THE BIG WALKS OF THE NORTH

Material revised and updated from THE BIG WALKS OF GREAT BRITAIN, published by Summersdale Publishers Ltd in 2007 (first published as THE BEATEN TRACK by Summersdale Publishers Ltd in 2001)

Summersdale Publishers Ltd
46 West Street
Chichester
West Sussex
PO19 1RP
UK

www.summersdale.com

Printed and bound in Great Britain

ISBN: 978-1-84953-023-1

THE
BIG WALKS
OF THE NORTH

DAVID BATHURST

About the author

David Bathurst has been a keen walker all his adult life, and as well as his completion of numerous long-distance routes has also walked the entire coastlines of Sussex and Kent. By profession David is a solicitor and senior legal adviser to the magistrates sitting in Chichester and Worthing, and he has written several other books on a wide range of subjects. His chief claim to fame is the recitation of the four Gospels from memory in July 1998 and then the recitation of the complete surviving works of Gilbert and Sullivan from memory in August 2004.

By the same author

The Big Walks of Great Britain, Summersdale 2007
The Big Walks of the South, Summersdale 2010
Walking The South Coast Of England, Summersdale 2008

Contents

Contents

About this Book

Despite the increasingly sophisticated range of leisure pursuits and interests available to us, walking still enjoys huge popularity as a form of recreation. People like to walk for different reasons. Some do it simply for the health benefits, and aren't fussy where their walk takes them. Some like to have a definite objective, such as a place of historic interest or a hilltop. Some will want to use their walking to trace our rich industrial, social or cultural heritage. Some like to walk long distances as personal challenges and/or to raise money for deserving causes. And some walk for all these reasons. As the popularity of walking has increased, so has the number of 'name' long-distance walking routes across Great Britain, providing challenging, invigorating and often exciting walking to and through numerous places of immense scenic beauty and historic interest. In short, all the reasons people like to walk come together in the walking of a long-distance route. The purpose of this book is to provide an overview of what can be described as the Big Walks, namely the top long-distance walking routes, in the north of Great Britain. Included either in this book or in the companion volume covering the south of Great Britain are all 15 of the National Trails of England and Wales, the four Scottish National Long Distance Walking Routes, and the Coast To Coast Walk which although without official National Trail status is one of the best-loved routes in the Great Britain. They are all tremendous walks, all with their distinctive character. There's the Speyside Way, for instance, through the heart of Scotland's whisky country; the Great Glen Way taking you from the foot of Ben Nevis to the jaws of the Loch Ness Monster; the Coast To Coast Walk, following in the footsteps of that doyen of walkers, Alfred Wainwright; and the Pennine Way, the ultimate walking challenge in Great Britain and the father of all Big Walks. Each has its store of treasures, waiting to be explored and to provide an unforgettable tapestry of magical walking memories.

This book aims to provide a succinct and light-hearted description of each route covered, providing information as to the nature and relative difficulty of the terrain, highlighting places of scenic and historic interest and offering advice to those contemplating the challenge. It does not pretend to give every route detail, but to be a reference work providing an accessible and user-friendly guide to the relative merits of each Big Walk so you can decide which one you like the look of the most from the detail given. And if for whatever reason you are unable to undertake any of them, you can enjoy following each route from the comfort of your armchair. A chapter is given over to each route: each chapter begins with the route length, overall assessment of difficulty, and highlights of the walk to be described. The walk is then broken down into sections. There is no magic in the section divides: the aim is for each section to start and finish at a place that is reasonably easily accessible by road or rail, and to equate to what a fit walker should be able to accomplish in a day. Where a section is very long, it will be because of the lack of amenities or transport opportunities available on it. Mileages are given for each section and cumulative mileages given in brackets throughout the narrative. All this will assist in the planning process. Please note that every effort has been taken to ensure the accuracy of the information in the book, so that you know exactly what you're taking on, but inevitably there are changes to routes and land use which could not be anticipated at the time of writing.

Becoming a Big Walker

Bearing in mind the shortest route in this book is 73 miles, and the longest is 255 miles, you'll quickly appreciate the magnitude of the task facing you should you decide to take one of them on. You may be an experienced rambler who simply wants some focus for your walking, in which case you may be able to tackle any of these Big Walks with ease and with little need to peruse the rest of this introduction. But if your idea of a long hike is the 200-yd walk up the road to buy a carton of milk, you clearly have some work to do before tackling even the easiest of the described routes. You need to get properly fit. Don't pigeonhole it with all your other New Year's resolutions (come New Year's Day, it's bound to be pouring with rain or freezing cold anyway). Start now! Begin by aiming for 30 minutes' brisk walking every day – don't skip it one day and tell yourself you'll make up for it the next, as the chances are you won't. Having established the minimum, make time to take yourself off on longer walks, up to say three or four hours at a stretch, aiming ultimately to manage a full day's walk. Where you go is up to you – you may be happy tramping round the vicinity of your home town or village, but you may wish to explore further afield. You might, of course, hate it (in which case you probably wouldn't be reading this book). On the other hand, you may get hooked. Romantic evenings out are ditched in favour of intensive studies of Ordnance Survey maps. Weekend shopping trips revolve around visits to outdoor shops in search of a particular brand of hi-tech bootlaces. You actually read the care instructions that come with a new pair of gaiters. You startle fellow commuters by trying out new walking boots with your suit when hurrying to catch the 7.39. You start subscribing to a walking magazine and are able to answer a few clues of the walker's crossword. You no longer feel self-conscious in a bobble hat. You bore your dinner guests with statistical and photographic records of your most recent walking endeavours. And the present that excites you most on Christmas morning is a gift-wrapped multi-pack of perfumed sneaker balls.

THE BIG WALKS OF THE NORTH

Whether you've become an obsessive or just an enthusiast, once you've achieved the necessary levels of fitness you may be ready for your first Big Walk. Remember, though, that tackling any of the walks in this book will require several days' hiking, over terrain which may be more demanding or inhospitable than any you've tackled from home. There's no reason why the whole of any Big Walk needs to be done at once – not everyone will have the resources to do, for instance, the Pennine Way in one go. Indeed you may prefer to do your first one in segments, maybe just a day or two at a time, only increasing the number of consecutive days' walking when you're sure you are ready for it. It's a good idea to start with one of the easier walks such as the Great Glen Way or the Speyside Way, where not only is the terrain less demanding than on other Big Walks but transport links are always reasonably accessible. Remember, though, that even the easier Big Walks have their remote stretches with no access to wheeled transport, and if you don't feel up to negotiating them, you need to think again. Once you've successfully completed the shorter and easier walks, you can start thinking about one of the stiffer challenges in this book. We all have different levels of fitness – a 12-mile walk will be a half-day stroll to some and a never-ending slog to others – so ascertain your level before committing yourself. Then and only then should you get down to the exciting business of planning your travel arrangements and your accommodation, which of course will be a matter of personal taste. The Internet and local tourist information offices will give you all the information you need on that aspect. You also need to think about when to go: you may conclude that there is never a right time to walk, with unpredictable weather and short days in winter but crowds and inflated prices in summer. Unless and until you are an experienced and confident walker, and better able to cope with the unexpected, the summer months with longer days and better weather are undoubtedly to be preferred.

Equipment

Having decided on your Big Walk, and when you're going to do it, the next question is what to wear and what to take, and this will depend very much on the nature of the terrain and length of your walk. There's a huge market for walking equipment of all kinds, the claims made in support of the various available products growing seemingly more overblown and pretentious with the passing years. Before parting with large amounts of money, prioritise and consider what you really need. Footwear is of prime importance. Those trusty walking brogues you purchased from a backstreet gents' outfitters in Macclesfield in 1957, and which haven't needed as much as a new pair of laces since, may be quite adequate for an easy day's pottering on the Great Glen Way but will be totally useless for a winter day's assault on the West Highland Way. The choice of footwear is huge, so rather than befuddle your senses by scanning the 30 pages of walking boots in your monthly walking magazine or a million pages of the things on the Internet, seek advice from a reputable outdoor wear shop. Just beware of being talked by target-driven salesmen into buying any number of expensive but unnecessary accessories, from pocket hand warmers to luxury loganberry-flavoured foot gel, at the same time. Clothing is also important: if it's cold or there's rain about, a decent breathable waterproof jacket is a must, and in cold weather you will also need gloves as well as plenty of layers. In hot weather, you must avoid sunburn so loose fitting long-sleeved shirts and trousers are better than T-shirts and shorts (which in any case are, shall we say, less than flattering on those of a certain age or above), and you shouldn't forget a sunhat. As to what to take with you, water is a must, especially in warm weather: thirst (dehydration) is to be avoided at all costs, so drink lots, especially early in the day. Even if you're hoping to find a pub or cafe en route, have a supply of high-energy food as well — bananas or dried fruit are to be preferred to chocolate. For day-long walks, a small day pack to carry your supplies may be all you need, but for several consecutive days, even if you're B & B'ing or hostelling rather than camping, you'll need a much bigger backpack capable of containing all you need for your trip including changes of clothes, toiletries, maps and essential food, drink and emergency supplies (see below). If once you've packed your rucksack you find you can't lift it off the floor, don't panic. Remove all the stuff you really feel you can do without. If having done that you find you still can't lift it off the floor… then you can panic. That said, bag-carrying services do operate on some of the walks described in this book, enabling you to enjoy your Big Walk unencumbered. Failing that, you can always go along to weight-training at your local gym. And it's as well to remember Sod's law of backpackers – it'll always be the item you need the most that finds its way to the most inaccessible corner of the rucksack.

Highs and Lows

The lows first. Embarking on a big walk does carry certain risks. The route descriptions provide bracketed mileage indicators so you can work out how far it is from one significant location to another, and you can therefore get some idea of how far you may need to walk in one day to be sure of reaching somewhere with an adequate range of amenities. There are some very lengthy amenity-less and remote sections; St John's Town of Dalry to Sanquhar on the Southern Upland Way is just one example of a section of route where you could find yourself in real difficulty if you were insufficiently fit to complete the walk in a day. Some of the climbs and descents are very steep, with the attendant risk of accident and injury; mist or heavy rain can transform a benign landscape into a hostile wilderness; the simple act of missing a signpost and drifting off course could leave you stranded, miles from anywhere, at nightfall. You need to minimise these risks. Pace yourself carefully, planning to do slightly less than you think you can manage in a day. Start the day with a decent breakfast including lots of high-energy food. Have with you proper mapping of the route. (The Aurum Press and Cicerone Press guides to individual routes contain all the mapping you'll need.) Equip yourself with a compass but make sure you know how to use it first. If you can't comprehend even the English part of the 60-page multilingual instruction manual, and were unable to concentrate on the outdoor shop assistant's impromptu lesson as you were worried your lunch hour was almost up, maybe it's best not to attempt any of the tougher walks, especially in the winter months. Make sure someone knows where you're going to be walking and where you're aiming for. Have a mobile phone (although a signal can't always be guaranteed) and local taxi firm numbers with you. Keep not only an emergency food supply but first aid materials, a torch and a whistle as well. And, prevention being better than cure, consider cancelling your walk if the weather is bad. On a more prosaic note, even if you never put yourself in danger, your resolve may be tested by blisters, aching muscles, or just general fatigue. Don't force yourself to carry on if you really can't bear to – remember, it's not an Army endurance test, and the path will still be there next year – but don't give up too easily either. A sudden great view, a nice meal, even just a beer or a pot of tea, can transform your whole attitude to the walk, and give you the impetus to complete the journey.

Having dwelt for a few moments on the negatives, let's finish on a positive note. To accomplish a Big Walk, even one of the lesser routes in this book, is no mean achievement. If you've got people to sponsor you to complete it, you may make a nice sum for charity (doubtless wishing the person who sponsored you 50 p a mile had signed his name at the top of the form, thus setting the standard for others to follow, rather than the person who sponsored you 50 p to complete the whole walk). You may make some great friendships that will last the rest of your life. You'll get to see some fantastic scenery, some beautiful towns and villages, and, if you're observant, a huge variety of plant life and wildlife. Having completed one Big Walk, you'll be hungry for more, and find you've fresh impetus to rise to new walking challenges. And you'll have learnt a lot of valuable life lessons. The virtues of self-reliance, patience and determination to complete the course. The knowledge that in our technology-dominated society the simplest things are the best – a dewy valley in the morning sunshine, a snow-capped mountain top, a babbling stream refreshed by last night's rains. And acceptance of the inevitability with which the pub your friends recommend as the best they've ever been to, and which you've made a two-mile detour off the path to visit, has been turned into a block of luxury flats.

Happy walking.

The Yorkshire Wolds Way

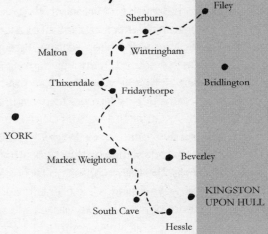

Designation: National trail.
Length: 79 miles.
Start: Hessle, East Riding of Yorkshire.
Finish: Filey Brigg, North Yorkshire.
Nature: An undulating walk through the unspoilt chalk uplands known as the Yorkshire Wolds in eastern Yorkshire.
Difficulty rating: Moderate.
Average time of completion: 5–6 days.

The Yorkshire Wolds Way, one of the shorter routes in this book, is of comparatively recent origin. The idea for such a route was first mooted in 1968

HIGHLIGHTS OF THIS WALK:

- **Humber Bridge**
- **Comber Dale**
- **Londesborough**
- **Millington Dale**
- **Thixen Dale**
- **Wharram Percy**
- **Filey Brigg**

and the trail officially opened in October 1982 following extensive negotiations with landowners. However, walkers tramping the Yorkshire Wolds are in fact following in prehistoric footsteps; a Gallic tribe known as the Parisii is known to have settled here, and a number of prehistoric routes crossed the Wolds. Later, the Romans built a road from Brough to Malton which passed through the Wolds in preference to the gentler lowlands. For a long time the Wolds have been associated with sheep-rearing, though in more recent times large areas have been intensively farmed, and much farmland will be crossed along the Way. You may notice some of the dew-ponds which were dug by farmers to provide a supply of water to their animals.

But although others have been here before, you will find a refreshing sense of stillness and solitude on this national trail. Although there are a few stiff climbs, the terrain poses no technical demands for the walker, and the waymarking is excellent throughout. The Way avoids large centres of population, but villages and small towns are never too far away, and with a little forethought it should not be difficult to plan. The scenery, while unspectacular, is still delightful, with the uneven contours of the rolling hills producing a constantly changing landscape.

The most distinctive and endearing feature of the Wolds are their dry valleys, created by erosion of the chalk hills. The trail passes through several of these valleys on the route, many clothed with attractive tree plantations. The chalk grassland contains many colourful wild plants and flowers including scabious, hawkbit, salad burnet, crosswort and harebell. I had the good fortune to walk the Way on a succession of golden autumn days, where the lush green pasture coating steep slopes rising above me complemented the blaze of colour from the pockets of deciduous woodland. It was ample compensation indeed for having to stand or sit on the floor for the whole of the train journey from London to Doncaster en route for the path, and a meagre breakfast at a Hull hotel.

Hessle to South Cave (12.9 miles) via Welton

ENJOY: Humber Bridge, Welton Dale, Brantingham

It is a short train ride from the vibrant city of Hull to the start of the walk at Hessle, the official start being situated opposite the Ferryboat Inn on the west side of Hessle Haven. The first few miles of the trail consist of a walk alongside the estuary of the Humber, formed by the meeting of the Ouse and Trent rivers, and flowing into the sea below Spurn Head east of Hull. Almost immediately you pass beneath the magnificent Humber road bridge; opened in July 1981, it is the world's longest single-span suspension bridge with a span of 4628 ft and twin towers that are 535 ft high. The Way continues beside the Humber, following an awkward course along a shingle beach, then immediately beyond North Ferriby turns right and proceeds, just west of north, through a strip of woodland called Long Plantation and over the busy A63. The strip of woodland extends north-westwards, the route following through the middle of the woods and climbing away from the Humber. You cross a minor road then drop to the lovely village of Welton (6.6) which contains a pond, a stream running beside the main street, an early nineteenth-century stone pump, and several attractive houses including the eighteenth-century Welton Hall and Welton Grange. Perhaps Welton's chief claim to fame, however, is that its Green Dragon Inn saw the final capture of the highwayman Dick Turpin.

The Way turns right in the village and proceeds north-eastwards along Welton Dale, the first of the many lovely dry valleys on the route, with steep wooded slopes rising on either side. Close by is the Raikes Mausoleum, dating back to 1818. You rise out of the Dale and emerge in more open country, passing the splendid ivied grey-brick Wauldby Manor which contains a chapel in its garden, then turn more sharply north-east to reach a wider track. The route turns left onto this track and soon passes straight over the Welton–North Newbald road onto a narrower metalled road which goes south-westwards and drops down to Brantingham. Just before reaching the village centre, the Way turns right onto a footpath which descends to the village church, set in a valley amongst fir trees. Instead of taking the footpath, you may prefer to continue down into Brantingham; to the south-east of the village is the Victorian Brantinghamthorpe Hall in a parkland setting, and in the village itself is a Gothic memorial composed from fragments of the 1862 Hull Town Hall. Pevsner describes it as 'one of the most lovably awful things in East Riding'.

The walk from Brantingham to the next village of South Cave is fiddly but most rewarding. Turning right onto a metalled road to pass the church, the Way proceeds through the lovely wooded Brantingham Dale, bears left onto the track, then at Woodale Farm turns right. There is another stiff climb to Mount Airy Farm along the left-hand edge of the lovely Woodale Plantation, then by Mount Airy Farm you join a track, turning left onto it then quickly right, dropping down the open hillside to reach a road at the north-eastern extreme of South Cave (12.9). This is the largest habitation reached since leaving Hessle; among its attractive houses are Cave Castle (converted into a hotel) of 1802, and a market hall dating back to 1796.

South Cave to Londesborough (13.4 miles, 1.2 extra miles for Market Weighton loop route, not included in total or subsequent cumulative mileage) via Goodmanham and Market Weighton

ENJOY: Comber Dale, Newbald, Goodmanham, Market Weighton

The Way turns left onto the road, then shortly right off it following a footpath, then turns right onto a track which goes uphill past Little Wold Plantation to the left. The views from here to the Humber are spectacular. You are now beginning to pull more decisively away from the great estuary and its nearby communities, and the next section is quite delectable. The track reaches a T-junction with a wider track at the hilltop, and here you turn right. You then begin to descend, turning left onto a path which passes into Comber Dale with a glorious prospect of rolling hills and woodland, all quite unspoilt; this is Wolds Way walking at its very best. You drop down to proceed briefly onto the course of the now defunct Barnsley–Hull railway, through that most traditional of Yorkshire Wolds Way landscapes, with steep banks rising on both sides. At first only the bank to the left is wooded, but soon the Way turns left off the old railway to head north-westwards through East Dale, with thick woods covering the banks on either side. You climb out of the woodland into more open country, passing a triangulation point at just over 530 ft, the panoramic views only marginally spoilt by the sight of the cooling towers of Drax power station in the distance. Soon you reach the B1230 Howden–Beverley road, following it briefly then going forward to reach a minor road which in turn you again follow briefly. Just past the next crosseoads rake a footpath which heads initially north then north-west through the unwooded dry valley of Swin Dale.

You then drop down to emerge at a minor road linking North Newbald with Beverley. Although the Way bears right, North Newbald is quickly reached by turning left here and is well worth a visit. It contains a delightful cluster of greystone and whitewashed cottages on streets with such quaint names as The Mires and Rattan Row, a stream running between banks bright with flowers, a mid-twelfth-century church which has been called the most complete Norman church in the Riding, and the intriguingly-named Gnu Inn. It is not immediately obvious how it got its name (could it have been intended to be called the Gun, but the signwriter misspelt it?) but lovers of English popular song will at once recall the Gnu of Michael Flanders and Donald Swann. A low-spirited walker anywhere might endeavour to revive himself with a rendition, but may care to temporarily cease at the approach of other walkers who will not have the benefit of the imaginary backing of the London Symphony Orchestra or the Berlin Philharmonic.

Soon after turning right onto the minor road, the Way turns left and climbs to meet another road, turning right and then again left to follow track, path and road in a northerly direction to meet the A1079 York–Hull trunk road. On this section you pass the excellent viewpoint of Newbald Wold, just under 475 ft high. The Way goes straight over the A1079 then immediately branches left off the minor road onto a track to pass the hamlet of Arras. Immediately to the south-west, on either side of the A1079 crossing, is an Iron Age barrow cemetery with over 100 small round barrows, and nearby is the site of a Roman amphitheatre. Beyond Arras, the Way follows a footpath heading north-westwards across rough grassland, then descends. The going can be quite slow and not hugely rewarding, but improves as you arrive at another delightful dry valley and meet the Hudson Way. Named after the nineteenth-century railway magnate George Hudson, this is a footpath linking Market Weighton with Beverley, using a substantial section of the old York–Pocklington–Market Weighton–Beverley railway, which shut in 1965.

You now have a choice. You may follow a road to Goodmanham, this being the more direct route, or you can turn left onto the Hudson Way to reach Market Weighton via an alternative *loop* route. The latter route is the obvious choice if you are seeking overnight accommodation in this pleasant, unspoilt town. Of its many fine buildings, of which several date back to the eighteenth century, the red brick Londesborough Arms is arguably the best. To leave Market Weighton via the loop route you must take the road leading north-westwards from the church towards the A1079, then as the built-up area ends, you turn right across fields to reach the A163 Selby–Driffield road. You go straight over onto a track past the site of Towthorpe village, on alongside Towthorpe Beck, and then over a minor road onto a drive through Londesborough

Park to reach the direct route at a junction of drives in the park (extra mileage for detour: 1.2 miles). The *direct* route, meanwhile, proceeds easily along the road from the Hudson Way crossing to Goodmanham (23.9).

Goodmanham

Goodmanham is regarded as one of the earliest sites of Christianity in Britain; a window in the squat little Norman church – not the first Christian building on this site – commemorates the conversion to Christianity in AD 627 of Coifi, the pagan High Priest of Goodmanham, and his destruction of the pagan temple of Woden which is believed to have stood where the church stands now.

The Way turns sharp right by the church and follows a track north-westwards to reach the A163, crossing straight over and then turning left off the track into Londesborough Park, eventually being met by the alternative route. You now proceed straight through the village of Londesborough (26.3) which contains a pretty church, some fine eighteenth-century red brick houses and a seventeenth-century almshouse. Londesborough Hall, historically the village's grandest building, has been pulled down, but there remains a pleasing red brick Victorian mansion in Londesborough Park. The estate was purchased by George Hudson in 1845; at that time he was planning the York–Market Weighton railway and went as far as to plan it with a private station for himself at the edge of the estate at Shiptonthorpe, a few miles to the south-west. The railway has long since gone, and Londesborough and its surroundings have taken on a new air of beauty and timelessness, suggestive perhaps to today's visitor of a likely setting for a Sunday teatime television adaptation of a Jane Austen or George Eliot novel, with no danger of insensitive interruptions by advertisements for cut-price furniture superstores and anti-dandruff shampoo.

Londesborough to Thixendale (17.7 miles) via Nunburnholme, Huggate and Fridaythorpe

ENJOY: Millington Dale, Huggate, Thixendale

The Way leaves Londesborough by following a metalled road that heads north-westwards to Partridge Hall, turning right briefly onto a minor road east of Burnby, then shortly bearing left onto a footpath to Nunburnholme (28.8). Nunburnholme, which derives its name from the twelfth-century Benedictine nunnery that once stood here, is a pretty place in a tranquil valley setting; it has an attractive stream running beside it, and a church with an Anglo-Saxon cross shaft that is at least 1,000 years old. The church minister from 1854 to 1895 was Francis Morris, who also found time to write *The Natural History of British Birds*. The Way turns left onto the village street then right at the church to continue north-westwards, first along a path, then on a road, and then a track through Bratt Wood and across an open hillside to reach the B1246. You cross straight over this road. However, a left turn will take you to the town of Pocklington, with excellent connections for the city of York, whilst a right turn leads to the pretty village of Warter, which contains thatched cottages, a pond and a large park, and is the site of a twelfth-century Augustinian priory. It also marks the finishing post of the Kiplingcotes Derby, a horse race which supposedly started in 1519 and is claimed to be the oldest horse race in the world.

Beyond the B1246 you continue north-westwards on the hillside, passing Jenny Firkin Wood and Kilnwick Percy Hall, superbly situated in a park which also contains large lakes and a Norman church. Beyond Jenny Firkin Wood the Way turns right and climbs steeply uphill to begin the walk above the dry valley of Millington Dale, which I regard as the loveliest section of the route. At the hilltop you turn left and head north-eastwards, enjoying tremendous views across Yorkshire which on a good day might include York Minster. Soon after gaining the hilltop you could detour to Millington with its enchanting part-Norman church, but at the cost of losing all the height already gained. On two occasions it is necessary to drop steeply to the dale bottom and then rise equally precipitously up again, but the surroundings are so lovely that it is worth the effort. Although the valley walls are not as thickly wooded as some already seen, there are plenty of trees and bushes to decorate the steep slopes, and at one point near to the route hereabouts there is a small lake where, unusually, one of the many underground Wolds chalk streams has broken to the surface.

Eventually you reach the head of the dale and turn left onto a road, then at a T-junction you go straight over onto a path heading north, reaching nearly 650 ft. Not only is this the highest point reached so far, but there is a real sense of remoteness. The route turns north-east and then south-east, crossing a minor road, joining a track and passing Glebe Farm to reach a T-junction of tracks. The Way turns left here, but by turning right you immediately reach the village of Huggate (37.4). Huggate contains some fine buildings including the former rectory, Kirkdale House, and a part-sixteenth-century Manor House. Its church contains a fourteenth-century west tower; a board in the church dated 9 October 1826 lists the names of a jury empowered to impose fines for such misdemeanours as harbouring vagrants, or 'suffering swine or geese to be in the streets between Old May Day and Old Lammas.'

Having turned left at the T-junction above Huggate, the Way heads north-east along a track, then turns left onto a path and heads north-westwards into the next dry valley, Holm Dale. There is a steep drop into the valley, then a climb up to the head of the dale where you join a track and follow it northwards to reach Fridaythorpe, the halfway point of the national trail. It is necessary to turn right onto the A166 York–Bridlington road then left along the village street past the church. Fridaythorpe (39.9) is a pretty village with a green, two large ponds and St Mary's Church, which has a twelfth-century south doorway described by Pevsner as 'utterly barbaric' because of its profusion of columns, carving, rope motif, rosettes, scallops – 'any old thing that was going'. Beyond the church, you turn left onto a track, which descends steeply to the dry valley of West Dale and then, passing Ings Plantation, climbs to the head of the dale at Gill's Farm.

Crossing straight over a minor road, there is then a very steep descent into Thixen Dale. The Way negotiates a hairpin bend, swinging southwards then, on reaching the valley floor, turns right onto a footpath heading northwards through what is a quite delightful dale. The flat, dry valley bottom provides comfortable walking whilst hills decorated with mini-plantations rise up on each side. You reach a road and turn right onto it, still in the valley, then go forward into Thixendale village (44). This lovely village, claimed by some to be the prettiest in Yorkshire, stands at a junction of a series of impressive dry valleys. Although the church, school and vicarage were all built around 1870, some houses in the village, notably Raisthorpe Manor and Round The Bend, date back to the eighteenth century. It has a delightfully tranquil atmosphere and, like Londesborough, enjoys a timeless quality. At the time of my visit, however, it was not without some amenities, which included a shop that also served as a tearoom and a filling station with a single petrol pump standing smartly on the forecourt outside it. The harsh commercial realities of modern life have forced village shops to become more and more versatile in the range of services offered to the customer; in the twenty-first century you may expect to find the village store providing not only bars of chocolate and cartons of fruit juice, but dry-cleaning, photocopying, faxing and perhaps even web access and e-mailing facilities, whilst attempts to make a simple telephone call from the village kiosk to a taxi firm ten miles away may continue to be completely frustrated by the mechanism's inexplicable aversion to 10p or 20p pieces.

Thixendale to Sherburn (18.5 miles) via Wharram-le-Street and Wintringham

ENJOY: Wharram Percy, Duggleby Howe

The Way turns right in the village on a track which climbs out of the valley to Cow Wold, heading north-westwards. There follows a quite delightful descent on good paths into Vessey Pasture Dale, with splendid views to the valley and the steep banks on each side. You then follow the dale in a direction just east of north, the ground rising steeply, and at the hilltop you turn right onto a track, heading eastwards and soon reaching the head of Deep Dale. This is well-named, with the steep banks on each side, dotted with small trees and bushes, plunging spectacularly to a narrow valley floor. Through the valley it is possible to view the ruined church of Wharram Percy, and an alternative route turns left off the main route to reach it, although it is easily reachable from the main path as well. The main route continues along the hilltop and passes a strip of woodland to the left, while beneath your feet is Burdale Tunnel on the old Malton to Driffield railway line. Very soon the Way turns left onto a metalled road, from which there are tremendous views to the Derwent valley and beyond. Soon there is a junction with a track where you turn left and walk past the ruined village of Wharram Percy, veering right beyond the ruins to arrive at a lane just below Bella Farm. Here you turn left.

Wharram Percy

The village once contained water mills, manor houses and accommodation for workers on the land and their animals. Then, some 500 years ago, the landowners decided that more money was to be made from sheep than from crops, and the peasants were thrown off the land. Only the church survived, but despite attempts at maintenance and restoration, it also crumbled and is now unsafe for worship, though parts of the eleventh-century tower and other later additions can still be seen.

You continue north-westwards along the lane, then, when this swings to the right, you go straight on along a footpath to reach Station Road, turning right to arrive in Wharram-le-Street (49.3), the church of which has a part-Saxon tower that is reputedly the oldest of any Wolds church. You turn left in the village onto the B1248, but by crossing straight over the B1248 and following the road, it is possible to visit the village of Duggleby. To the south-east of the village is Duggleby Howe, a gigantic round barrow which, at 20 ft high and 120 ft in diameter, is one of the largest of its type in Britain. When excavated it revealed the cremated or buried remains of many bodies, together with the flint and bone implements of a late-Neolithic people. The Way soon leaves the B1248, turning right and heading north. It crosses over the B1253, then shortly afterwards bears left to Wood House Farm and then right onto a track going uphill and north-eastwards. You pass Settrington Wood and then skirt another strip of woodland, going forward to a minor road crossing and the excellent viewpoint at Settrington Beacon, with good views across the Derwent Valley. Still heading north-east, you pass through an area of woodland, descend sharply and continue through open country. As the track swings to the north-west, the Way turns right along a path that heads south-east, offering views over a stream to the village of Wintringham (55.7). You turn left onto a track to reach the centre of the village, and then right, taking a road which leads past the large church. The church, one of the largest Wolds churches, has a Norman chancel and handsome Jacobean pews, but its finest feature is its stained glass, believed to be Flemish and dating from the fourteenth century, with 32 medieval saints filling the tracery lights of the aisles.

Continuing along the road beyond the church, the Way proceeds uphill through woodland, heading north-eastwards, then leaves the woods and turns right onto a track heading east. For much of the next five miles you continue in an easterly direction, staying on top of a north-facing escarpment. Initially there is woodland to your left, but after crossing a road that leads northwards to West Heslerton the walking is more open, with excellent views across East Heslerton Brow to the Derwent valley and beyond. If you have the time it may be worth detouring to West Heslerton, with its large, stuccoed part-eighteenth-century Hall. In due course you arrive at, and turn left onto, a road heading downhill towards Sherburn (62.5), a pretty village with several fine old houses, including the eighteenth-century Brewery House, a part-Norman church containing several pieces of Anglo-Saxon sculpture and a village cross presented by Sir Tatton Sykes the younger. Like his ancestor, Sir Christopher Sykes, Sir Tatton Sykes was one of the greatest benefactors in the history of the Wolds, financing the building and restoration of numerous churches and other buildings in the area. His discovery of the fertilising value of bonemeal – he noticed the grass grew better where his foxhounds had gnawed their bones – also helped him to gain the epithet of Farmer's Friend. Famous as a jockey and pugilist, Sir Tatton was known as one of the 'three great sights of Yorkshire,' the others being Fountains Abbey and York Minster.

Sherburn to Filey Brigg (16.9 miles) via Ganton, Muston and Filey

ENJOY: Ganton Hall, Stocking Dale, Filey, Filey Brigg

The Way does not enter Sherburn village but turns right onto a path just short of it. You turn right onto the next road to climb Sherburn Brow, and left onto a path which contours the Brow then drops and continues north-eastwards near the foot of the escarpment above Potter Brompton to reach a road leading down to Ganton. The Way turns left onto the road, passing the Victorian red brick Ganton Hall with its lovely parkland, then turns right onto a path that skirts the village (65.5). Like Sherburn, it is worth taking time to explore the village centre; its main street, with a stream running beside it, is lined with whitewashed chalkstone and pantile cottages dating back to the eighteenth century. From Ganton, the Way heads out into the country again, and after climbing back up the hillside on a succession of field-edge paths you gain the top of the escarpment and head due east to reach the B1249. The Way crosses the B1249, but by detouring to the left along the road you will reach Staxton with its seventeenth-century Stirrup Inn and more attractive chalkstone houses, while to the right is Willerby Wold, with its long barrow, 4 ft high by 133 ft long.

The Way heads just north of east from the B1249 and then south-east over Staxton Wold, passing round the edge of an RAF station. After what has been an unexceptional few miles, there is now a return to more traditional Wolds Way fare, with a succession of dry valleys to enjoy. You descend steeply into Cotton Dale, then turn left and climb steeply uphill again before proceeding north-eastwards above Lang Dale and, beyond a minor road crossing, Raven Dale. Because bulls run on the flat valley bottom, paths were specially created along the safer dale tops, although two steep descents and two very demanding climbs are still necessary on this section. It is interesting to compare these virtually bare green hillsides with the thickly wooded slopes much earlier in the route. The Way drops down into Camp Dale and climbs out of it again, passing a small pond on the valley floor and now heading south-eastwards, away from the ultimate goal. There is then a further descent to Stocking Dale where you swing left up the valley, resuming a north-easterly course. This is the final dry valley of the Yorkshire Wolds Way, and with its plantations and steep banks it is one of the prettiest.

Climbing to the head of the dale, and passing just below a strip of woodland, you emerge at a minor road. The Way crosses straight over, but a detour to the right along this road takes you to Hunmanby. This is a most attractive little town with a twelfth-century church, many chalkstone buildings, two fine seventeenth-century houses (Batworth Cottage and the Old Manor House) and several eighteenth-century houses. Francis Wrangham, who was minister here in the early nineteenth century, was a great bibliophile and he often entertained the greatest of clerical eccentrics, Sydney Smith (himself once a Yorkshire parson), who came to borrow books from him. One assumes that Smith may have used some of them to assist him in his preaching, but he still adopted a somewhat fatalistic attitude towards the task of addressing his congregation, acknowledging that, 'When I am in the pulpit, I have the pleasure of seeing my audience nod approbation while they sleep.'

Having crossed the Hunmanby road, the Way follows a track past Muston Wold Farm, with superb views to the North Sea, Filey and Flamborough Head. The route then forks right and drops down to the A1039, turning right onto the road to reach Muston (75.2). The village boasts an early nineteenth-century hall and, at 8–9 Hunmanby Street, a chalkstone house with cruck framing – a rarity in the East Riding. Turning left in the village, you follow a path north-eastwards, crossing the A165 Scarborough–Hull road, then as you reach the outskirts of Filey you swing to the right to arrive at the A1039; turn left onto it and follow it into the town centre (76.7). Filey has had a long association with fishing, but its long sands have also turned it into a popular seaside resort. It contains a number of interesting features, including the Norman church of St Oswald, regarded as easily the finest in the north-east corner of the East Riding, the early eighteenth-century houses of Church Street and the nineteenth-century Crescent which Pevsner suggests gives the town a 'distinctive, refined character'. It also boasts an old smugglers' inn, T'Aud Ship, complete with secret panels and hollow beams. The Way proceeds through the middle of the town then heads towards the beach, dropping down a flight of steps at the north end near the lifeboat station to reach Coble Landing, a popular mooring point for the distinctive flat-bottomed fishing craft known as cobles. To the right you can see the majestic headland of Flamborough, and to the left is the end of the Yorkshire Wolds Way at Filey Brigg. The Way now heads resolutely for that objective, climbing onto the

Pampletine cliffs which give fine views to Scarborough and beyond. It is a short walk along the clifftop to a junction of paths, where there is a splendid stone monument into which has been carved the names of various Yorkshire Wolds Way locations, thus giving you a chance to recall some of the highlights of the walk.

The Way actually does turn left at this path junction and continues beside the sea to link up with the Cleveland Way just beyond Club Point. It is here that the Yorkshire Wolds Way ends (79.4). However, a far more satisfying conclusion to the walk is to turn right by the monument and walk along the clifftops to reach Filey Brigg itself (purists wishing to claim they have completed the whole trail can of course retrace their steps and then go out to the Brigg). The Brigg consists of a reef of rocks which juts into the sea for nearly a mile, and when the seas are stormy the sight of waves crashing against these rocks is indeed an awesome one. If conditions permit, it is possible to descend onto the reef. Those to whom its origins have been attributed include not only the Devil but the skeleton of a dragon that died after its jaws became glued together with Yorkshire parkin. Walkers wishing to celebrate their completion of the Way with a helping of this delicacy at one of the tearooms in Filey, please take note.

The Cleveland Way

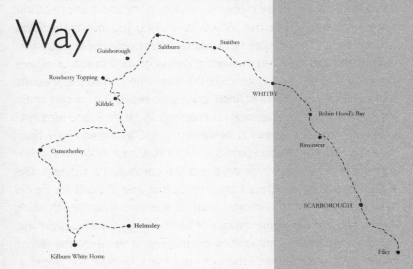

Designation: National trail.
Length: 108 miles.
Start: Helmsley, North Yorkshire.
Finish: Near Filey Brigg, North Yorkshire.
Nature: A route of two halves; a
traverse of the fringes of the North York
Moors along the tops of the Hambleton
and Cleveland Hills, then a section of
coastal walking including some of the
most spectacular cliff scenery on the east
coast of England.
Difficulty rating: Moderate, but
strenuous in places, particularly the
Cleveland Hills.
Average time of completion: 8 days.

**HIGHLIGHTS OF
THIS WALK:**
- **Kilburn**
- **White Horse**
- **Hasty Bank**
- **Roseberry**
- **Topping Staithes**
- **Whitby**
- **Robin Hood's Bay**
- **Scarborough**

THE BIG WALKS OF THE NORTH

The Cleveland Way is one of the older national trails, opened in May 1969. It can be divided into two distinct sections. The first is an inland walk which includes the superb moorland scenery of the Hambleton and Cleveland Hills. The second is a coastal walk on which you will encounter not only excellent cliff scenery but also the bustling towns of Whitby and Scarborough, and beautiful villages including Staithes and Robin Hood's Bay. The route is extremely well signposted and well defined, posing no real technical demands, although considerable stamina is required to tackle some sections, especially that between Osmotherley and Clay Bank Top where there is a lengthy overlap with the Coast to Coast Walk.

The wildlife and plant life on the route contains the richness and variety one would expect from a walk that encompasses a tramp over splendid moorland and coastal scenery. The North York Moors provide three fine species of heather – ling, bell heather and cross-leaved heath – as well as cloudberry, crowberry and dwarf cornel, with their orange, black and red fruits. Grouse are plentiful, and you may also see the curlew, meadow pipit, merlin, common lizard and green-and-black caterpillar of the emperor moth, while the coastal section may bring sightings of the oystercatcher, plover, cormorant, tern, shag and dunlin.

What perhaps characterises the Cleveland Way is its splendid open walking and consequently wide, sweeping vistas, both inland and on the coast, making binoculars a must. The factor most likely to spoil the walk in summer is a light mist known locally as 'roak', which drifts in from the sea on summer days and can quite significantly wreck the good visibility needed to enjoy the journey. All the more infuriating, then, to learn that friends enjoying a holiday in the Dales barely an hour's drive away have been basking in glorious sunshine throughout. In good weather, however, it is a most satisfying and enjoyable walk, and indeed if you still yearn for more when you reach the end, you can immediately join the Yorkshire Wolds Way, which links up with the Cleveland Way.

The Cleveland Way

Helmsley to Sutton Bank (10.2 miles) via Cold Kirby

ENJOY: Helmsley, Rievaulx, Sutton Bank, Kilburn White Horse

The Way begins in the charming town of Helmsley, the focal point of which is the ruin of a castle which was built in the early twelfth century although its oldest surviving buildings go back to around 1200. The marketplace in the town contains several attractive houses, some dating back to the sixteenth century, as well as a good range of amenities of which you would be well advised to take advantage as there is nothing more guaranteed until Osmotherley, a full day's walk away. You start out at an impressive monument with the National Trails acorn motif carved into it, this being reached by following a track heading westwards off the B1257 more or less opposite All Saints church. The Way then continues along this track, which becomes a pleasant footpath that gently rises through open country and follows the edge of a wood, still heading roughly westwards. There are fine views back to Helmsley and its castle ruin.

The Way continues to follow the path, which temporarily enters woodland, dropping and then rising again to join a track and continue along the edge of a steep wooded escarpment, known as Whinny Bank. Soon, close to the site of a village rejoicing in the unusual name of Griff, you enter the wood and drop steeply down the escarpment to reach a road, turn left onto it, and follow it, coming to a bridge over the river Rye. Immediately before the bridge you should turn right to detour up to Rievaulx Abbey, a Cistercian foundation which was colonised in 1131. There is more left standing at Rievaulx than at any Cistercian abbey in England except Fountains in the Yorkshire Dales, and although there is little remaining from the time of foundation, a great deal of the early thirteenth-century work still stands.

After crossing the Rye bridge you continue along the road, soon passing Hagg Hall on the left. Shortly after Hagg Hall the road bends sharply to the left, and just beyond the bend the Way turns right onto a track which passes beside three lakes, and then bears right to begin its passage towards an area of woodland marked on the map as Blind Side. However, you soon bear left off this track on a path through the woods, shortly turning right on a route which climbs out of the woodland and develops into a wider track that leads to the village of Cold Kirby. Its remote feel contrasts starkly with the lush, homely surroundings of Rievaulx. The Way passes the nineteenth-century church of St Michael and proceeds through the village on a metalled road, turning first left onto a track. This leads to a path that in turn continues to the edge of a wooded area then turns right, passing Hambleton House and coming to a lane. You turn left onto this lane and follow it to arrive at the A170 by the welcome Hambleton Inn, crossing straight over onto another lane before bearing right onto a path. This proceeds through woodland to emerge at the first highlight of the journey, the viewpoint of Sutton Bank. Suddenly, after walking through somewhat nondescript upland terrain, you are faced with a glorious panoramic view across a huge area of Yorkshire.

Here you have a choice. If pressed for time, you could immediately turn right to reach the A170 and cross it to begin the glorious promenade along the top of the escarpment which is the western rim of the wild Hambleton Hills. However, the definitive route of the Cleveland Way includes the detour along the tops of the cliffs of Roulston Scar, involving a left turn at Sutton Bank and a tremendous walk that leads to one of Yorkshire's more distinctive landmarks, the Kilburn White Horse, before backtracking to Sutton Bank, crossing the A170 and going forward to the impressive visitor centre (10.2). Although the views from the White Horse are stupendous – York Minster is clearly visible on a good day – you will be right above the horse and the view is not as good as if you were seeing it from far below. Indeed, when I walked the Way I was convinced I had been standing triumphantly on the horse's forelegs, but when I made a return visit two months later I found I had in fact been standing on its nose. The horse, dating back to 1857, is 314 ft long and 228 ft high, the outline having been cut by the village schoolmaster John Hodgson and his pupils. Teachers might reflect that if the national curriculum and Ofsted had been around in 1857, the horse would probably never have been cut at all.

Sutton Bank to Osmotherley (11.4 miles) via Sneck Yate

ENJOY: Gormire Lake, Black Hambleton Moor, Osmotherley

Having made the Kilburn White Horse detour, you now need to retrace your steps – no hardship in view of the magnificent scenery – to Sutton Bank (10), and cross the A170. Then begins an exhilarating high-level march over the Hambleton Hills, with wild moorland and woodland to the right and the great swathe of the Vale of York stretching out to the left. After passing high above Gormire Lake, the route follows a well-defined path that stays close to the escarpment edge, first alongside woodland, then past the impressive rocks of Boltby Scar, across a metalled road at Sneck Yate Bank, through a piece of woodland, and shortly thereafter onto a track that forks, the route taking the right fork past High Paradise Farm to reach an important crossroads of paths just beyond the farm. The Way goes left to proceed north-westwards on an excellent track which passes along the right-hand edge of a forest and then strikes out onto open moorland, with Little Moor and Arden Great Moor to the right and Kepwick Moor to the left.

You then curve gently northwards as you continue on to Whitestone Scar, between Arden Great Moor and Kepwick Moor. Here you reach another path junction, the Way heading left over Black Hambleton Moor, and again passing the right-hand edge of a forest, rising to over 1,300 ft. Superb views now begin to open up ahead as well as to the left, with industrial Teesside clearly visible to the north. Now the long descent towards Osmotherley begins.

Shortly after leaving the forest behind, you drop down to a metalled road and, beyond that, a car park; bearing left here, you take a path which drops steeply down through the heather, passing to the right of two lakes and, at Oak Dale, joining a track leading to a metalled road. Crossing the road, you join a track that leads to Whitehouse Farm, beyond which the track turns into a path that heads westwards downhill to cross Cod Beck. There follows a climb through the woods and then a field walk, still heading westwards, into Osmotherley (21.6).

This is a delightful place, with attractive stone cottages round its triangular green and a church with a fine Norman doorway. The steep streets of the village have cobbled pavements and grassy verges lined with trees and flowers. John Wesley, the founder of Methodism, preached in the eighteenth-century Methodist chapel; in North End, there is the old pinfold, or pound, in which stray animals were impounded until their owners paid a fine. Wherever walkers stay in Osmotherley, they may well find fellow guests are doing Wainwright's Coast to Coast Walk, which meets the Way a mile north of the village. Those who have come from St Bees on that route will have accomplished over 140 miles, compared with the Cleveland Way walker's more modest 21.6, and may well therefore feel entitled to assume an air of smug superiority. There will always be walkers whose achievements outstrip yours so it is best, when engaging in conversation with fellow hikers, not to trumpet your own exploits too loudly. Otherwise you risk provoking them into regaling you with tales of their own extraordinary and intrepid adventures, diminishing your own paltry efforts to the level of a lunch-hour stroll to the newsagents to top up your supplies of Pot Noodle.

The Cleveland Way

Osmotherley to Clay Bank (11.6 miles) via Scugdale

ENJOY: Scugdale, Carlton, Cringle Moor, Hasty Bank

The Cleveland Way leaves Osmotherley by proceeding from the village green up North End, turning left onto Ruebury Lane and ascending gradually. The lane begins as a metalled road but becomes an unmetalled track that offers magnificent views westwards. You reach an area of woodland, immediately meeting a path that comes in from the left; the Way goes on ahead, but by turning left here you may visit Mount Grace Priory. This is the point where the Coast to Coast Walk meets the Cleveland Way and will continue with it for the next 14 miles, and the Lyke Wake Walk follows the same route for those miles. The Lyke Wake Walk was originally a 40-mile route along which local people used to carry the coffins of their deceased to bury them at sea. It has now become a challenge walk and people who complete it nowadays within 24 hours are eligible to join the Lyke Wake Club, membership of which entitles them to a small badge in the shape of a coffin.

The Cleveland Way, together with the other routes, continues through the wood on a good path, heading north-eastwards to pass the television booster station on Beacon Hill. Soon afterwards, you emerge from the wood and swing in a more easterly direction. There follows a fine stretch of open walking across Scarth Wood Moor, the path losing height first gradually and then more rapidly, descending to reach a metalled road. The Way crosses straight over onto a very good woodland path, which drops down into the attractive valley of Scugdale. On arrival in the valley, you reach a gated lane and turn right, following another excellent path up the wooded valley for about three quarters of a mile, then turn left onto a path which crosses a tributary of Scugdale Beck and reaches a metalled road. You join this road, crossing Scugdale Beck immediately and climbing up to a T-junction with the Swainby–Scugdale Hall road at the hamlet of Huthwaite

Green. The Way crosses straight over this road, taking a path to the right of a telephone kiosk up the facing hillside. In just under half a mile the Way turns sharply right up an extremely steep woodland path, emerging from the woods and striking out across Live Moor, heading eastwards.

The next six miles are the most exciting on the Cleveland Way, as the very good path, proceeding in a generally easterly or north-easterly direction, negotiates the Cleveland Hills, a succession of moors involving a number of lung-testing ascents and knee-jarring descents. The views throughout are glorious; there are the wide plains stretching for miles to the left, and on the right are the beautiful heather uplands of the North York Moors. The first ascent, to the 1,025 ft summit of Live Moor, sets the scene, but although arduous it is by no means the toughest. From Live Moor the Way continues on over Carlton Moor, descending steeply off it to reach a metalled road. By detouring to the left down this road you will reach the pleasant village of Carlton, with its pretty Alum Beck, old cottages and sloping orchards and gardens, but the route continues on the obvious track over the road. Refreshments may be available here and even the fittest walker should take advantage of them, as there is nothing more for many miles. The Way then climbs onto Cringle Moor, described by Wainwright as the finest elevation yet reached along the escarpment, and you should pause at Cringle End near the summit, where there is a view indicator and seat.

There is another steep drop, another big climb to the summit of Cold Moor, another big descent, and then the finest climb of all, up onto Hasty Bank past the cluster of pinnacled rocks known as the Wain Stones, with some scrambling required to complete the ascent through the stones. A superb high-level walk follows, and it is quite anticlimactical to drop steeply down to the B1257 just south of Clay Bank car park (33.2), marking the end of this wonderful sequence of ascents and descents. You should note that although the car park is well used, there are likely to be no amenities available and the nearest village, Great Broughton, lies a couple of miles to the north. As you trudge down to the car park you may well be overtaken by those endeavouring to complete the Lyke Wake Walk in the quickest time they can, unencumbered by rucksacks and clad in the lightest possible gear, hopping nimbly and confidently up and down the almost vertical slopes.

Clay Bank to Slapewath (19 miles) via Kildale

ENJOY: Urra Moor, Roseberry Topping, Highcliff Nab

After crossing straight over the B1257 there follows a long slog onto Urra Moor. The route, still well-defined, continues in a south-easterly and then a more easterly direction, passing the 1,491 ft triangulation point which marks the summit of Urra Moor, and inscribed stones known as the Hand Stone, the Face Stone and the Red Stone, thought to have been erected in the early years of the eighteenth century although there is some suggestion that they date back even further. Shortly beyond the Red Stone you reach a T-junction, meeting the clearly defined course of the old Rosedale Ironstone Railway (see description of the Coast to Coast Walk) and turning right onto it, very soon reaching the crossroads of paths known as Bloworth Crossing. Here, at last, the Cleveland Way parts company with the Coast to Coast Walk and the Lyke Wake Walk; the latter two routes go straight on, whilst the Cleveland Way goes left. Proceeding along another excellent track, the Way heads north-westwards along the edge of the escarpment known as Greenhow Bank, then swings north-eastwards over Battersby Moor. You now enjoy splendid views as the track carrying the Way turns into a metalled road which descends steeply, swinging north-westwards again to pass Park Dyke, arriving at a T-junction with another road and going right along the road into Kildale (42).

The Way turns left in the village to head for the railway station, then immediately right along a lane, going under the railway and past Bankside Farm, where you enter woodland. You follow the lane steeply uphill and at the brow of the hill you turn left, joining a track that heads westwards through the woods. You emerge onto Easby Moor and go forward, steeply uphill, to reach Captain Cook's Monument, in honour of the explorer who spent most of his childhood in the nearby village of Great Ayton. From here there are breathtaking views back to Kildale and the Cleveland Hills. Immediately beyond the monument you turn right along a path that heads north-eastwards, coming off Easby Moor to pass through woodland, descending briefly and then continuing along the west edge of Great Ayton Moor, passing along the eastern side of another patch of woodland. You then climb again and swing north-westwards, along a steep escarpment edge and then along the right fringe of Slacks Wood with the open moorland of Newton Moor to the right. Throughout this section of the Way there are magnificent views to the Cleveland Hills and the surrounding countryside.

At the top end of Slacks Wood there is a crossroads where there starts an official 'out and back' detour to Roseberry Topping, described as Yorkshire's Matterhorn. To make the detour, you take a left turn at the crossroads and then head just south of west to the gritstone-capped summit. The hill's terraced slopes have been caused by the alternation of adjacent beds of harder and softer rocks, making it a place of great interest for geologists as well as sightseers. The views are wonderfully wide-ranging, encompassing the moors, industrial Teesside, the villages of Great Ayton and Stokesley and the town of Guisborough. Though well-known as one of the most prominent natural landmarks in the North East and featuring in many of the panoramic views offered along the Cleveland Way, the quaint name given to this isolated conical hill may to those unfamiliar with the area be more likely to conjure thoughts of a sickly-sweet flavoured synthetic cream that adorned the nation's Sunday dinner tables in the early 1970s.

It is a real wrench to leave the summit and head back to the crossroads, going straight over and proceeding north-eastwards over Newton Moor and Hutton Moor along an obvious track with thick woodland to your left. There is no doubt that this section is something of a trudge, but patience is rewarded, for as you swing north-westwards to enter Guisborough Woods, you reach the rocky outcrops of Highcliff Nab, with superb views to Guisborough. Beyond the Nab you are faced with perhaps the least inspiring section of the Cleveland Way. You proceed initially through the long expanse of Guisborough Woods, passing an old quarry at one point, heading in a generally north-easterly direction along a good path, although care should be taken as there are numerous other paths in the wood. At length the woodland relents and you emerge into open land, arriving at a track. You turn left onto it, proceeding downhill, and soon turn right onto a path that heads eastwards through woodland to reach the A171 at Slapewath (52.2), the path seemingly going right past the village before turning sharply down to the road. The path can be muddy and the noise of the traffic on the A171 quite intrusive. By walking westwards along the A171 you can reach Guisborough; its most notable feature is its Augustinian priory, founded about 1120, although the oldest remaining features date back no earlier than the thirteenth century. St Nicholas church is worth seeing for its ornate Brus cenotaph, and the 1907 Methodist church might be inspected if only for the walker to decide if he thinks Pevsner was right to describe it as 'unforgivable'!

Slapewath to Staithes (13.2 miles) via Skelton, Saltburn and Skinningrove

ENJOY: Saltburn, Boulby Cliffs, Staithes

The Way turns left onto the A171 then shortly right onto a path that proceeds round the rim of a quarry to the left with woodland to the right. The old quarries hereabouts were once a lucrative source of ironstone and alum, first quarried here 400 years ago. Having rounded the quarry, you turn sharply right to head northwards with an area of woodland to the left, then right again north-eastwards past a triangulation point to Airy Hill Farm, joining a track here which leads down towards Skelton. You arrive at a road, going straight over and following a path over fields, turning right to follow a track briefly and then shortly left on a path that soon reaches the A173 in the centre of Skelton. Skelton is not a particularly attractive village but does boast a fine late eighteenth-century house called Skelton Castle, reflecting the fact that there was once a real twelfth-century castle here. Immediately south of the house is a remarkable old church with a three-decker pulpit, box pews and gallery, although in recent years it has fallen into disuse.

The Way crosses straight over the A173 through a modern housing estate – what a contrast to the glories of Roulston Scar, Hasty Bank and Roseberry Topping! – and then from the north-east edge of the estate follows a path northwards through fields and into woodland. As the houses of Saltburn begin to appear, you cross Skelton Beck and pass underneath an impressive brick viaduct carrying a freight railway, then stay on the left bank of the Beck through an area of woodland with more than one path from which to choose. With the suburbs of Saltburn encroaching, it is not such an idyllic scene as it might be.

At length you reach the sea front at Saltburn (57), with the dullest part of the Cleveland Way and also any real route-finding difficulties now at an end; the second half of the Way consists of a straightforward walk along the finest section of the east coast of England. Saltburn not only offers a good range of amenities and rail connections, but is a cheerful little resort with a good stretch of sands and a pier that dates back to 1868. Crossing the A174, the Way joins a coastal path heading eastwards with the sea on the left, climbing past Saltburn Scar and Hunt Cliff where there is the site of a Roman signalling station built in the fourth century to warn of Anglian and Saxon pirates. There is then a drop to the dunes of Cattersty Sands and the village of Skinningrove, which, with its vast ironworks, is sadly is no more attractive than its name. The Way then climbs again above Hummersea Scar and on past Boulby quarries, where ironstone, alum and jet have all been worked. The cliffs hereabouts, where it is said that the sixth-century Viking hero Beowulf is buried, are at 666 ft the highest on the east coast of England, with excellent views and easy walking.

After descending from the clifftops, the Way joins a track to pass through the hamlet of Boulby, continues alongside the cliffs of Bias Scar by means of a footpath, and then joins a metalled road to pass through Cowbar and arrive at the village of Staithes (65.4).

Staithes

With its maze of cobbled streets running steeply up from the harbour, itself protected by the high cliffs of Cowbar Nab and Penny Nab, Staithes is one of the most picturesque settlements on the Way, although it has always been a tough working village with long-standing associations with the mining and fishing industries. Captain Cook, whose monument was seen several miles back, worked as an apprentice grocer in the village until he signed on as a cabin boy in a Whitby ship. There are several fine old stone buildings in the village, especially in the High Street and Church Street with its Georgian houses and rockery-girt cottages. Between these two streets run a number of quaint alleyways with most unusual names that include Gun Gutter, Slip Top and Dog Loup. The latter is just about 18 inches wide, and well-built or well-equipped walkers may proceed along it with some trepidation; after they have endured the rigours of Black Hambleton and the precipitous descents off Cold Moor and Hasty Bank, it would indeed be a savage irony for their conquest of the Way to be scuppered by becoming wedged between two stone walls.

Staithes to Robin Hood's Bay (18.4 miles) via Runswick, Sandsend and Whitby

ENJOY: Whitby, Saltwick Bay, Robin Hood's Bay

Having left Staithes, the Way proceeds above the cliffs of Old Nab and on past the hamlet of Port Mulgrave with its harbour from which ironstone was once exported. Erosion is a serious problem on this stretch and walkers may be diverted from the cliff edge. You descend steeply to Runswick Bay, a holiday village which lacks the charms of Staithes, then walk along the beach for half a mile before climbing splendidly by a narrow beck and up some steep steps to regain the cliffs. From here you continue round the headland of Kettleness, which offers good views back to Boulby cliffs and forward towards Whitby. The Way stays on the clifftop as far as Deepgrove Wyke, then drops steeply to join the course of an old railway, which was used to take steel products, fish and agricultural produce to the Middlesbrough area. You follow the old line to the village of Sandsend, where you join the A174 and proceed beside it through East Row and alongside a golf course. Shortly beyond the clubhouse, you turn left onto a track which heads back towards the sea, and soon after passing under a footbridge, you bear right onto an obvious path that leads into Whitby (77).

This fishing port and seaside resort is an almost obligatory resting-place on the journey. Dominated by the remains of the thirteenth-century abbey – an earlier abbey was actually founded here in AD 657 – the town boasts a lively harbour and a jumble of steep alleyways and hillside cottages, converging on the River Esk, which flows right through the town. Captain Cook lived in the town as a young man, and another noted navigator, William Scoresby, departed from Whitby for the Arctic whaling grounds. The parish church of St Mary, with its Norman tower, triple-deck pulpit and one of the most complete sets of pre-Victorian furnishings in England, is approached by the 199 Church Stairs from which there is a splendid view of the town. The old streets are dotted with craft and antique shops, many of them offering items of jewellery made from jet, which is still found along the nearby cliffs. It comes from wood that has been washed out to sea, fossilised and then subjected to the pressure of water and silt.

Having climbed away from the Esk to leave Whitby near the abbey, you enjoy a splendid seven-mile walk to Robin Hood's Bay. Soon you pass the cliffs of Saltwick Nab and Black Nab, with the picturesque Saltwick Bay nestling between them, and after an easy start, the going becomes more undulating. The cliff scenery is stunning and constantly fascinating; indeed, the cliffs along the whole of the 20 miles between Whitby and Scarborough are a geologist's paradise. Shales, clays, sandstones and limestones all rise to the surface with their different colouring, the near-vertical limestone cliffs contrasting with the more rounded clay ones. At Maw Wyke Hole the Cleveland Way once again overlaps with the Coast to Coast route, last seen at Bloworth Crossing on the moors, and both journeys follow the cliff path all the way to Robin Hood's Bay. Although there is a considerable amount of up-and-down work, the views out to sea are ample reward.

Having proceeded in a south-easterly direction all the way from Whitby, the coast path swings south-west at Ness Point, from which it is a straightforward walk on to Robin Hood's Bay (83.8). Like Whitby, the village is a delightful jumble of narrow streets, passages and quaint old houses on a variety of levels, and is described as the most picturesque fishing village in Yorkshire. Though walkers attempting to reach Scarborough from Whitby in a day may feel the need to press on, it is an excellent place to stop and recharge the batteries.

Robin Hood's Bay to Scarborough North Bay (13.6 miles) via Ravenscar

ENJOY: Ravenscar, Hayburn Wyke, Cloughton Wyke

Beyond Robin Hood's Bay there is more wonderful cliff scenery, but erosion has sadly taken its toll and you may be diverted away from the cliffs as far as Stoupe Beck Sands, where there is a brief gap in the massive stone stacks, before making the long uphill slog to Ravenscar. There were plans in the 1890s to turn Ravenscar into a resort, and a groundwork of streets was laid out here as part of a planned development which never materialised, although some buildings were erected, including the Raven Hall Hotel. This was built near the end of the eighteenth Century and, prior to its becoming a hotel, George III was treated here by a Dr Willis for his supposed madness. It now stands proudly on the cliffs, commanding splendid views in an unspoilt setting, almost exactly halfway between Whitby and Scarborough.

Beyond Ravenscar there follows a fine 10-mile walk to Scarborough, close to the cliffs most of the way, although at Beast Cliff the Way goes to the landward side of a strip of woodland, and at Hayburn Wyke there is a steep descent to a wooded valley with an attractive footbridge and waterfall. Emerging from the woods, the walking becomes more open and the lovely inlet of Cloughton Wyke, where the path dips down again, provides scintillating sandstone cliff scenery. Excellent and straightforward clifftop walking follows, passing the headlands of Hundale Point, Long Nab, Cromer Point and Scalby Ness, but as you approach the latter you do become very conscious of the proximity of Scarborough. You descend to pass round the seaward side of Scalby Mills and beside North Bay (97.4), one of two large bays (the other being South Bay) that are separated by the promontory on which Scarborough's magnificent twelfth-century castle is built.

The town is full of fine buildings, most notably the parish church of St Mary which has twelfth-century origins, and the Grand Hotel, described by Pevsner as 'wondrous.' Its harbour is always busy, not only with pleasure craft but also traditional fishing vessels such as cobles and mules. It has been said that Scarborough is a fishing village and seaside town rolled into one, and it is easy for the visitor to see why as he observes not only the quaint streets of the old town but also the traditional trappings of a holiday resort, from cockle stalls to amusement arcades. It will be a brave walker indeed who chooses to gamble part or all of his train fare home in the casino, in the full knowledge that the capricious turn of the roulette ball will determine whether his journey home next day is in the comfort of a first-class seat in a Pullman lounge or wholly dependent on a golden-hearted truck-driver magically appearing in the Esso garage in Filey and responding favourably to his outstretched thumb.

Scarborough North Bay to Filey Brigg (10.2 miles) via Cayton Bay

ENJOY: Lebberston and Gristhorpe Cliffs, Filey Brigg

The Cleveland Way is not signposted through Scarborough (99), but the final leg of the route resumes in Holbeck Gardens to the south of the town, not far from Holbeck Hall, a hotel which collapsed into the sea owing to a cliff slip in 1993. The Way, still following the coastline, rounds the headland of White Nab and passes along the landward edge of an area of woodland, descending to Cayton Bay. As you follow round the bay, you will note that the scenery is somewhat marred by the presence of a holiday camp as well as the nearby A165 road. Things improve, however, as you climb again and regain the coastline to pass Lebberston and Gristhorpe Cliffs, fascinating for their offshore reefs and layered rocks topped with crumbling boulder clay.

THE BIG WALKS OF THE NORTH

The official route ends shortly at Newbiggin Cliff, at the boundary of the old North and East Riding of Yorkshire (107.6). This also marks the start of the Yorkshire Wolds Way, which most walkers will wish to follow on into Filey. However, there is no proper sign or other landmark to show the end of the route, and it really is a somewhat anticlimactical way to end a national trail of such beauty and variety. But never mind: Filey is just a short way away, and there are plenty of pubs and cafes for you to enjoy celebratory drinks and sweet treats. Even if they don't come with Roseberry Topping.

Hadrian's Wall Path

Bowness-on-Solway
Walton
CARLISLE
Steel Rigg
Chollerford
Heddon-on-the-Wall
NEWCASTLE UPON TYNE
Wallsend

Designation: National trail.
Length: 84 miles.
Start: Wallsend, Tyne and Wear.
Finish: Bowness-on-Solway, Cumbria.
Nature: A demanding but rewarding walk beside one of the most ancient and enduring man-made features in Britain, through often stunning countryside.
Difficulty rating: moderate, strenuous in places.
Average time of completion: 6–7 days.

Hadrian's Wall Path was added to the family of national trails in 2003 and is at the time of writing the only national trail to provide a coast to coast route across England. Admittedly, its start point at Wallsend is a few miles from the point at which the Tyne reaches the North Sea, and its finish point at Bowness-on-Solway nestles some

HIGHLIGHTS OF THIS WALK:
- **Segedunum,**
- **Brocolitia**
- **Housesteads**
- **Sycamore Gap**
- **Windshields Crags**
- **Great Chesters**
- **Thirlwall Castle**

distance from the meeting of the Solway Firth with the Irish Sea, but it still offers effectively a walk across England. It is also, as the path's name implies, a walk back to Roman times, as it traces the defensive wall begun by the Roman Emperor Hadrian between 122 and 126 AD and constructed to stop tribes such as the Picts mounting raids on Northern England; the Wall actually marked the northernmost limit of the Roman colonisation of Britain. Built with great skill to take advantage of the lie of the land, the Wall was guarded by troops and supplemented by a number of forts and smaller intermediate fortifications. On a number of occasions it was breached by the Picts and finally abandoned around the end of the fourth century; as a consequence, you may think it quite remarkable that two thousand years later so much of the Wall still remains, and although sightings of the Wall are very scarce indeed during the early and later part of the walk, large sections of the Wall combined with quite spectactular scenery can be enjoyed in the middle of the journey.

Contrasts between raw rural beauty and urban clutter are starker on this path than any other national trail, with correspondingly contrasting demands upon the mental and physical resources of the walker. Whilst some sections require proper walking equipment and mapreading skills, others need only the aptitude and fitness levels of a Sunday afternoon stroller. Moreover, it may only be the anticipation of grand, sweeping views from the noble stone remains around Housesteads and Windshields Crags that will keep you going as you stride through the grim suburbs of Newcastle with the only tangible evidence of links with the dim and distant past consisting of clumsily daubed graffiti proclaiming that Kevin Keegan Rules OK.

Wallsend to Heddon-on-the-Wall (14.9 miles) via Newcastle upon Tyne

ENJOY: Newcastle upon Tyne, Wylam Wagonway, Heddon-on-the-Wall

Wallsend is easily reached from Newcastle central station (in turn a short walk from the express coach station and the city centre) by means of the Tyne & Wear Metro, and it is a short walk south from the Metro station to the official start of the path close to the banks of the Tyne. Immediately you are confronted by a splendid fragment of the Wall on the site of the fort known as Segedunum, the most easterly of the forts built along the Wall at roughly seven-mile intervals. Much of this fort has been excavated and a fine museum has been built around the excavated stonework; one of the most interesting features of Segedunum is the bath house, reconstructed to look very much as it did in Roman times.

The national trail proceeds south-westwards from Segdunum along the course of an old railway which was part of the old Blyth and Tyne railway line, and the going is very easy and straightforward. The atmosphere is very urban in character, with extensive areas of housing to your right, while the Tyne lies to your left, separated from you by factories, shipyards and wharves; the somewhat depressed and depressing nature of your immediate surroundings may be confirmed by evidence of graffiti and petty vandalism around you. Your railway walk ends in a little park from which you proceed by means of a ramp to reach the bank of the Tyne, and now you can enjoy a straightforward walk beside this river, taking you ever closer to the centre of Newcastle, with the buildings of Gateshead clearly visible across the river to your left. You pass the impressive Ropery development and briefly leave the river to go round the edge of Spillers flour mill, then continue beside the Tyne and pass a number of very distinctive bridges over the river including the Gateshead Millennium Bridge and the noble steel-arched Tyne Bridge based on the same design as that of the Sydney Harbour Bridge. To your right are a number of very old houses including the distinctive timber-framed Bessie Surtees House, with the main shopping centre of Newcastle a few minutes' walk beyond. I first walked this section very early on a Wednesday morning, when few people were about; I returned to the same site the following Sunday evening during a Bank Holiday weekend when the quayside was thronging with scantily-clad clubbers and my now rather weatherbeaten hiking attire made me feel more out of place than a happily married heterosexual couple on the set of the Jerry Springer Show.

You continue along the bank beyond the bridges, the surroundings becoming less inspiring as you walk beside what were once working quays, but at length are forced away from the Tyne and must now cross a busy road junction before following first another section of old railway, the Scotswood, Newburn & Wylam, and then a public park. You cross over the A1 – thankfully a footbridge is provided – then make your way back to the old railway and follow it past the suburban district of Lemington, noting the very conspicuous Lemington glass cone. The going is fast and easy, ample vegetation gives at least the impression of rural walking, and there are shops at Lemington which are easily accessible from the route if you are in need of sustenance. Passing the site of the former huge Spencer steelworks, you cross a road and shortly beyond the crossing arrive back at the Tyne at Newburn Bridge. Now you can at last say you have left the big city behind you as you enjoy a really fine riverside walk in beautiful surroundings, with the village of Heddon-on-the-Wall clearly visible on the hillside to your right whilst to your left is the river and beyond the river are the woodlands bordering the little town of Ryton. As you proceed, you find yourself following the line of the former Wylam Wagonway, site of one of the first experiments with steam locomotion. George Stephenson's birthplace cottage, owned by the National Trust, is only half a mile

14/2

Ritchie, T

west of the trail along the Wagonway. Your enjoyable riverside stroll ends as you turn off the Wagonway and skirt the edge of sports playing fields, passing a golf driving range, then climb quite steeply to arrive at Heddon-on-the-Wall (14.9). This may be a convenient place to end your day's walk from Wallsend, now 15 miles back, especially as the village offers a shop, pub and excellent bus links to Newcastle. It also boasts a very fine section of the Wall and a section of what is known as the Vallum, a defensive ditch punctuated with earthworks running alongside the Wall.

Now the character of the walk changes, as from here to just beyond Brocolitia, some twenty miles distant, you will be walking virtually the whole time within sight or sound of the B6318. This was a military road begun in 1754 linking Newcastle and Carlisle, and one of a number of roads built by British troops who were sent to quell the Jacobite Rebellion in 1745 and who found communications systems inadequate; in many places it actually submerged the Wall itself, and as a result it has been condemned by some as institutionalised vandalism. Because the road followed the course of the Wall so closely, at any rate as far as wall-mile 33, a mile west of Brocolitia, it is inevitable that the national trail must stick with it (although it always uses parallel paths rather than staying on the tarmac), meaning that the next day or two's walking will be a blessing to those who need a compass to negotiate their way out of a wet paper bag.

Heddon-on-the-Wall to Chollerford (15.2 miles) via Port Gate and Wall

ENJOY: Vindobala, Vallum at Halton Shields, Heavenfield, Brunton Turret, Chollerford

The walk from Heddon-on-the-Wall beside the B6318 starts rather inauspiciously with a crossing of the very busy A69 but things soon look up as you pass the remains of the fort of Vindobala or

Rudchester, even though all you can see are earthworks in an otherwise ordinary field. Traces of the Vallum can be seen as you now press westwards, passing the hamlet of Harlow Hill and a group of reservoirs but all the while remaining faithful to the B6318. On you plod, passing the driveway to Matfen Hall, and going forward to the next hamlet, Halton Shields. Then comes the first real highlight of your walk from Heddon, when your path leaves the roadside and strikes out south-westwards round the left side of some woodland to arrive at some prominent Vallum earthworks with tremendous views across the surrounding countryside. Newcastle suddenly seems a very long way back.

Suddenly anticlimax sets in, however: you drop down quite steeply, and having passed just to north of Halton with its medieval castle remains and old church, you find yourself close to the B6318 again with no obvious further signs of the Vallum. Soon you arrive at Port Gate, where the B6318 meets the busy A68, a road which may strike a distant chord with Pennine Way veterans. Across the A68 at Port Gate is a pub followed by a very straightforward walk close to the B6318 with Chollerford just a couple of hours distant.

Beyond Port Gate the walking remains very straightforward and increasingly enjoyable. To begin with, although you are still parallel with the B6318, you are now a little further away from it, and soon you dive into an area of woodland. Forest tramping is not everyone's favourite kind of walking, but it comes as quite a welcome contrast to what has gone before and is undoubtedly refreshing in hot weather. Emerging from the woods, you continue on the south side of the road as far as the remains of Milecastle 24, one of many fortified gateways built at Roman mile intervals along the Wall. You cross the B6318 here and now enjoy one of the best pieces of walking so far, with tremendous views to the north which on clear days have been said to stretch as far as the Cheviots. The Roman ditch can clearly be identified and, with the B6318 just close enough to prevent any worries about going off course, it is all very enjoyable. You'll note from your OS map that there is a battle site to your right along this part of your walk; it is in fact the site of the Battle of Heavenfield, fought in the seventh century between Northumbria and an alliance between Gwynedd and Mercia.

Having been climbing almost constantly ever since the reservoirs just beyond Harlow Hill, and reached 800 ft above sea level, you now begin to drop down to the North Tyne valley. You cross back over the B6318 and almost immediately beyond the crossing you arrive at the first section of extant masonry Wall – called Planetrees – since leaving Heddon-on-the-Wall. Shortly beyond Planetrees you leave a wood then follow a minor road to join the A6079 just north of the village of Wall. No marks for originality with the name, but top marks for the availability of a pub. Turn right to follow the A6079 with a short detour to Brunton turret, one of the best preserved fragments of the Wall in existence, strongly recommended. Follow the A6079 to its junction with – you've guessed it, the B6318 – and then turn left to follow beside your old friend across the very splendid eighteenth-century Chollerford Bridge. The village of Chollerford (30.1) lies just over the bridge, and this offers not only beer but beds. An even more generous supply of both, however, can be found at Hexham, which is a brief bus ride away.

Chollerford to Steel Rigg (12 miles) via Housesteads

ENJOY: Chesters, Brocolitia, Sewingshields Crags, Housesteads, Cuddy's Crags, Highshield Crags, Sycamore Gap, Vindolanda

You bear left to follow the B6318 out of Chollerford, soon arriving at the entrance to the fort of Chesters; as with Segedunum, this is a splendid collection of excavations, the most impressive of which are the main bath house, the remains of the Roman bridge and the partly exposed guard house, and the setting is much lovelier than Segedunum. Beyond Chesters, you stick to the B6318 as far as the village of Walwick a short way further on, then take a somewhat circuitous route round Walwick Hall before returning to a familiar bill of fare, namely tramping parallel with and close to the B6318. However, this is now very fine walking indeed: there is a considerable climb, but your reward is a good section of the Wall and sweeping views over miles of beautiful countryside. You are now embarking on the best section of the whole walk. You cross the road to enter the sites of the Roman fort of Brocolitia, a temple to the Persian god Mithras known as the Mithraeum, and a well dedicated to the goddess Coventina. The course of the national trail considerably passes the sites of all three. Then it is back to B6318 duty, but at last, around a mile from Brocolitia, the path leaves the road. Route finding, however, presents no problems, and soon you reach a clear landmark, namely the woodlands surrounding the buildings of Sewingshields and the easily identified Milecastle 35. Beyond the woods, on Sewingshields Crags, you can enjoy a quite magnificent section of walking, with the Wall for company too. The waters of Broomlee Lough appear to your right, the rolling hills stretch seemingly for ever, and there is a sense of complete remoteness and timelessness as the path swings south-westwards with the Wall and makes for Housesteads. This is fantastic walking and for many it may be the best section of the entire national trail; the heavily wooded Housesteads Crags, seen from a distance, are one of the most enduring images of the Wall.

A long descent and crossing of Knag Burn is followed by an ascent to the Housesteads fort, known by the Romans as Vercovicium (the place of good fighters). Arguably this is the most famous of all the forts on the Wall, largely because so much of the original structure remains intact with well-defined ramparts still giving it the look of a fort, and it has become a massive tourist attraction – with the elaborate plumbing system a particular source of interest! Ironically it is not possible to access the fort directly from the path itself, and a detour will be necessary.

Magnificent walking now follows, as the national trail continues in switchback fashion past Cuddy's Crags (where the Pennine Way begins its overlap with the Wall), Hotbank Crags, Highshield Crags and Peel Crags to the road crossing at Steel Rigg (42.1), the approximate halfway point of the whole walk. The narrow road at Steel Rigg offers easy access to the nearby Once Brewed youth hostel and also the opportunity for a detour to Vindolanda, a fort that actually dates back to 85 AD and thus predates the building of the Wall, and contains some extremely interesting excavations including documents written in ink on wooden tablets.

Housesteads to Steel Rigg

Although the provision of stone steps reduces the harshness of some of the descents and ascents, the whole of the walk from Housesteads is still hard work, but it is fantastically rewarding, as the Wall remains with you much of the way, and there are superb views to Crag Lough immediately below the cliffs on which the Wall is built at Highshield Crags. One magical moment in the walk comes at Sycamore Gap between Highshield Crags and Steel Rigg; the sight of this very handsome tree, nestling in the narrow valley between two monster hillsides, will soften the heart of any walker who is cursing his decision to spurn the chance of an extra Mars Bar at Housesteads.

Steel Rigg to Walton (16.3 miles) via Greenhead

ENJOY: Windshields Crags, Aesica, Walltown Crags, Thirlwall Castle, Gilsland, Birdoswald

Proceed westwards from the road at Steel Rigg, and now climb onto Windshields Crags, arriving at the summit of the path at well over 1000 ft above sea level. Tremendous walking now follows, the Wall remaining beside you, as you descend steeply to another road then climb onto Cawfield Crags. Slight anticlimax sets in as you descend to a lake which stands on the site of old quarry workings.

Beyond the lake is a road, and by turning left down the road you will come to the B6318 and a most welcome roadside pub, though it has to be said that at the time I patronised it it appeared to cater more for the well-heeled customer than for walkers. The national trail goes over the road and forward to the site of Aesica or Great Chesters fort, which includes the only original altar still surviving in situ on the Wall. Beyond Aesica is a section which could be quite soul-sapping at the end of a long day, through rough moorland with none of the glorious craggy scenery you have been enjoying, and a lot of rather demanding uphill work. Some traces of the Wall or its ditch can be seen, but there is none of the interest of the previous section. However, all that changes when beyond a farm track crossing you embark on a promenade over Walltown Crags; seemingly from nowhere you find yourself enjoying more of the same delectable fare of a few miles back, with another great section of Wall to enjoy and fabulous views. The course of the national trail is not obvious and the best advice is to aim for the highest ground, thus giving you the best views.

You descend to another old quarry, which has been converted into an attractive country park – you may be lucky enough to find a drink or ice cream here – and a little way from the park, just off route, is the fort of Carvoran and the Roman Army Museum with illustrations of all aspects of life as a soldier on Hadrian's Wall. Then it is straightforward quick walking down to Holmhead and the magnificent ruin of the fourteenth-century Thirlwall Castle, most of the building material of which was taken from Hadrian's Wall. A short distance to the south of Holmhead, where incidentally the overlap with the Pennine Way ends, is Greenhead (48.7), which boasts a youth hostel in a converted chapel.

Visitors' books

I stayed at a bunkhouse in Holmhead and found unlikely entertainment in the visitors' book and a lengthy somewhat adverse comment therein about the standard of accommodation provided, provoking the owner of the establishment into an even more verbose spiel defending herself against the various accusations. Visitors' books can provide much amusement to subsequent signatories, although it is perhaps wise for the traveller not to use it as an opportunity for boasting about the great effort that brought him here, for fear that his assertion that he is over halfway across Hadrian's Wall may be topped by the walker attempting his 80th journey up the Pennine Way, or the sad masochistic soul who has just accomplished his 838th mile across England wearing nothing but swimming trunks and flipflops and pushing a pram loaded with the complete leatherbound works of William Shakespeare.

Between Thirlwall Castle and Gilsland the walking is comparatively uninteresting, although railway buffs will enjoy their first encounter with the Newcastle–Carlisle railway line since viewing it across the Tyne near Ryton many miles back. The initial walking is disappointingly fiddly for anyone wanting to get a few quick miles under their belt after a Greenhead youth hostel breakfast, but at Gilsland things really perk up again: the village itself, at one time developed as a spa, is most attractive and there is a fine section of walking close to the railway and past the remains of another milecastle. Once beyond Gilsland you can enjoy a lovely walk through the valley of the River Irthing beside another fine section of Wall, then after a brisk climb you reach the Roman fort of Birdoswald, with its hilltop setting providing an ideal defensive position. Now dominated by a nineteenth-century tower built in the style of the much older tower, its most interesting features are the gateways; there is also an extremely good museum and visitor centre, and the fort's situation is magnificent, with beautiful views across the surrounding countryside.

Now the going becomes quicker as you make progress westwards and indeed from here you enjoy a really good fast section of hilltop walking, close to and parallel with a section of Wall that was constructed of turf and known as the Turf Wall. You cross the Wall Burn and then after a short walk through woodland, you embark on an equally swift section of walking beside the hilltop road. Shortly you reach the Pike Hill Signal Station which pre-dates the Wall – it is worth pausing here to enjoy the view as there is nothing quite as good as this to come – and from here it is a short roadside walk to the charming albeit amenity-less hamlet of Banks. You ascend from the village and now enjoy an agreeable march westwards through farmland with the extensive Walton Wood to your right, at length arriving at a metalled road.

At the time of writing the trail follows the quiet road to the village of Walton (58.4). Although the trail opened in 2003 this short section has still not been finalised.

Walton to Carlisle (11.1 miles) via Crosby-on-Eden

ENJOY: Crosby-on-Eden, Eden river walk, Carlisle

Having had a well-earned drink at the pub at Walton, assuming it's open, you now head for Carlisle, proceeding resolutely south-westwards. Almost at once you pass through a beautiful wood, then keeping close to the line of the Wall, go forward to the equally picturesque Cam Beck and on through unspoilt farmland to the sprawling and sadly unmemorable village of Newtown. There follows one of the least inspiring sections of the whole walk, relieved only by the sight of some earthworks near the hamlet of Bleatarn; you are still walking in the steps of the Romans, the path following the line of the Wall with the ditch to the right, but gone is the magical scenery. The surroundings are quite uninteresting and it is a relief when at last you are directed just east of south along Sandy Lane, cross over the A689 by means of a footbridge, and then head westwards along the line of the old Roman road Stanegate, past the fine Crosby Mansion and very handsome church, to reach the centre of Crosby-on-Eden. There is a pub here, The Stag, which will be particularly welcome if you have been tramping non-stop from Greenhead or Gilsland, and turning left off the village street, you are directed down to the beautiful River Eden, a nice surprise after the somewhat nondescript scenery of the last few miles.

A very attractive riverside walk follows, but all too soon you are forced away from the river and as the Eden turns resolutely southwards you are directed westwards to the village of Linstock. The village boasts a castle that is actually one of the pele-towers to which families retreated for safety when threatened by border raids, but there are no amenities to speak of, and the course of the Wall is now some way to the north-west (your right). Beyond Linstock there is a long road trudge, only enlivened by the bridge crossing of the M6 and the pretty village of Rickerby with a folly consisting of an isolated tower in a field to the right of the road. Just beyond Rickerby you enter a park, now on the edge of Carlisle, and find yourself united with the Eden beside which you proceed all the way to the centre of the city; in due course you arrive at a bridge carrying a road across the Eden, and this is the best place to leave the route if you wish to sample Carlisle's ample amenities.

Carlisle

Carlisle (69.5), situated just a few miles from the Scottish border, has an unsurprisingly chequered history. Known by the Romans as Luguvalium, this settlement was raided by the Picts and Scottish tribes; much later, in 1092, William Rufus built a castle here as a stronghold against the Scots but on three separate occasions during subsequent centuries the Scots gained control of the city. The castle has been restored and is one of the town's principal attractions, but there are many other things of interest to see including the medieval walls, the fourteenth-century Guildhall, a Jacobean mansion named Tullie House which is now a museum, and a cathedral which dates back to 1123 and boasts a splendid Early English choir.

Carlisle would in many ways be a splendid place for your walk to end. Instead, the walker is still faced with nearly 15 miles to go and could in fact be forgiven for deciding to give them a miss, especially when told that most of the walking is trudging along the flat, there is very little of the Wall to see, and buses back to civilisation from the end of the route are scarce. Oh yes – and part of the route could be submerged at high tide.

Carlisle to Bowness-on-Solway (14.7 miles) via Beaumont, Burgh-by-Sands

ENJOY: Burgh-by-Sands, Solway Firth

The final leg of the national trail begins with another promenade beside the river Eden, and with the city's castle close by, the surroundings are agreeable enough. Soon you pass beneath the main London to Glasgow railway line and continue past a sewage works and power station, but thankfully the surroundings improve and the riverside walking becomes more enjoyable, with some up and down work in the shade of trees, culminating in the pretty village of Grinsdale. Here you leave the river and strike out across farmland; as you walk you are, believe it or not, still following the line of the Wall, with the Vallum discernible to your left, but it all seems an eternity away from Sycamore Gap and Walltown Crags. You climb onto a bank which affords good views of your surroundings, then descend to the next village, Kirkandrews-on-Eden, just beyond which you are reunited with the riverside.

A peaceful riverside ramble follows, and although it seems a shame to be signposted shortly away from the river, you are rewarded with the very pretty village of Beaumont with a part-Norman church built on a mound from which the village gets its name. Then comes another tramp of about a mile and a half through farmland towards Burgh-by-Sands, along an obvious path through fields; ironically the national trail here overlaps with the

Cumbrian Coastal Way although you are not following the coast or even the river at this point! On a hot day this may seem quite a laborious piece of walking and you may be tempted to drink from the refreshing-looking waters of Powburgh Beck which is crossed just before Burgh-by-Sands is reached. It is probably not a good idea to do what I did, and yield to that temptation, however thirsty you may feel; the discomfiture you might experience at having to knock on a local resident's house to fill a water bottle wondering whether you will initially be mistaken for a burglar, meter reader or Maltese timeshare apartment salesman is probably preferable to the fear, as you nurse a violent upset stomach the following day, of how much chemical waste, cattle effluent and raw household sewage has found its way into your digestive system.

Burgh-by-Sands is a very long straggly village and the start of a lengthy road walk in a westerly direction. You pass the splendid twelfth-century village church which was built on the site of the old Roman fort of Aballava, incorporated Roman stones into its structure, and has a particularly impressive fourteenth-century fortified tower. However after continuing along the main street past attractive old houses, and striking out into the countryside again, the surroundings becomes uninspiring with no real evidence of the Wall or the Vallum, the course of both of which lie to your right. Meanwhile, the Eden has, well to the north of Burgh-by-Sands, flowed into the Solway Firth which separates the northern reaches of Cumbria from south-west Scotland. You carry on along the road and pass a road junction immediately north of the village of Longburgh, but could now find yourself in difficulty. The route continues westwards along a road through the saltmarshes immediately south of the Solway Firth to the next village of Drumburgh, and it is susceptible to flooding where high tides combine with adverse winds; it is not a problem that occurs frequently, but when it does, it will render the road impassable, and it is best to check with the Tourist Information office before you set out.

Assuming the way ahead is clear and dry, you are encouraged to continue along the edge of the road rather than along the parallel grassy bank; this is in the interests of preserving the bird ecology of the Solway Marshes, a Site of Special Scientific Interest. It is a good two and a half mile walk from the Longburgh junction to Drumburgh and although they are fast miles they are hardly breathtaking ones; the interest is to be provided to your left, with great views to the northern Lakeland mountains, dominated by the easily recognisable Skiddaw. Drumburgh is not entirely without interest – it actually boasts a fortified house known as Drumburgh Castle with altar stones from a Roman temple as garden ornaments – and it is here that your road trudge ends, for the path planners have mercifully directed the national trail along the Cumbria Coastal Way in a south-westerly direction, and then north-westwards towards Glasson along paths through farmland.

Glasson is a straggly village but has what could be a life-saving pub, then for a time it is back to farmland tramping along the line of the Vallum, so at least you can feel there is some focus to your footslogging. You then cross over the coast road that you last saw at Drumburgh, and now head towards the Solway Firth beside which you walk for roughly half a mile as far as Port Carlisle, which has another pub and also a most useful path-side teahouse. Somwhat anticlimactically you are now forced onto the coast road again, drifting slightly away from the waterside and the course of the Wall and Vallum further inland still, but soon the road returns to the water's edge and you can enjoy beautiful views across the Firth to southern Scotland as you approach your final destination, Bowness-on-Solway. Though the Roman defensive system extended further alongside the Firth to what is now Maryport it is here, at Bowness-on-Solway, that the Roman wall ended, albeit there is no trace of the Wall to be found today – the sea has seen to that. However, the official end of the path (84.2) is attractive indeed, in a landscaped area immediately above the sea, and the village itself, developed within an old fort, is charming.

At the time of writing a bus, numbered AD122 for hopefully obvious reasons, runs daily during the summer months from Bowness-on-Solway all the way to Newcastle, taking a route that incorporates many of the sights you will have enjoyed during your national trail walk and reuniting you with your sometime bosom pal: what else but the B6318.

The Coast to Coast Walk

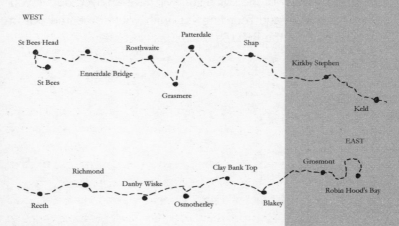

WEST

St Bees Head

St Bees

Ennerdale Bridge

Rosthwaite

Patterdale

Grasmere

Shap

Kirkby Stephen

Keld

EAST

Grosmont

Robin Hood's Bay

Richmond

Danby Wiske

Clay Bank Top

Reeth

Osmotherley

Blakey

Designation: None.
Length: 191 miles.
Start: St Bees, Cumbria.
Finish: Robin Hood's Bay, North Yorkshire.
Nature: Wainwright's classic walk across
Northern England from coast to coast,
including sections of the Lake District, the
Pennines, the Yorkshire Dales and the North
York Moors.
Difficulty rating: Strenuous, occasionally
severe.
Average time of completion: 12–14 days.

Whilst many long-distance footpaths owe their
origins to a group of enthusiasts, the Coast to

**HIGHLIGHTS OF
THIS WALK:**
- **Haystacks**
- **Borrowdale**
- **Helm Crag**
- **Helvellyn**
- **Kidsty Pike**
- **Nine Standards**
- **Keld**
- **Richmond**
- **Hasty Bank**
- **Robin Hood's Ba**

The Coast to Coast Walk

Coast Walk is without question the brainchild of a single individual, Alfred Wainwright, whose beautifully-illustrated guides to the Lakeland fells have become bestsellers amongst walkers and visitors to the Lake District. Having failed to enjoy his walk up the Pennine Way – at that time the only 'official' long-distance route in existence in England – he set about creating his very own long-distance route over kinder terrain. His stipulations were that it should be in the north of England, with which he was already familiar, and should have a definite start and finish point, thus providing a worthy objective for the walker whichever way he went. By drawing a line on a map between St Bees Head, one of the most spectacular points on the west coast, and the attractive village of Robin Hood's Bay on the same latitude on the east coast, he not only succeeded in meeting his requirements but found a route that contained what he believed to be some of the finest scenery in Britain. He finished the planning in 1972 and published a book describing the route in 1973. Although he expressed a hope that his planned path would avoid trespass or invasion of privacy, certain sections were found to cross land on which there was no public right of way, with the result that the many walkers who decided to follow his route were in fact trespassing in some areas! Where this happened, the National Park Authorities and other similar organisations were able to work together to re-route the walk over the nearest public rights of way, or arrange with landowners that Wainwright's original route could continue on a permissive basis.

Wainwright was at pains to point out that his chosen route (which in any event incorporated a choice of paths at many points) was in no way the definitive crossing from coast to coast. Moreover, at the time of writing there is no sign of the Coast to Coast being accorded national trail status. The fact remains, however, that his route has been adopted by a vast number of walkers, and although it is a challenging, demanding walk that requires physical fitness, proper equipment and good navigational skills, it is walked considerably more than many national trails. It is now one of the most popular routes in Britain, beloved of walkers for its completely unspoilt scenery of tremendous beauty (it passes through three National Parks), immense historical interest, and great variety of terrain, animal life and plant life. It should be borne in mind, however, that waymarking is very sketchy in places.

St Bees to Ennerdale Bridge (14 miles) via Cleator

ENJOY: St Bees, Fleswick Bay, Dent Fell, Nannycatch Beck

St Bees is a most attractive village from which to begin the walk; the Priory Church, built on the site of a seventh-century nunnery, has some features which date back to 1150 and there is a grammar school dating back to 1583. From the village centre it is a pleasant walk down the lane to the sea wall where the journey across England begins, and Wainwright suggests that as an opening ritual, walkers should dip their boots in the Irish Sea before getting going. There follows a splendid four-mile cliff walk, heading initially (and perhaps incongruously) slightly west of north, following the clifftops for the most part and dropping down just once to the beautiful rock scenery of Fleswick Bay before rising again. The cliffs themselves, huge stacks of red sandstone, are magnificent and there are excellent views northwards to Whitehaven and beyond, and seawards to the Isle of Man.

Once past St Bees Head and lighthouse, you swing round to the east and then leave the cliffs above Saltom Bay, bidding farewell to the sea for another ten days at least. The route heads south-eastwards along well-defined tracks to the pretty village of Sandwith, but after leaving Sandwith there follows a rather fiddly four and a half miles, all the time heading south-east. You continue along narrow tracks, crossing two roads linking Whitehaven with St Bees, then descend and trudge across fields to pass under the Carlisle–Barrow railway close to Stanley Pond. You join another lane to climb out of the valley, cross the busy A595, and go on to reach Moor Row, half a mile east, by road and cycle track. An alternative route bypasses Moor Row to its north and east using a cycleway. You follow the Egremont road, heading southwards, out of Moor Row before turning left, heading south-eastwards, joining a lane to reach Cleator (9). Turning left briefly along the A5086, you soon turn right to exit from this nondescript village of dull grey stone, descending to Blackhow Bridge and then following a lane to Blackhow Farm. The walking improves with a stiff climb to the 1,131 ft summit of Dent Fell, giving splendid views to the Isle of Man and to some of the Lakeland fells.

Still heading east, the route drops south-eastwards from the summit to a forest known as the Uldale Plantation, then emerges and drops steeply down to the valley. It then turns sharply north-eastwards past the delightful ravine of Nannycatch Gate, with the slopes of Raven Crag and Flat Fell immediately to the left. You continue beside Nannycatch Beck, the valley narrowing as Flat Fell Screes are passed, and climb to a road beside the Kinniside Stone Circle, of recent rather than prehistoric origin. It is then a simple walk alongside the road, heading north, to the pretty village of Ennerdale Bridge (14), the gateway to Lakeland. This first section is reasonably easy and you should therefore arrive at Ennerdale still feeling fresh and excited about the challenges ahead.

Ennerdale Bridge to Rosthwaite (14 miles) via Black Sail

ENJOY: Ennerdale Water, Black Sail Hut, Grey Knotts, Borrowdale (optional: High Stile, Haystacks)

Leaving Ennerdale, you initially follow roads then a path leading you to Ennerdale Water and a lovely path walk along the southern shore. The going, on a rocky path, is quite rough, particularly as you negotiate the promontory known as Angler's Crag and pass a small headland known as Robin Hood's Chair. After passing through an area of woodland you reach the eastern shore of the lake, and from there the route proceeds briefly north-eastwards through fields to reach a forest road. The going is then extremely easy, as the route continues south-eastwards along the road for four miles or so, past Low and High Gillerthwaite and through the massed conifers of Ennerdale Forest roughly parallel with the River Liza. Gaps in the trees reveal superb views to Pillar and the awesome Pillar Rock on the right.

You leave the forest road almost immediately south of Wainwright's beloved mountain Haystacks, proceeding to that remotest and most romantic of youth hostels, Black Sail Hut (23). Beyond Black Sail Hut, you must be careful not to get sucked down to the valley bottom again but instead contour the hillside immediately beyond the hostel, there being no footpath to speak of. Eventually you reach and ford Loft Beck, then turn left to go parallel with it, following a recently improved path very steeply uphill. This is the sternest climb yet, and good preparation for tough work ahead. As you pause for breath, you should look back to the magnificent valley you are leaving behind, with Great Gable, Brandreth and Pillar soaring up beyond. Eventually the ground levels out, and you reach a metal post marking the former Brandreth Fence. If you felt very energetic you could leave the main route just beyond High Gillerthwaite, turning left and climbing to the summit of Red Pike, then continuing south-eastwards along a magnificent ridge of mountains including High Stile, High Crag and Haystacks. Passing the delectable Innominate Tarn, the alternative way continues in the same direction to the head of Loft Beck, here meeting the main route. Heading north-eastwards, the route then contours the hillside topped by Grey Knotts at a height of just under 2,000 ft. The views are spellbinding, including the twin lakes of Buttermere and Crummock Water, beyond which Grasmoor is clearly visible. On a clear sunny day it is a place to linger, and the binoculars should be kept handy for sightings of golden eagles and peregrines.

Proceeding onwards, the route meets the Honister–Great Gable footpath and drops to an old tramway (*not* going forward to the old quarry road), turning right and heading due east downhill, initially gently and then precipitously. At length it emerges at the youth hostel and old quarry sheds at the head of Honister Pass on the B5289. You briefly join the road but soon forsake it to follow either along or beside an old toll road. In due course you leave it, negotiating a crude hairpin bend to drop down to Borrowdale and the pleasant and popular village of Seatoller. Turning left to proceed through the village car park, you join an attractive path that snakes through Johnny's Wood, with the River Derwent now visible to the right; the going becomes rough and a chain is provided at one point to negotiate an area of rocks. Soon after passing Longthwaite Youth Hostel, the Derwent is crossed and it is then a simple field walk northwards to reach Rosthwaite (28), the principal settlement of Borrowdale which is one of the loveliest parts of Lakeland with its green fields, attractive stone villages, a fine river leading to Derwent Water, and of course its mountain backcloth. After your day's adventures you'll feel you've earned your overnight rest here, and can permit yourself just a touch of schadenfreude from motorists you see struggling to find parking space in the village for their cars, people-carriers and caravans. Borrowdale is a magical place and the walker with time to spare may wish to enjoy the luxury of a bus ride to Keswick and back through the dale before continuing.

Rosthwaite to Patterdale (18 miles) via Grasmere

ENJOY: Stonethwaite, Lining Crag, Helm Crag, Grasmere, Tongue Gill, Grisedale Tarn, Brothers' Parting (optional: Helvellyn, Striding Edge)

From Rosthwaite you follow a well-defined path that heads south-eastwards, heading for Lining Crag and ultimately Grasmere. The going, past the delightful hamlet of Stonethwaite and alongside firstly Stonethwaite Beck and then Greenup Gill, is easy at first, but as you approach and pass Eagle Crag, the gradient becomes stiffer. You will find pauses for breath become more and more necessary, but as you rest you can admire the view back to Borrowdale, a sight of bewitching beauty. There is a steep scramble up on to Lining Crag, where hands as well as feet are necessary to make progress, but the reward is a stunning view to the northern end of the Lake District, including Bassenthwaite Lake and Skiddaw.

The path becomes indistinct now, the direction only marginally east of south, as you cross a marshy area and pass the summit of Greenup Edge, marked by an iron stanchion. On a clear day the way ahead is obvious, a clear path being seen to head south-eastwards down the hillside to the head of Far Easedale Gill, with the prospect of Grasmere and its verdant surrounds beyond. If the summit of the pass is blanketed in mist, then unless you are skilled in compass reading (and have a compass to hand), you must rely on intelligent guesswork. After a rough descent to the head of the gill, Wainwright's recommended route turns to climb on to the ridge immediately to the left, and proceeds to Grasmere via the ridge. The alternative is a straightforward descent on a path beside Far Easedale Gill, which is the obvious bad weather route. The ridge walk encompasses three mini-peaks, namely Calf Crag, Gibson Knott and finally Helm Crag; the going is not always easy, the path well-defined but weaving sinuously through the areas of grass and rock. The views are spectacular, and include Helvellyn, the Langdale Pikes, the long ribbon of water that is Lake Windermere, and even the sea. Of the three peaks on the ridge, Helm Crag is the noblest, with its intriguing and grotesque rock formations; indeed its summit rocks have been likened by some to a lady playing the organ! There is a very steep descent southwards from Helm Crag into the valley to reach the path following the alternative route, and this in turn joins a road which leads into Grasmere (38). One of the major tourist spots in Lakeland, Grasmere is most famous for gingerbread, the annual August sports, and of course Dove Cottage, the home of William Wordsworth at the start of the nineteenth century. It is also a most useful place for replenishing supplies before heading resolutely north-eastwards towards Patterdale.

Leaving Grasmere you use minor roads to go forward past the youth hostel to the A591, crossing it and following a clear path ahead to embark on the Grisedale pass route. The going is gentle at first, but below Great Tongue you have a choice between a long steady ascent or a shorter sharper one. The former is by way of path to the right of Great Tongue, alongside Tongue Gill and its impressive cascades. The latter proceeds to the left of Great Tongue, up an extremely steep grassy path running alongside Little Tongue Gill, then above a fringe of rocks the path levels out and swings to the right to meet the other path. Both then go forward to the summit of the pass, through a mass of rocks and boulders with the summit of Seat Sandal to the left and Fairfield to the right. The summit brings with it an immediate view to the hitherto invisible Grisedale Tarn, the route proceeding along the right side of it to the base of Tarn Crag. Nearby is a rock known as Brothers Parting, where William Wordsworth said a last farewell to his brother John, the event being commemorated by verses on a tablet affixed to the rock.

From here the approved route proceeds easily and unerringly downhill through Grisedale, keeping Grisedale Beck below and to the right, with glorious views to Ullswater ahead. There is an alternative path along the right-hand side of the beck which may be preferable in bad weather. You go forward to join a road briefly, then strike out south-eastwards on a path which heads into the delightful Glenamara Park, veering north-eastwards to reach Patterdale (46). One other possible route from Grisedale Tarn to Patterdale for energetic walkers with time and the weather on their side is as follows. Turn left by the tarn, ascending to skirt the 2,810 ft summit of Dollywaggon Pike and then proceeding onwards to the summit of Helvellyn, one of Lakeland's Big Four at a summit of 3,118 ft. It is then necessary to walk along the rocky ridge of Striding Edge, one of the most spectacular walks in the country, before dropping gradually to Grisedale to meet the main route and go forward with it into Glenamara Park. On a clear day this latter alternative will be a tempting proposition indeed, with magnificent views across huge areas of Lakeland and beyond. On a wet or misty day you will simply be mightily relieved to have made it to Patterdale even using the main route.

Patterdale to Shap (16 miles) via Haweswater Reservoir

ENJOY: The Knott, Rampsgill Head, Kidsty Pike, Whelter Beck, Shap Abbey

Having crossed over the A592 in Patterdale, you climb at first gently then arduously southeastwards along Boardale Hause. Having taken care to fork on to the right hand path, you continue to climb steeply and it is a relief when the path levels out to provide magnificent views back to Helvellyn, Patterdale and Brothers Water. There follows an exciting high level walk on an excellent path, reaching two forking paths at the head of Dubhow Beck and taking the lower of two. Soon the path swings round the northern end of Angle Tarn, a useful landmark in mist, and proceeds boggily but clearly by the eastern side of the tarn, rising slightly to Satura Crag. Here it is important not to veer eastwards on to Rest Dodd; the correct route, heading south-east all the time, stays close to a wall, descending slightly and then rising steeply towards the Knott, the ground still extremely juicy.

The route aims for the Knott's eastern shoulder, the ground eventually levelling out and the going underfoot becoming clearer. Magnificent walking follows, with the summit of Rampsgill Head immediately to the east, and the 2,718 ft summit of High Street straight ahead. The Coast to Coast does not make the climb to this fine peak, but at Twopenny Crag turns left and there is then a tremendous ridge march to Kidsty Pike, its summit clearly visible at the ridge end. To the right, and separating Kidsty Pike from High Street, is the great ravine of Riggindale. The arrival at the 2,560 ft Kidsty Pike (52) marks a key moment on the walk; this is the highest point on the whole route, the last point which offers a grandstand view of Lakeland, and the beginning of the end of your association – on this trip – with the Lake District. On a clear day the views are magnificent, with many major Lakeland peaks including Hevellyn, Pillar, Coniston Old Man and Blencathra on show.

Progress eastwards down to Haweswater Reservoir looks straightforward on the map, but the descent, after an easy start, is extremely steep; there are numerous drops requiring the use of hands as well as feet, if limbs are to survive intact. Eventually you reach the waterside and turn left to follow an excellent path by the west shore. After a brief climb to Birks Crag – the site of an old fort – and descent again, the going is very quick, with delightful surroundings including pleasant woodland and the impressive crossing of Whelter Beck. Eventually the steep hillsides to the left relent somewhat, and the path drops down to a road where you turn left. Soon you reach the hamlet of Burn Banks then turn right along a path to reach a road crossing of Haweswater Beck. You cross to follow a path on the south side of the beck, heading eastwards, then forsake the beck, continuing eastwards; from here you swing first south-eastwards to pass Rawhead, then cross a metalled road and swing north-eastwards to descend over common land to the pretty Lowther river bridge at Rosgill.

From here you take a path that passes near to the confluence of the Lowther and Swindale Beck, heading southwards to pass the farm at Good Croft and then crossing Swindale Beck by means of a charming packhorse bridge. A field path heading south-eastwards takes you uphill to a metalled road, and you briefly join it, shortly turning left again and walking downhill through a field – still heading south-east – to reach the imposing ruins of Shap Abbey, which dates back to the twelfth century. Having endured a few miles of fiddly route-finding, you will be relieved to join a metalled road leading to the village of Shap (62) in just over a mile. At the end of this road, you turn right on to the main street (the A6 in fact) and into the village centre. Before the advent of the M6 the village served as a useful stop for motorists, as reflected by its wide range of amenities, but it now has the feel of a quiet backwater. Although there are good views back towards Lakeland, the pointed peak of Kidsty Pike being particularly prominent, it has little of architectural merit, the seventeenth-century market hall being the only building of real note in the village. It is remarkable however, for the length of its main street which may hold some interest for students of local history and planning policy, but rather less fascination for the weary walker who, having walked all the way to the very bottom of the village in search of his night's lodgings, finds them to be situated at the very top.

Shap to Kirkby Stephen (22 miles) via Mazon Wath

ENJOY: Robin Hood's Grave, Orton, Severals, Smardale Bridge, Giants' Graves, Kirkby Stephen

This section involves much easier walking over the limestone-rich Westmorland Plateau, but with a constant view to the fells, most notably the Howgills ahead and to the right. You leave Shap by means of a road heading eastwards off the main street opposite the King's Arms; soon you cross the main London–Glasgow railway, then strike south-eastwards, first along a lane, then a succession of field paths and tracks to the tiny hamlet of Oddendale, crossing a footbridge over the M6 and then passing a limestone quarry. At Oddendale the route swings southwards, going just to the east of a stone circle, then shortly after passing the walled enclosure and barn known as Potrigg, there is a left turn and you head in a more south-easterly direction again. There follows a fine moorland walk along the side of Crosby Ravensworth Fell, the route well waymarked as it crosses an old Roman road and Lyvennet Beck and proceeds without difficulty to the Orton–Crosby Ravensworth road.

There are two mini-valley crossings; at the second, a short detour to the right brings you to an ancient cairn described inaccurately as Robin Hood's Grave. On arriving at the road you could, if pushed for time, simply turn right and proceed to the cattle grid where there is a junction with the B6260 coming down from Appleby. However, Wainwright's recommended route involves crossing the first road and following a path that swings in a southerly direction to run between the two roads along a dry valley bottom, to reach the road junction. The approved route now heads west of south to reach Orton before swinging eastwards to follow the B6260 then leaving it to arrive at Knott Lane via a field path. Orton is the only settlement of any size near the route between Shap and Kirkby Stephen; it is a charming village with tidy terraces of old cottages, a field serving as a village green with streams crossed by many little bridges, a church with a fine tower, and a former manor house built in the seventeenth century. If you prefer to take a short cut round Orton, an alternative route leads south-eastwards off the approved route shortly beyond the B6260 through a field to the east of Broadfell Farm, turning left on to a drive and left again on to a metalled lane which passes three more farms. Just beyond the last, a left turn takes you along a path to Knott Lane(where the approved route is rejoined. Go straight over to pass to the left of a prehistoric stone circle and across fields, heading east, to the farm at Acres; here you bear left, following a lane past the farms of Sunbiggin and Stoneyhead Hall, and going out on to Tarn Moor. You meet two crossroads of paths in close succession, turning right at each and proceeding downhill to turn left on to a road and pass Sunbiggin Tarn, a favoured spot for waterfowl. You bear right onto a road and shortly left to bear southwards then south-eastwards along a path across Ravenstonedale Moor, arriving at a road and bearing left then shortly right to join a path going eastwards to Ewefell Mire.

You go forward across Ewefell Mire (which is not as bad as it sounds) and past Bents Farm, then beside Bents Hill and past the prehistoric village settlement of Severals, of which there are few obvious traces. There is then an unexpectedly steep descent towards Scandal Beck, the path turning south-westwards to drop down to cross it by means of the charming Smardale Bridge. Veering eastwards and then north-eastwards, the route initially follows a cart-track heading uphill, with fine views to an old railway viaduct. You should look out for the long mounds to the left of this section, known as Giants' Graves; they are not graves of giants, nor are they thought to be burial mounds. One theory is that they were platforms used for stacking bracken, another that they were coney-beds or rabbit warrens. You continue on a clear path, heading north-eastwards and steadily uphill across the moorland of Smardale Fell and Limekiln Hill; the rewards for your efforts are your first views to the Eden valley, a sign that Kirkby Stephen is not far off. Continuing in a predominantly north-easterly direction, and using a mixture of roads and paths, you now head downhill to pass underneath the Settle to Carlisle Railway. Just to the right of the path, immediately beyond the underpass, are traces of the earthworks of another prehistoric settlement.

Rather bitty but undemanding field-walking then follows, the route heading north-east and downhill to pass under two disused railways towards the Green Riggs Farm buildings. Here you join a lane that leads to the first of just two towns on the route, Kirkby Stephen (84), the lane emerging by the main street.

Kirkby Stephen

Kirkby Stephen is an attractive town, with several Georgian houses including Winton Hall, built in 1726, and a thirteenth-century church dedicated to St Stephen, approached through a stone portico built in 1810 by a naval purser, John Waller. The church contains a stone carving of the Norse devil Loki, thought to be one of the earliest Christian symbols of the Devil in human shape. The town has a wide range of amenities (viewers of Wainwright's TV series about the route may remember his tucking into a generous fish supper at the town's Coast To Coast fish and chip shop!) and is a most welcome halt on the journey.

Kirkby Stephen to Keld (12 miles) via Hartley

ENJOY: Nine Standards, Wain Wath Force, Keld, Swaledale

Having loaded the rucksack with provisions – there are no shops on or near the route for the next 23 miles – you leave Kirkby Stephen, bound for the halfway mark of the Coast to Coast at Keld, by following an alleyway off the marketplace down to cross Frank's Bridge over the river Eden. There follows a pleasant riverside walk eastwards, keeping the river to the right, and from here it is easy walking gently uphill through a field, still heading east, and then along a lane to the pretty village of Hartley. You cross a stream and reach a metalled road, turning right on to the road and following it uphill for just over two miles, past the somewhat unsightly Hartley Quarries. The going is extremely easy and it is good to get two quick miles under the belt before the real hard work begins.

Soon after passing Fell House Farm and crossing Hartley Beck, the metalled road peters out, giving way to an unmetalled track heading south-east past sheep pens. There follows a splendid march along an excellent track on to Hartley Fell, the views getting better all the time. The next objective is the conquest of the distinctive Nine Standards summit cairns which are now excitingly visible ahead. Some guidebooks may direct you to opt for one of a choice of routes now, depending on the time of year, with a view to minimising erosion in the area. The suggestion is that winter and early spring walkers miss the Nine Standards altogether, heading along footpaths first south-eastwards then south-westwards past the Tailbrigg pot holes, a section of the B6270, and then a track and path beside the left bank of Ney Gill. Walkers at other times may (it is suggested) proceed straight uphill along a very good path to reach the Nine Standards cairns, providing tremendous views particularly across the Eden Valley. After an exhilarating high level march via Nine Standards Rigg to White Mossy Hill, the choice is then (according to the season) between a south-easterly descent via Coldbergh Edge to the track/path leading to Ney Gill, or a steep often squelchy downhill trudge via Whitsundale Beck to arrive at Ney Gill. All that said, your choice may be dictated by the prevailing conditions, and nobody could blame you for opting for the winter route if bad weather rendered the ascent to Nine Standards both arduous and, in terms of likely views from the top, unrewarding.

The route fords Ney Gill soon after the reuniting of the three 'strands', and then continues eastwards to reach a narrow metalled road, turning left on to it to reach the farm at Raven Seat. After crossing Whitsundale Beck, you join a path which for the next couple of miles heads south-eastwards along the hillside, with splendid views to the beck on the right as it passes through a deep ravine. Having negotiated walled pastures just beyond Raven Seat, the walking becomes more open as it passes the huge sheepfold called Eddy Fold and drops down to Smithy Holme Farm and on along a cart-track. As the track swings to the right to drop to the B6270, the route turns off left to run along a path parallel with that road while just over the river, which is to your left, are the impressive limestone cliffs known as Cotterby Scar. Looking down, a pretty waterfall called Wain Wath Force soon becomes visible.

At length you reach a road and you now keep to tarmac, including a portion of the B6270, to reach Keld (96), the halfway point on the Coast to Coast, and the point where it meets the Pennine Way. It is also the gateway to the Yorkshire Dales National Park. Keld consists of a small assembly of farm buildings and cottages, a hall and a chapel (rebuilt in 1860) all round or near a rustic square. Another chapel, a youth hostel and a few other buildings stand beside the B6270. The charm of the village lies not only in its pleasant buildings but also in its timelessness – the scene here has altered little in centuries – and, of course, its magnificent setting amongst Pennine fells beside the River Swale. Wainwright comments that, at Keld, there is always the music of the water, and proof of this can be found in no less than four fine waterfalls close by: not only Wain Wath Force but Catrake, Kisdon and East Gill Forces. Amenities are severely restricted; although there are a few bed and breakfasts as well as the youth hostel, there is no shop or pub in the village, and after the bustle of Kirkby Stephen the quietness and isolation is palpable. I selected a bed and breakfast a mile and a half north of the village (reached by following the Pennine Way) in the most unspoilt and timeless surroundings one could wish for, although to be fair this atmosphere was somewhat marred by the farm owner's teenage son who that evening whiled away a good two hours winning the Monaco Grand Prix and bringing about the bloody end of a ruthless serial killer by means of the PlayStation plugged into the television.

Keld to Reeth (11 miles) via Blakethwaite

ENJOY: East Gill Force, Crackpot Hall, Swinner Gill, Old Gang Smelt Mill

From Keld village square, a well-marked footpath heads south-eastwards, soon reaching another junction of paths where the route, now following the same course as the Pennine Way, turns left and drops down to cross the Swale. There is then a brief climb to a junction of paths with the beautiful waterfall of East Gill Force immediately to the right. The Pennine Way bears left to head towards the Tan Hill Inn, whilst the Coast to Coast turns right to cross the water and follows a clear track south-eastwards, with splendid views to the Swale. You now have a choice. The Wainwright-approved route takes the 'high road' to Reeth and this is described more fully below. If however you have fallen in love with the Swale and prefer a riverside route to Reeth, continue along the track which heads south-eastwards to be reunited with the river and remain close beside its left bank past the little village of Ivelet and on to Gunnerside, crossing the B6270 here; you then stay in or close to the valley, the Swale close by to your left. You pass but do not visit the villages of Feetham and Healaugh and continue all the way to Reeth, meeting the Wainwright-approved route here.

Wainwright's approved route across the moors and past the many old mineworkings of Upper Swaledale is as follows. You turn left off the clear track mentioned above and proceed past the ruins of the once handsome residence of Crackpot Hall; it is important to take the upper of two paths beyond the ruins, proceeding north-eastwards to reach a bridge over Swinner Gill.

Having crossed the Gill by the bridge, the route continues eastwards, going steeply uphill beside another stream known as East Grain, but the rough walking soon gives way to an excellent track heading eastwards across the moors. The moorland scenery within the Yorkshire Dales National Park, and its bird life, are magnificent, and you should keep your eyes peeled for kestrel, merlin, lapwing, curlew and golden plover. It is a shame to leave this track at the point that it swings southwards towards Gunnerside. The route heads north-eastwards steeply downhill through grass and heather on a path that is far from obvious on the ground, and again signposting cannot be guaranteed. You drop to Blakethwaite Smelt Mill where you'll certainly wish to pause to inspect the old workings, then swing sharply southwards onto a level green track before turning sharply northwards, rising steeply again.

Lead mines

The ruined smelting-mill here is just one of a number of old lead mine workings hereabouts, and several more reminders of the area's important industrial past will be seen in the next few miles. Many of the mines date back to the seventeenth or eighteenth centuries, but the industry collapsed at the end of the nineteenth century and farming has become the principal occupation in the area.

You then resume your predominantly eastward progression along a somewhat surreal landscape. As you do so, you will pass what are known as 'hushes' – ravines cut by mineral prospectors to enable water to strip the vegetation, thereby allowing the subsoil to be examined in the hope of finding a vein. You go by the Old Gang Mines and cross Flincher Gill to Level House Bridge, then veer in a more south-easterly direction. You pass the distinctive tower and other ruins of the Old Gang Smelt Mill and continue on to Surrender Bridge, where you meet a road. You go straight over the road and after passing another ruined smelt mill, head just north of east across a moor to negotiate the ravine of Cringley Bottom, dropping steeply to a beck and then rising equally precipitously. There are then three easy miles to Reeth along well-defined tracks heading south-eastwards and then eastwards across pastures, passing a number of farms. After the rugged moorland terrain, the surroundings now seem gentler as a gradual descent is made towards the Swale. At length, you join a narrow lane which heads south-eastwards more decisively downhill, joining the B6270 and turning left on to that road to enter Reeth (107) which is blessed with ample amenities for the visitor. Standing at the meeting point of Swaledale and the formerly industrial Arkengarthdale, and described as the capital of Upper Swaledale, the village consists of an assembly of grey stone houses round a large irregular green. The most difficult part of the Coast to Coast is now behind you.

Reeth to Bolton-on-Swale (19 miles) via Richmond

ENJOY: Marrick Priory Church, Marske, Whitcliffe Wood, Willance's Leap, Richmond, Easby Abbey

From Reeth, follow the B6270 briefly south-eastwards, bearing right across the meadows to cut a corner and join a riverbank. You cross the B6270 and proceed along a riverside path to a road onto which you turn right and which you follow for just over half a mile as far as Marrick priory church. The original priory, thought to be either Benedictine or Cistercian, was founded in the 1150s and the church was built in 1811 out of materials from the priory, although the walls of the former chancel remain outside the church. At the church you leave the road, and follow a good path north-eastwards through attractive woodland to reach the pretty village of Marrick. The path leads to a road that follows through the village, turning right on to a road just past a house with a most peculiar sundial.

You soon leave the road and for just under two miles proceed through a succession of fields, heading first downhill to the attractive cottage at Ellers and a charming bridge over Ellers Beck, then uphill to regain the Fremington–Marske road. Concentration is needed along this section, as the path is not clear on the ground and it is important to identify the stile or gate that will allow progress through to the next field. A useful marker is the 1814 monument to Matthew Hutton, a 60 ft obelisk just off route to the right not far from Hollins Farm beyond Ellers. Turning right on to the Fremington–Marske road, there is then a steep descent along the road to the lovely village of Marske, one of the prettiest on the whole route. The little church of St Edmund has a Norman doorway and some box pews; there is an eighteenth-century hall, a fifteenth-century bridge over Marske Beck, and several attractive stone cottages.

The Coast to Coast Walk

Ignoring the signposted Richmond road heading off to the right, you continue on the road uphill past the church, turning right at a T-junction of roads onto another Richmond-bound road. This is followed for just under half a mile, after which the route turns right on to a path heading north-east to cross Clapgate Beck. It then goes steeply uphill, still heading north-east, to an unusual white cairn marking the junction of the path and a farm track, immediately below the dramatic limestone cliffs of Applegarth Scar. You head eastwards then north-eastwards along the track past a succession of farms, all with Applegarth in the title; the track is indistinct in places and there are a few stiles to negotiate, but just past East Applegarth Farm you join a much clearer track, heading into Whitcliffe Wood. You pass the steep slopes of Whitcliffe Scar on the left, and observe on the hilltop the monument known as Willance's Leap, commemorating the remarkable deliverance of a horseman who fell from the spot whilst riding in 1606.

Having passed through Whitcliffe Wood, heading south-eastwards, the track emerges to give a magnificent view of Richmond and the surrounding countryside. It is then a very easy and satisfying walk on to Richmond, the track becoming a road which proceeds unerringly downhill to this beautiful and historic town, with the best range of amenities on the walk. Wainwright invites walkers to tidy themselves up a bit as they approach Richmond in the hope of meeting a 'sweet lass of Richmond Hill' or two, but after seven days' hard walking you may have long since passed caring about your personal appearance, and will settle for making yourselves sufficiently presentable to attend the town's chemist to be served much-needed additional supplies of blister pads.

Richmond

Richmond (119) is one of the most attractive towns in Yorkshire. It is dominated by the massive eleventh-century castle keep but there are many other notable buildings including the Georgian Theatre, one of the oldest in England, the medieval Holy Trinity Church which now houses the Green Howards' Regimental Museum, the fifteenth-century Greyfriars Gateway, and the eighteenth-century Culloden Tower in the 35-acre estate of Temple Lodge. The cobbled marketplace contains several fine eighteenth-century buildings including the Town Hall and the King's Head Hotel, and almost every street leading from the marketplace contains houses of historical interest.

The Coast to Coast Walk, taking whatever route through Richmond is desired, drops down to the fine eighteenth-century Richmond Bridge, crosses over and then turns left for a lovely walk beside the Swale, leaving the river as it curves to the left. You then proceed through a wood and past Priory Villas to reach the A6136. Beyond this road you have to join a lane leading past a sewage works, but there are good views over the Swale to the ruin of the twelfth-century Easby Abbey, described by Pevsner as one of the most picturesque monastic ruins in the county. The route then follows a grassy bank heading south to reach the river at a sharp bend, and there follows a most picturesque woodland walk close to the river, followed by some fiddly field walking south-eastwards past the ruin of Hagg Farm. Eventually you reach the pleasant village of Colburn, which contains a rebuilt Tudor mansion and separate Manor Hall. After passing along its main street the route uses a mixture of tracks and footpaths to head eastwards, with the Swale never far away to your left.

At length you drop steeply to pass underneath the very noisy A1 and then continuing beside the Swale to Catterick Bridge. The original bridge dates back to the fifteenth century although the medieval structure is hidden by refacing and widening. You cross the bridge and continue by means of a path along the north bank of the Swale, bearing left to the B6271 as the river bends sharply to the right. You turn right along the B6271 then first right down a lane and shortly left along another lane to reach Bolton-on-Swale (126), crossing straight over the B6271 and heading for the church with its large and imposing tower of pale pink sandstone. The churchyard has a remarkable commemorative obelisk to a local man named Henry Jenkins who, if the wording on a black slab in the church is to be believed, lived to be 169. Moreover, he is reputed to have swum across the Swale when he was 100!

Bolton-on-Swale to Osmotherley junction (16.5 miles) via Danby Wiske

ENJOY: Lazenby Hall, Arncliffe Hall, Mount Grace Priory, Osmotherley

Having continued on the road past the church, the route turns off to follow a pleasant course south-eastwards through fields along a path beside Bolton Beck, first on its west bank and then its east bank, to reach a road at the hamlet of Ellerton Hill. You turn left briefly onto the road, then right beside the buildings of Ellerton Hill and down to the B6271. Turn left to follow this road past the entrance to Kiplin Hall as far as a sharp right bend, where you turn left (effectively straight on) to leave the tarmac. Footpaths take you south-eastwards to bring you back to the B6271 which you don't in fact join; you turn sharp left here up a lane, bearing right to follow further paths to Brockholme Farm, turning right onto a lane and then left to follow field paths past High Brockholme. Eventually, you reach a T-junction with a road, bearing left to proceed to Danby Wiske (132). The route carries on into the village, which one has to say sounds more picturesque than it is, although there is an interesting church with a Norman doorway, an early fourteenth-century chancel, a thirteenth-century north arcade and an early fourteenth-century memorial effigy. East of the church is the probably seventeenth-century Lazenby Hall which is worth a look if time is not pressing. In his books about the route, Wainwright makes great play of the fact that when planning the route he looked forward to a pub meal here but all he could get to eat was a bag of crisps from a surly landlord, and it was thus with delight that he was able to inform his viewers in the TV series that meals here were now available. When I arrived at the pub one lunchtime in late March, however, I found it locked and deserted, so don't hold your breath. Beyond Danby Wiske you continue along the road in a vaguely easterly direction, crossing the main London–Edinburgh railway and bearing left onto field paths to reach the A167 at the hamlet of Oaktree Hill, the site of the Battle of the Standard between the English and the Scots in 1138. After crossing the A167 you now head eastwards towards another big road crossing, the A19, using a mixture of roads and paths through heavily farmed and scenically uninspiring countryside. Having crossed the Northallerton-Middlesbrough railway, you veer firstly south-eastwards then north-eastwards past Harlsey Grove Farm and Sydal Lodge. At least now there are good views ahead to the Cleveland Hills which spur you on over the river Wiske, past Brecken Hill Farm ruins, then past two further farms. At length you reach the extremely busy A19. There is no bridge and you must take your life in your hands as you cross straight over and proceed south-eastwards along the minor road immediately opposite, to reach the twin villages of Ingleby Arncliffe and Ingleby Cross (141).

The road drops down to the A172 Thirsk–Stokesley road, crossing straight over and proceeding south-eastwards, heading uphill to reach Arncliffe Church and Hall. The church was rebuilt in 1821 except for the Norman west doorway, and inside there are box pews and two fourteenth-century effigies. The Hall was built in 1753–4, and contains some of the most spectacular rococo plasterwork in the country. Beyond the Church and Hall, a farm is passed and the lane turns sharp right; the Coast to Coast goes straight on through a field into woodland, reaching a forest road which you join, heading south-westwards close to the edge of the forest with lovely views through the trees. A turn to the right provides the possibility of a detour to the fourteenth-century Mount Grace Priory, described by Pevsner as the best preserved Carthusian monastery in England. In due course you reach a T-junction of paths (142.5), and the point at which you meet the Cleveland Way. Both Coast to Coast and Cleveland Way go left, but by detouring to the right you can reach Osmotherley which is about a mile away. There is a good range of amenities here and you may be fortunate enough to find a tearoom.

Tea rooms

The sight of a tea shop will gladden any walker's heart, particularly if the tea shop owner understands the needs of walkers and enjoys meeting and talking with them about their travels. Where this is so, it is likely that the thirsty hiker – quite unfussy about the quality of the brew provided it is hot and wet – will enter and be immediately bidden to sit wherever he wishes, with no pressure placed upon him to sample the culinary delights that may appear on the food menu. In certain establishments, however, particularly those wishing to boost revenue or attract a better class of customer, the sweaty traveller may be made to feel less than welcome. He may not only be forced to don a sleeved top and remove his muddy boots before the staff deign to speak to him, but may also be forced to queue before being permitted to sit. Then, having sat down, he will then be forced to choose between closely-prescribed set menus from which no deviation is permissible under any circumstances, and which make no attempt to disguise the management's aim of relieving him of as much of his cash as possible (*£2.50 supplement for smoked salmon sandwich, optional 10 per cent service charge added to all bills*).

Osmotherley junction to Lion Inn, Blakey (19.5 miles) via Bloworth Crossing

ENJOY: Live Moor, Carlton Moor, Cringle Moor, Cold Moor, Hasty Bank

From the T-junction above Osmotherley to Bloworth Crossing, the Coast to Coast follows the same route as the Cleveland Way. The chapter devoted to the Cleveland Way fully describes this part of the journey, via Beacon Hill, Scarth Wood Moor, the attractive valley of Scugdale, the hamlet of Huthwaite Green, and the ascent on to the Cleveland Hills. There is a real roller-coaster walk over Live Moor, Carlton Moor, Cringle Moor, Cold Moor and Hasty Bank before the final big ascent on to Urra Moor and the joining of the old Rosedale Ironstone Railway.

At Bloworth Crossing the Cleveland Way parts company with the Coast to Coast, the former turning left off the old railway while the latter (with the Lyke Wake walk) goes straight on, following the old railway. The railway was constructed in 1861 to convey high-grade iron ore mined on the Rosedale hillsides some way to the south-east, and although passengers were occasionally carried, the line was only ever used by freight trains. However, ironstone production declined after the turn of the century and the line shut in 1929. The old trackbed now allows fast, easy walking for the next five miles, negotiating a number of bends before heading more resolutely south-eastwards. There is fine moorland scenery all around, the heather a quite magnificent sight when in full flower in the summer, and to the right there are excellent views down the more verdant valley of Farndale. Birds to look out for are the curlew, merlin and grouse, the latter easily identifiable with its cries of 'Go back! Go back!' Four miles beyond Bloworth Crossing the track comes on to High Blakey Moor, swinging to the left to pass round the head of Blakey Gill, and here the Lion Inn comes into view; this is indeed a welcome sight for those who have walked from Ingleby Cross or Osmotherley today. Soon after the track has swung to the right again beyond Blakey Gill, you leave it by turning left and climbing slightly to reach a metalled road immediately beside the Lion Inn (162).

Blakey to Grosmont (14 miles) via Glaisdale

ENJOY: Great Fryup Head, Beggar's Bridge, East Arncliff Wood, Egton Bridge, North York Moors Railway

Turning left on to the road at the inn, you follow the road up to the Young Ralph Cross, turning right here onto another road which passes a monument known as White Cross or Fat Betty. Continue south-eastwards along the road for roughly a mile, bearing left onto a signed track over the heather to shortly reach another road. Turn left onto it, then at the top of a gentle hill, bear right onto a clear path. You head eastwards past Trough House and there follows a grand walk on a good path that passes round the head of Great Fryup Dale. The track swings to the north-east and crosses Glaisdale Moor, reaching a road. You follow the road for about a mile, again heading north-eastwards and enjoying fine views to Great Fryup Dale to the left and Glaisdale to the right. Just before a white Ordnance Survey column, you branch north-eastwards along a good track across Glaisdale Rigg, eventually descending towards Esk Dale. The walking is as fast and easy as that between Bloworth Crossing and the Lion Inn, with good views to both Glaisdale and Esk Dale. The track becomes a road and you go forward to meet a T-junction, at which you turn right to pass through the village of Glaisdale (171). The main part of the village is strung out along a steep hillside, commanding splendid views down into the deep wooded heart of Esk Dale, and as you descend towards the river Esk along the road you will note terraces of typically Victorian cottages, built to house workers at the village's three blast furnaces. At length you reach the railway station on the left, leaving the road just before the railway bridge and turning right on to a woodland path. By passing under the bridge, however, you can view Beggar's Bridge; one of the best-known landmarks in this part of Yorkshire. A packhorse bridge, built in 1619 and unaltered ever since, it is said to have been built by Thomas Ferris, a poor youth who used to wade or swim over the Esk to court the daughter of the squire of Glaisdale. The squire did not approve of the liaison so Ferris left the dale to seek his fortune. He returned a wealthy man, married the girl and built the bridge to symbolise their love and to enable later generations to cross the river dryshod.

The route now heads south-eastwards on a beautiful path through East Arncliff Wood, with both river and Whitby–Middlesbrough railway visible through the trees. After a mile you reach a metalled road, and turn left on to this road to proceed across the Esk into Egton Bridge, the lush meadows and trees presenting an amazing contrast to the remote moorland you passed only an hour or so back. The village contains many pretty cottages, an imposing manor house, and the nineteenth-century Roman Catholic Church of St Hedda with a richly decorated altar made in Munich, and fine tableaux depicting the Stations of the Cross. The Postgate Inn, a useful stop for weary walkers, is named after a local priest, Father Nicholas Postgate; hanged in 1679 for baptising a child into the Roman faith, he was one of England's last Catholic martyrs. Like Glaisdale, the village also has a useful railway station on the Whitby–Middlesbrough line. Just before the church you turn right off the road to proceed eastwards along the estate road of the manor; this was once a toll road, and a list of charges still stands at the toll bar by the estate road, easily visible (but thankfully not applicable) to today's walkers. Keeping the meandering River Esk to your right, and remaining on the estate road, you swing to the left, pass under the railway and continue north-eastwards to reach the Egton–Grosmont road. You turn right along the road, shortly crossing the Esk and soon reaching Grosmont (176).

Apart from the nineteenth-century church of St Matthew, containing what Pevsner describes as a 'fussy' interior, there is little of architectural interest, and disappointingly few amenities, amongst the austere grey stone buildings of the village. Grosmont's main feature of interest is the railway station on the North York Moors Railway re-opened as a preserved steam railway after being axed from the main rail network many years ago. There is no doubt that the sight of steam locomotives – of which arguably the most impressive is the Sir Nigel Gresley – pulling majestically out of the station, is a thrilling one.

Grosmont to Robin Hood's Bay (15 miles) via Hawsker

ENJOY: Little Beck, Falling Foss, Maw Wyke Hole, Ness Point, Robin Hood's Bay

The route sticks to the main road through the village and, having crossed the railway, follows the road as it climbs extremely steeply uphill. You shortly fork right and at the next junction fork right again, climbing a 1 in 3 gradient and continuing along Fairhead Lane. From the lushness of Eskdale you now suddenly find yourself on the moors again, climbing to the 900 ft height of Sleights Moor. The official route describes a semi-circle away from and back to the moor road, to visit two sets of stones, the Low Bride Stones and High Bride Stones. Leave the road by a car park to turn left along a moorland path taking you to the A169 onto which you turn left and which you follow for a quarter of a mile until you reach bridlepaths going off to the left (north-west) and right (east). Turn right here.

The route then follows the bridleway eastwards, heading downhill; in due course it becomes a lane, and then meets a road coming in from the left; you join the road continuing eastwards to drop down to the delightful hamlet of Little Beck in a wooded valley. A stream (Little Beck) is crossed, and almost immediately afterwards the Coast to Coast route turns right off the road to take a path heading south-eastwards through woodland, keeping Little Beck to the right. The path is quite undulating, and although well-defined it can be extremely muddy. In just under a mile after leaving the road, the path rises to reach the Hermitage, a huge lump of rock out of which an impressive stone shelter has been carved. The going now gets easier, and soon you will see the magnificent waterfall of Falling Foss to the right, its wooded setting enhancing its charms. The path passes immediately to the left of a building known as Midge Hall, near the waterfall, and crosses a footbridge over May Beck. You follow beside or close to the beck, contuing south-eastwards, and at length reach a metalled road beside a car park. Veering north-eastwards you follow the road for half a mile or so then beyond New May Beck farm you proceed on a path that heads north-eastwards over Sneaton Low Moor and then due north to reach the B1416; you follow this briefly eastwards, then turn on to a path and strike out north-eastwards across the moors once more on a well-defined path that is marked by a line of posts.

In due course, the moorland gives way to pastures, and as this happens you swing slightly west of north, descending through fields to reach a lane which you follow to meet a road. Road walking now follows, first just west of north then north-eastwards past Mitten Hill Farm and across the A171 to reach Hawsker (187), an attractive village with a useful range of amenities although so few miles now remain that you may be happy to press on. You exit from Hawsker along the B1447 that is signposted to Robin Hood's Bay, and very soon, when the road bends to the right, you proceed straight on down a lane past Seaview caravan site. There's tremendous excitement now as you descend along a clear path north-eastwards to arrive at the North Sea, with the tremendous cliff scenery of Maw Wyke Hole immediately to the left.

On reaching the cliffs you turn right and again join the Cleveland Way for the final miles to Robin Hood's Bay. The next two miles are exhilarating as you follow a well-defined coast path on a platform high above the North Sea, and as you round Ness Point, you see journey's end ahead. It is without doubt the finest ending to any of the routes described in this book, all the more so because the objective has been so well-defined from the start – a walk from coast to coast. At length the path leads to a road which proceeds past rows of houses to reach a T-junction with the road that has come from Hawsker. The route turns left on to this road, and then shortly left again down a road that leads into the main village street of Robin Hood's Bay (191). This descends precipitously through the old part of the village, and straight down to the North Sea, where your first task must be to obey Wainwright's command and place your boot into its salty waters. Robin Hood's Bay, as well as marking the end of the walk, is an extremely picturesque spot in its own right; it is a maze of steep streets and passages with houses on many levels, and the old church of St Stephen has some splendid features including box pews, three-decker pulpit and gallery. There are many places to obtain celebratory refreshments, and a wealth of attractive little shops, several of which sell Coast to Coast souvenirs – little mementos of a magnificent walk across England. Before staggering back up the hill to catch a bus back to Whitby or Scarborough – from where there are excellent bus and rail connections to all parts of the country – you may be tempted, as I was, to obtain a certificate of successful completion of the walk. In fact, these are rather too easily available, so don't feel too surprised when you see them being shamelessly flaunted by customers clad in footwear which would have rendered them barely capable of accomplishing the 200-yd walk from the pay and display car park.

The Pennine Way

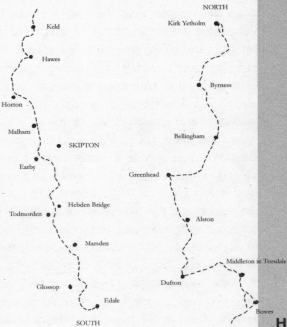

Designation: National trail.
Length: 255 miles by the direct route,
258 using the Bowes Loop. (Note: these
are the mileages that have been calculated
by the Countryside Agency, which are
also used as the basis for mileages for
individual sections in the description that
follows. Alfred Wainwright's Pennine Way
Companion reckons the total mileage to
be around 270.)
Start: Edale, Derbyshire.

**HIGHLIGHTS OF
THIS WALK:**
* **Kinder Downfall**
* **Stoodley Pike**
* **Gordale Scar**
* **Malham Cove**
* **Pen-y-Ghent**
* **Hardraw Force**
* **Tan Hill Inn**
* **High Force**
* **High Cup**
* **Hadrian's Wall**
* **Housesteads**

The Pennine Way

Finish: Kirk Yetholm, Scottish Borders.
Nature: A walk up the Pennine and Cheviot ranges of northern England, through some of the wildest and most remote upland terrain in the country.
Difficulty rating: Severe.
Average time of completion: 18–21 days.

The Pennine Way is the father of all long-distance footpaths in Great Britain. It is the oldest and arguably most famous trail of the British Isles and although not the longest, it is the most technically demanding and the most satisfying to achieve. It also has the most chequered history. Eighty years ago, much of the land over which the present route passes was strictly private. Understandably, many countryside lovers at that time were wanting far greater access to areas of outstanding natural beauty, and in 1932 thousands of them deliberately flouted the laws of trespass by walking in the hills around Kinder Scout, which now forms the southern end of the Pennine Way. The Kinder Trespass caused considerable embarrassment to the Establishment, whose attitudes to walkers were considerably less sympathetic than they are today. Then in 1935, one Tom Stephenson wrote an article in the *Daily Herald* which proposed a continuous route across the Pennines. It took a further 16 years for his suggestion to gain ministerial approval, and after that came lengthy and often bitter negotiations with local landowners before the route was complete. Finally, in 1965, a ceremony on Malham Moor marked the official opening of the long-distance route linking Edale in the Peak District with Kirk Yetholm on the Scottish border.

The route has become extremely popular over the years – so much so that there has been very considerable erosion in some areas, resulting in re-routing and extensive path repair. Purists could argue that it is not a true Pennine Way in that firstly it starts some way into the Pennine range and finishes in the Cheviots, well beyond the Pennines, and secondly it does not keep to the main Pennine watershed (the highest ground of the Pennine chain where both west-flowing and east-flowing watercourses begin), but often descends to lower-lying ground on either side. However, it is the variety of landscapes that make the route so interesting and rewarding, ranging from the peaty moorland of the Peak District and the Cheviots to the dramatic limestone outcrops of Malham; from the noble splendour of Hadrian's Wall to the pastoral charm of Wensleydale, and from the formidable heights of Great Dun Fell and Cross Fell to the awesome falls of Hardraw and High Force. Each type of landscape brings its own distinctive wildlife and plant life. On the moors you will walk amongst bogbean, marsh cinquefoil, cotton grass, crowberry and bilberry, be bidden by the grouse to 'go back' and watch as curlews, golden plovers and hen harriers hover overhead. The limestone country of Yorkshire offers purple saxifrage, juniper and hart's tongue fern, and on entering the primrose and cowslip-clad pastures of the Dales you may spot a merlin on a fence post, scanning the surroundings for potential prey. If you examine the crags of Hadrian's Wall you may find bell heather, rock-rose, wild thyme and tormentil while ring ouzels and jackdaws fly around you, and you may be accompanied on your journey through the Cheviots by skylarks and meadow pipits.

There is no doubt that the Pennine Way is a considerable undertaking, requiring a great deal of planning and preparation, and experience of hill walking and navigation. Most walkers will need three weeks to complete it, and that in itself calls for a high level of fitness as well as proper advance planning and an adequate financial outlay. It is important not to be so carried away with the idea of 'doing the Pennine Way' that you lose sight of your own personal limitations. If you possess neither camping equipment nor navigational skills (including the ability to use a compass) you should think very seriously about whether to attempt the route, especially on your own. It is true that the walk is not quite the formidable proposition it once was. Many of the worst surfaces have been replaced by proper flag paths; bag-carrying services vie with each other to provide the best deal for transporting your rucksack or luggage from one accommodation to the next; mapping of the Way seems to improve year by year, with numerous excellent maps and guides available; and the mobile telephone makes it much easier to summon assistance if required. Nevertheless, the terrain is tough, and demands the utmost respect. There are many sections where not only the signposting, but the path itself, is non-existent, and the Way itself is either over steep hills and fells or across treacherous moorland wildernesses where slimy quagmires wait eagerly to suck in not only your boots but most of the lower half of your body. In bad weather, you can lose all sense of direction and a straightforward walk across a field to a stile may turn into a nightmarish struggle that sees you floundering spectacularly off course. At times, you really will feel like giving up, and sadly there are all too many aspiring Pennine Way walkers who have done so. There is no shortage of accommodation along the Way but there are long stretches with none at all, including the first 16 and the last 29 miles. These rather gloomy comments are not intended to deter would-be walkers but to serve as a warning, and if you are adequately prepared, you will enjoy a unique walking experience to be treasured forever. It should be added that civilisation and company is generally never too far away: the Pennine Way has been called a giant pub crawl, and even small communities along the route offer everything the walker needs, from sumptuous bar meals washed down by real ale, to the shelf in the convenience store offering the latest hi-tech foot powder, blister cream or other supposed remedy which even though it may not do the slightest bit of good, will at least make hikers feel better about putting their boots on again next morning.

Edale to Crowden (16 miles) via Kinder and Bleaklow

ENJOY: Kinder Downfall, Wain Stones, Torside Reservoir

The Way starts in the pretty village of Edale, a popular centre for walkers, and easily accessible from other parts of the country with its convenient railway station on the Sheffield–Manchester line. To get to the start of the route, you need to make your way to a cluster of buildings known as Grindsbrook Booth by the Old Nag's Inn, a justifiably popular watering-hole. You turn westwards away from the buildings, along a lane, then proceed gently over fields, slightly south of west, to the hamlet of Upper Booth, from which you turn right on to a metalled road, follow this as far as Lee House, heading north-westwards, and then continue along a good path in the same direction.

At length you reach the stiff ascent on to Kinder, known as Jacob's Ladder. It derives its name from a certain Jacob Marshall, a packhorse driver who is said to have scrambled up the hill by the shortest route so he might have time to smoke a pipe while his ponies took a more gentle but far longer ascent! Above Jacob's Ladder you continue westwards along a wide path beside a broken wall, turning right to Swine's Back, then right again to head just east of north. You pass Edale Rocks and the triangulation point at Kinder Low – 2,077 ft high! – and, enjoying fine views to the Derwent valley, proceed beside the escarpment crest, passing through an area of boulders and gravel to reach the spectacular waterfall Kinder Downfall.

As you head towards the Downfall, you have on your right Kinder plateau, an awesome wilderness of featureless, largely pathless, peat moorland and one of the most frightening tracts of country you are ever likely to see. The peat is actually an accumulation of black, undecayed plant debris, which formed as a result of a 2,000-year period of wet weather in prehistoric times. It is unpleasant to walk on, holds huge quantities of rainwater, and, to make matters worse, erosion of the peat has produced 'hags' or steep-faced islands, separated from their neighbours by 'groughs' or watercourses which cut through the peat and invariably run straight across the walker's direction of travel. The Way used to proceed to the Downfall directly across the plateau, having ascended from Edale by way of Grindsbrook Clough, until serious erosion problems forced the route to be diverted on to what was formerly just a bad weather alternative. The current route, however, poses no such problems, and in clear conditions the Downfall should be reached without difficulty. In windy conditions and when the waters are in full spate, this is a truly spectacular sight, the wind causing the water to be blown high into the air above you. At the Downfall you change direction, heading north-westwards through more boulders and gravel, dropping to Ashop Head and climbing again to Mill Hill, where you swing north-eastwards again and continue in this direction for three miles to reach the often snowed-up A57 Snake Road via Glead Hill and Featherbed Moss. This walk is now straightforward, as an excellent flag path (a line of flagstones) has been laid for walkers, but in days gone by this section was one of the most treacherous on the whole route, and many hikers – particularly those who had struggled over the old route on the Kinder Plateau – have called it a day here. Barry Pilton, writing in *One Man and His Bog*, recalls meeting a man on Kinder who told him that the Snake Road was where 75 per cent of all walkers gave up the Pennine Way, 'when the hypothetical path crosses a very real bus route!'

You cross straight over the Snake Road (the unusual name is derived from the presence of a serpent in a local family crest) and continue north-eastwards. You cross an old packhorse route of Roman origin called Doctor's Gate, then proceed along a shallow trench known as Devil's Dike, swinging slightly west of north to ascend towards the 2,060 ft Bleaklow Head. At the time of writing, parts of this path have been flagstoned, but not all, and the going, across further peat moorland, can be most unpleasant in places.

Close by are the Wain Stones, an extraordinary formation of grit stone that resembles two faces engaged in a kiss. The rock from which the grit has been created is known as millstone; isolated blocks of coarse millstone have been scoured and shaped by the wind and weather, resulting not only in the Wain Stones but many other curiously-formed outcrops on these soggy moors. Beyond Bleaklow Head you swing north-eastwards briefly, then turn north-westwards, beginning the long descent into Longdendale.

The route swings westwards to follow the north bank of the peaty stream of Wildboar Grain, soon reaching its confluence with Torside Clough, crossing this watercourse and continuing just north of west, initially contouring Clough Edge then turning in a more northerly direction to drop steeply to the Longdendale valley floor. Dropping to a farm road, you turn left on to it and follow it as far as the B6105 Woodhead–Glossop road, crossing straight over this on to a causeway that separates Torside Reservoir on your right from Rhodeswood Reservoir on your left. Having passed both reservoirs, you turn right on to a well-defined track through woodland, heading north-east across the A628 and then remaining roughly parallel with that road and the north-west-facing fringe of the Torside Reservoir. The Way shortly turns left off the track to head north-westwards towards Laddow Rocks, but by detouring on along the track you reach the youth hostel at Crowden (16). This is the first accommodation opportunity since leaving Edale 16 miles back, and a place for walkers to lick their wounds and exchange stories of the first day of their big adventure.

Crowden to Standedge (11.4 miles) via Black Hill and Wessenden

ENJOY: Laddow Rocks, Wessenden Lodge

Having rejoined the route, you have an easy enough start, proceeding north-westwards towards the impressive gritstone formations that are known as Laddow Rocks. To your right is Crowden Great Brook, which is never far away as you follow a good path, crossing Oakenclough Brook and climbing steadily. Beyond Laddow Rocks you swing north-eastwards and continue in that direction towards Black Hill, striking out onto open moorland; for a while you follow the left bank of Crowden Great Brook, then proceed along a flag path to Dun Hill and thence to the summit of Black Hill. This used to be another ghastly stretch of the route, but although the horrors have been somewhat mitigated by the flag stones, the 1,908 ft Black Hill itself remains a peaty morass around a triangulation pillar. Indeed, the Royal Engineers triangulation team had such a difficult time erecting the pillar that the summit has been nicknamed Soldier's Lump! Even in pleasant conditions, the surroundings are hardly hospitable or especially aesthetically pleasing, but in wet or misty weather, it is a place to escape from as quickly as your legs and the terrain underfoot will allow you to. There are actually plans to re-route the Way to avoid the summit, which may or may not have come to fruition at the time of publication of this book. From the summit you head northwards then swing north-eastwards downhill past Black Dike Head, before turning north-westwards along a flag path which continues downhill. You cross over Black Dike and Dean Clough, then climb slightly, crossing Reap Hill Clough and arriving at the A635 Holmfirth–Greenfield road. (Fans of *Last of the Summer Wine* may like to note that the series is shot in and around Holmfirth, some four miles along this road to the right.) You turn right on to the road and follow it briefly, then turn left on to the Meltham road.

Shortly after joining the Meltham road, you turn left on to an excellent path that proceeds north-westwards downhill to Wessenden Lodge. This is a welcome break in the struggle across peat moorland. You keep the reservoirs of Wessenden Head and Wessenden to your left, with a fine backcloth of hills behind, as you descend to the Lodge, set snugly amongst the trees, but just before reaching the Lodge you turn left and follow the western end of Wessenden Reservoir. Beyond the reservoir you pass a waterfall and, now high above a brook, you proceed north-westwards alongside Blakely Clough, heading slightly uphill. You continue along the bank, now heading just south of west up on to Black Moss. As the ground levels out, the Way turns right and proceeds in a generally north-westerly direction, passing between Black Moss Reservoir and Swellands Reservoir, and thereafter following a flag path downhill to the A62 at Standedge Cutting (27.4). It is at Black Moss Reservoir that you will be reunited with the course of the former route, which proceeded north-westwards from Black Hill and from the A635 followed a dismal course through a peat wilderness, of which White Moss was the worst section. Alfred Wainwright, in his *Pennine Way Companion* that many walkers use to guide them up the route, says there is a good Lancashire word that well describes the ooze of mud and mire so prevalent on this first section of the Way, namely 'slutch'. To quote Wainwright: 'Say it slowly, with feeling, and you have the sound of a boot extricating itself from the filthy stuff.' With the next easily accessible accommodation some 11 miles further up the route, many walkers will turn right along the A62 and then a minor road down to Marsden, some three miles away; refreshments and accommodation may also be available by following the A62 to the left.

Standedge to A646 for Hebden Bridge (14.8 miles) via M62 crossing

ENJOY: Millstone Edge, Blackstone Edge, Stoodley Pike

The Way proceeds north-westwards from the A62, initially along a sandy track and then uphill on to Millstone Edge where, among the rocks, you will find the Ammon Wrigley Memorial Stone, named after a much-revered writer and local poet. Still heading north-westwards, progress is initially very straightforward as you walk along a dry track on the edge of an area of peat moorland, swinging briefly north-east at Northern Rotcher before turning north-west again, this being your general direction all the way to the A58. You continue over the moors, dropping to Oldgate Moss, then after passing Little Moss you cross the A640 Milnrow–Huddersfield road, and proceed upwards to Rapes Hill, descending and then rising again to White Hill. The going could be quite juicy as you come off White Hill, but improves as you go forward to the A672 Oldham–Halifax road by way of Axeltree Edge. Crossing straight over the A672, you pass Bleakedgate Moor Wireless Telegraphy station and very shortly after that you cross the M62 trans-Pennine motorway beyond which you head via Slippery Moss and Redmires to Blackstone Edge. This section, passing over more hideous peat moorland, has been greatly improved in recent years, but it used to be a diabolical stretch of route. On the occasion I walked it, one of my new-found walking companions became completely stuck here, requiring assistance to be extricated.

The huge boulders of Blackstone Edge provide a welcome contrast to the peat moorland, and from now on the going becomes a great deal easier. You head northwards on a good path as far as the Aiggin stone, an old guide stone, then turn left along a Roman road and shortly right on to a path that curls round Blackstone Edge moor, alongside a watercourse known rather unromantically as Broad Head Drain. You then head downhill to the A58 Littleborough–Halifax road (34). You bear right on to the A58 then shortly left, proceeding north-westwards along a reservoir road for some three miles, passing firstly Blackstone Edge reservoir, then the reservoirs of Light Hazzles and Warland. The going is the easiest so far, and there are excellent views to the town of Littleborough and its surrounding hills; after the great wildernesses experienced further back, it is somehow reassuring to know that civilisation is not too far away. Finally, just beyond Warland Reservoir, you turn right and proceed first just south of east then north-eastwards alongside

Warland Drain. The imposing monument of Stoodley Pike should now be clearly in view and, leaving Warland Drain at Langfield Common, you head north-eastwards towards it, along a good clear track. At Withens Gate you pass a track leading to Mankinholes Youth Hostel, a useful stopping-place for those for whom a further three-mile slog to the flesh pots of the Calder Valley is too much.

The Way continues to Stoodley Pike, a monument 125 ft high which was built in 1856 as a replacement to a monument constructed following the defeat and exile of Napoleon. There is a viewing balcony inside, offering an excellent panorama on a half-decent day. From Stoodley Pike you head eastwards, then swing north-eastwards and begin to descend into the Calder valley, hitting a farm road at Lower Rough Head, and proceeding north-westwards through Callis Wood – the first area of woodland since the start of the route – to cross the Rochdale Canal and river Calder and reach the A646 (42.2). Two towns lie within easy reach of the Way at this point: Todmorden three miles to the left, and Hebden Bridge a mile to the right. Of these, Hebden Bridge is the more interesting, its mills and grey terraced houses recalling the area's proud industrial past, and it could now almost be described as a giant museum piece. It is an easy detour from Hebden Bridge to the fascinating village of Heptonstall with its narrow streets of dark stone houses, the lovely cobbled Weavers' Square, and a sixteenth-century Cloth Hall. The village was once the centre of the handloom weaving trade and one could easily visualise the packhorses clattering through the little thoroughfares, having struggled up from the Calder. The octagonal Methodist church, founded by John Wesley in 1764, is one of the oldest Methodist churches, while the Anglican church of St Thomas dates back to the 1850s, having been built to replace a much older church that suffered heavy storm damage. The vicarage is built on the site of a cockpit – not the pilot's seat in an aircraft, but an area used in the Napoleonic Wars for cockfighting!

A646 to Ponden for Haworth (10.7 miles) via Colden

ENJOY: Heptonstall Moor, Top Withens, Haworth

Two fairly mediocre miles follow, as you undertake the long climb out of the Calder valley. You turn right onto the A646 then shortly left, passing under the Bradford–Manchester railway and following a track roughly north-westwards uphill past Dew Scout Farm. Just beyond the farm you turn sharp right, then shortly left uphill past Popples Farm and Scammerton Farm, heading just west of north. You cross a metalled road, continue northwards over Pry Hill, descending to cross Colden Water and climbing again, picking up a lane that leads north-westwards into Colden, which sadly is no prettier than its name. Crossing another road, you continue north-westwards along a partially walled footpath to Long High Top, swinging north-eastwards to Mount Pleasant farm. Here you reach Heptonstall Moor with some relief, and strike out north-westwards across the heather moor, crossing over Clough Head Hill. The going is excellent, with walkers further motivated to make fast progress by the prospect of the Pack Horse Inn which is now imminent! After a two-mile walk across the moor, you turn sharp right to continue just east of north, past the eastern edge of Lower Gorple reservoir, across and then along the east bank of Graining Water, and forward to a metalled road at Widdop. By detouring right you will reach the Pack Horse Inn, but the Way goes left, following the road north-westwards, shortly bearing right on to a reservoir road, heading north-eastwards – your direction of travel almost all the way to Ponden Hall.

You proceed past two Walshaw Dean reservoirs, keeping them to your left. Before reaching the top end of the second, however, you turn right, away from it, and head on to the open moors, climbing quite steeply initially, but being rewarded with a fine moorland march, enjoying excellent views back to Stoodley Pike. You pass Withins Height, having gained 1,000 ft since the Calder valley, and go forward to a now ruined house named Top Withens, whose windswept, romantic moorland setting is reputed to have inspired Emily Brontë when she wrote *Wuthering Heights*. Beyond Top Withens you begin to descend, following an excellent track past Upper Heights Farm, then turning left to follow a path past the farms of Buckley and Rush Isles, now heading north-westwards. Just beyond Rush Isles Farm you reach a junction with a lane on to which you turn left, but by detouring right and then right again on to a road, you reach Haworth and its Parsonage, home of the Brontë sisters. The town's steep main street is most attractive, although fearfully busy at holiday times, the crowds attracted not only by the Brontë connection but by the Keighley and Worth Valley Railway, where the film of *The Railway Children* was made. The Way, however, eschews the delights of Haworth and having joined the lane beyond Rush Isles Farm it proceeds alongside Ponden Reservoir to Ponden Hall (52.9), a fine seventeenth-century farmhouse which is reputed to be the inspiration for Thrushcross Grange, another important location in the novel *Wuthering Heights*. Wherever you stay the night in this area, you are almost guaranteed to have Emily Brontë's masterpiece in your thoughts even though, for the less culturally inclined, any manifestation of this may be confined to a dodgy rendition of Kate Bush's eponymous hit record after a few too many in a Haworth hostelry.

Ponden to Thornton-in-Craven (11.5 miles) via Cowling

ENJOY: Lothersdale, Pinhaw Beacon

Beyond Ponden Hall the Way continues along a path which, having passed the head of Ponden reservoir, arrives at the Colne–Keighley road. You turn left onto this road then shortly right, proceeding uphill through fields parallel with Dean Clough and then along a walled farm track, turning left onto another road at Crag Bottom. You follow this road to the left then at Crag Top turn right, striking out across Oakworth Moor and Ickornshaw Moor, the outstanding landmark on which is the 1,453 ft Wolf Stones, just to the left of the route on the moor's south fringes. Flagstones have helped to ease what used to be quite an arduous passage over this moorland. As the Way continues across the moor it gradually descends, and as you lose height you should look out on your right to the gritstone summit of Earl Crag, decorated by two impressive monuments.

You proceed somewhat circuitously round a number of ruins just beyond Andrew Gutter – a reminder of the sad decline of agricultural communities in the wake of the Industrial Revolution – but after passing Lumb Head Beck progress is straightforward, along a walled path which arrives at the A6068. You turn left on to it and shortly right to follow a path into the village of Ickornshaw, one of four little villages all strung together but with precious few amenities. In theory you could turn right on to the village street and then left at a T-junction into Gill Lane, passing the pretty Cowling church and the eastern end of the hamlet of Middleton. The Way, however, turns left off Ickornshaw village street almost at once, and follows a field path past the western end of Middleton to reach Gill Lane. You follow Gill Lane as far as the hamlet of Gill, and at the delightful Gill Bridge you turn left and strike out across rolling fields and meadows, climbing all the while. There are good views back across Cowling to the monuments on Earl Crag. You reach a metalled road, turning right and then immediately forking left to follow another road downhill, soon turning left again on to a path that drops to Surgill Beck. There is a climb to Wood Head Farm at which you join a lane that leads to the lovely village of Lothersdale, where picturesque cottages are grouped round an old textile mill in a wooded valley. There is a useful pub here where you can celebrate the end of 20 rather bitty miles' marching and look forward to some really great walking ahead.

You leave Lothersdale along a lane heading northwards from beside the inn, but when the lane peters out you continue uphill, keeping alongside a wall, in due course reaching the Colne–Skipton road. You cross over it and briefly join a lane, which ends at Hewitt's farm, and again you keep alongside a wall, going forward on to Pinhaw Moor and arriving at the 1,273 ft Pinhaw Beacon, a really fine viewpoint with spectacular views to Airedale and the town of Skipton. With some reluctance you set off again, actually heading a little south of west to pick up a quarry road. Here you return to north-westward travel, going forward on the quarry road to meet a road junction, and proceeding straight across to join the metalled Elslack road. Follow it over Elslack Moor; to your right is one of the largest patches of woodland seen so far on the route, containing the tiny Elslack reservoir. After about half a mile you bear left, initially across the rather juicy moorland of Park Hill and then through pleasant pastures, descending all the time. At Brown House you pick up a farm road which passes under the old Colne–Skipton railway to reach the A56 at the pretty village of Thornton-in-Craven (64.4), the gateway to one of the lowest-lying and gentlest sections of the route and the prospect of some superb walking beyond. I recall one particularly cruel twist of Fate that befell a Pennine Wayfarer walking this stretch a day or two ahead of us; having survived the rigours of Bleaklow, Black Hill *et al*, she was forced to abandon her walk after being bitten by a dog on Ickornshaw Moor. Dogs can be somewhat unsettling for long-distance walkers as it can never be predicted until the last minute whether they will studiously and disdainfully ignore you, sniff inquisitively but harmlessly around you, or start tearing large chunks out of you. And as a particularly aggressive-looking specimen bounds towards you, the promise of the owner that 'he won't hurt you' seems somewhat unconvincing when the owner's general look of helplessness suggests he is in fact incapable of controlling so much as a hibernating tortoise. For those surviving unscathed, Thornton-in-Craven offers a reasonable range of amenities, and by turning left on to the A56 you will in a mile and a half reach the little town of Earby, which has many more.

Thornton-in-Craven to Malham (10.6 miles) via Gargrave

ENJOY: Leeds and Liverpool Canal, Hanlith, Malham, Gordale Scar

The Way crosses more or less straight over the A56, initially following Cam Lane and then proceeding through fields, veering slightly west of north as it passes Langber Hill and arrives at the Leeds and Liverpool Canal. In the nineteenth century this enjoyed extensive industrial use, but like many canals in other parts of the country, it has now been revived as a tourist attraction, populated by pleasure craft. A quite delightful walk north-eastwards ensues along the towpath, and there is the possibility of a detour to the pretty village of East Marton, though with only two miles walked, it may be too early in the day to patronise the village inn. To reach East Marton you will need to get on to the A59, which crosses the canal by means of an unusual double-arched bridge, the extra arch being needed to facilitate the passage of the busy roadway above. Shortly beyond East Marton the route bears right and now heads in a north-easterly direction to Gargrave. Soon after leaving the canal you pass round the edge of a small woodland area and turn right on to a lane, then as the lane swings left you leave it and continue north-eastwards over pasture. The Way is not clear on the ground and there are numerous gates and stiles, making progress slow and potentially confusing in mist. You follow briefly alongside Crickle Beck and then climb gently on to Scaleber Hill, where there is a good view to Airedale with the welcome sight of Gargrave immediately ahead. You soon turn right on to a farm road and follow this across the railway – the famous Skipton–Carlisle line – then immediately after crossing the railway, you turn right along a path that takes you into Gargrave (68.7). This is an obvious stopping-place, with shops, refreshments and accommodation.

Having crossed the river Aire and the busy A65, you leave Gargrave by way of West Street, following a lane that heads north-westwards towards Bell Busk. You pass an area of woodland known as the Mark Plantation, and at the end of it you turn right, continuing in a north-westerly direction through open country, again with no obvious path on the ground, on to Eshton Moor. After crossing the moor you arrive at the river Aire, and from here virtually all the way to Malham the Way follows alongside the river, heading northwards through the meadows. Initially you stay on the left bank, looking northwards, then at Newfield Bridge you switch to the right bank, soon reaching the little village of Airton. Delightful walking through meadows and parkland, still on the right bank, takes you to the pretty village of Hanlith, with its mill and millpond. You turn right beside Hanlith Bridge along a lane, but soon turn left and return to the river which you follow as far as Malham (75).

Malham

It is said that if you make it to Malham you will complete the whole route. Hopefully the easy walking you have done from Thornton onwards will allow you time to linger in this remarkable village, historically famous for its sheep sales, and boasting a fine assembly of limestone cottages, many of which are several hundred years old. Walkers' needs have been well catered for by the Buck Inn and the Lister's Arms, which has the date 1723 above the doorway, and today the village offers a full range of amenities, catering as it does for not only walkers but tourists and geologists. Close to Malham are two remarkable limestone features, namely Malham Cove and Gordale Scar; Malham Cove, a cliff 280 ft high, will be seen by Pennine Way walkers heading northwards from the village but a detour is needed to visit Gordale Scar, a mile eastwards. This is a massive cleft in towering and overhanging limestone walls, with waterfalls plunging down a ravine 250 ft deep in places. Suddenly, all the geology they tried to teach you at school comes breathtakingly to life, as you see it for real rather than in the pages of an insufferably tedious textbook, the reading of which as early evening homework served as a poor substitute for a cup of hot Bovril in front of *The Perils of Penelope Pitstop*.

Malham to Horton-in-Ribblesdale (14.4 miles) via Malham Tarn

ENJOY: Malham Cove, Malham Tarn, Pen-y-Ghent, Hunt Pot, Hull Pot

Leaving Malham, you begin innocuously enough by following the Settle road north-westwards, but soon turn right to follow alongside Malham Beck and head towards the formidable limestone cliffs of the Cove, from which the beck emerges. Shaped as it is like a section of an immense amphitheatre, it is intimidating in its scale and steepness. It is worth walking to the base of the cliff, where there once poured a waterfall higher than Niagara. However the Way leads you to the left to follow a stepped path to the top, where another surprise awaits you in the form of a magnificent limestone pavement which you follow parallel with the cliff edge before turning left and heading north-westwards again. Those without a head for heights would do well to stay well back from the cliff edge, as it is unprotected and dangerous; furthermore, the pavement itself is uneven and should be walked on with care. With those caveats in mind, you will find this to be the most exhilarating walking on the route so far. Having turned left, you proceed over what is known as the Dry Valley, an area of lush green grass overshadowed by weathered limestone formations.

You swing north-eastwards among the rocks of Comb Hill, and pass Water Sinks, where the stream that has issued from Malham Tarn further north disappears underground. Shortly you arrive at a metalled road, turning right on to it, and left on to a path that heads just east of north to another road. You turn left on to this road, and follow it as it swings north-westwards round the edge of the National Trust-owned Malham Tarn, a serene and beautiful piece of water, and one of only a small number of natural lakes in Yorkshire. Situated amongst limestone, which does not hold surface water, the Tarn is only able to exist because it lies on a bed of Silurian slate, which is impervious to water. In the woodland that borders the lake, and passed by the Way, is Malham Tarn House, now a field study centre and reputedly the place that Charles Kingsley, who often stayed here as a guest, was inspired to write *The Water Babies*, one of the best-loved children's stories of all time, published in book form in 1863.

Not far beyond Malham Tarn House, just before Water Houses, you turn right and head northwards through open country, keeping a wall to your left. In a mile, near Stanggill Barn beyond the wall to the left, you head north-westwards to pick up a farm road, turning right on to it and following it to the hamlet of Tennant Gill. You then begin the long and arduous ascent of Fountains Fell, heading north-westwards all the way. Fountains Fell is not the loveliest of mountains – its side has been disfigured somewhat by old mine workings, of which only one colliery building remains – and there is no great satisfaction in reaching the extensive fell top. The igloo-shaped colliery building and two tall cairns, referred to as stone 'men' by guidebooks, are the only real features of interest as you near the summit. The early part of the climb is quite easy, but as you climb towards and then pass the 2,000 ft mark, crossing a number of watercourses including Tennant Gill itself, the limestone gives way to millstone grit and the going, although never very steep, becomes rougher underfoot. Indeed in very wet conditions, with soggy or flooded ground, you may be in very real danger of becoming a water baby yourself. You only have yourself to blame if you choose to walk the Pennine Way not in a pair of £129.99 water-resistant Gortex boots but in a pair of water-welcoming boots you picked up for a tenner from the Sunday morning car boot sale or purchased in a High Street chain store on the recommendation of a Saturday shop assistant whose idea of long-distance walking is a 300-yd trudge to the bus stop and if asked what Gortex was would hazard a guess that he was Arsenal's new signing from Bulgaria.

The view north-westwards from the summit of Fountains Fell, when you finally get there, is dominated by Pen-y-Ghent, which is the next major objective. You leave the summit cairn and head slightly south of west, descending rapidly, then turn north-westwards to follow alongside a wall, soon arriving at a metalled road, turning left on to it and following it south-westwards, passing Rainscar House. At a cattle grid you turn right and walk north-westwards up to the buildings of Dale Head farm, then beyond the farm you continue north-westwards along a good path that is bound for Horton. The Way too is destined to reach Horton, and in bad weather there may be merit in following this path all the way. However, at the limestone crater known as Churn Milk Hole, the official route bears right to begin the ascent of Pen-y-Ghent, one of the highlights of the Way. The ascent is fairly gentle to begin with, but as you gain height the going becomes very much steeper, and it is an exciting scramble through the boulders of limestone and gritstone to the grassy 2,273 ft summit. On a clear day the view is absolutely fantastic, with several mountains and hills visible, including Pendle Hill, the Howgill Fells, Whernside and Ingleborough. These last two, with Pen-y-Ghent, make up what are known as the famous Three Peaks, the conquest of which in a single day's journey is now an established challenge walk of 24 miles.

For Pennine Way walkers, however, it is downhill all the way to Horton, with no more climbing required. You head just north of west and begin your descent, which is initially very steep, then at 1,900 ft – look out at this point for the purple saxifrage in the springtime – you turn almost due west, making slightly gentler progress downhill through the grass and heather. As you do so, you pass Hunt Pot, a limestone pothole which is only 15 ft long but 200 ft deep, and you should take great care as you look down into the abyss. Just beyond Hunt Pot you swing a little north of west to reach a rough walled lane known as Horton Scar Lane, then turn left, south-westwards, on to the lane, and follow it to Horton (89.4). However, by detouring right at the point you reach the lane, you will soon reach another, more spectacular pothole known as

Hull Pot, only 60 ft deep but 300 ft long, and boasting a waterfall after heavy rain.

Horton (or, to give the village its full title, Horton-in-Ribblesdale) is not a tourist honeypot like Malham behind you, or Hawes, just ahead; although it boasts an ancient church and views of the river Ribble, its workmen's cottages and Victorian terraces remind you that this has for a long time been an important quarrying area. The setting of the village is tremendous, with Pen-y-Ghent rising up on one side and Ingleborough on the other, and there is opportunity for rest and refreshment in the village. Those wishing to call a temporary or permanent halt to their Pennine Way walk here may note that the village also has as a useful railway station on the famous Settle–Carlisle line. Arguably the village's most celebrated rendezvous point is not the pub but the Pen-y-Ghent Cafe, the base for many rigorous walking expeditions including the Three Peaks Walk. After we had walked here from Malham safely and in glorious sunshine, our tea and Kit Kats were consumed in a celebratory frame of mind, but one could well imagine would-be climbers and fellwalkers sitting here over mugs of stewing tea for hours on end, waiting with growing frustration for the rain and mist to relent, with nothing to do but apply themselves afresh to the Observer Two In One Jumbo Crossword.

Horton-in-Ribblesdale to Hawes (13.7) via Cam Fell and Dodd Fell

ENJOY: Ling Gill, Wensleydale

Having reached Horton, the Way turns right on to the village street, and shortly right again up another walled lane known as Harber Scar Lane, heading just east of north and then northwards, steadily gaining height. You keep a wall to your left and proceed along a lovely packhorse road, the going straightforward and comfortable. You pass more potholes including Sell Gill Holes, which open into a

210 ft deep underground chamber, an open chasm called Jackdaw Hole, the ominously-named Cowskull Pot, the 180-ft Pen-y-Ghent Long Churn, and beyond that, Canal Cavern. You continue just east of north over Rough Hill, then turn left, off the packhorse road, and proceed in a roughly westerly direction to the buildings of Old Ing, where you turn sharp right onto the Settle–Hawes packhorse road, proceeding most pleasantly just west of north, passing Dry Laithe Cave, otherwise known as Calf Holes.

You go forward to the sixteenth-century bridge crossing of Ling Gill; just below the bridge, the water cascades down a spectacular limestone gorge which is visible from the Way. You continue northwards uphill to Cam End, where your route meets the Roman road from Ingleton to Bainbridge, and at this important junction of old roads you turn right and continue over Cam Fell, still gaining height; you are now proceeding north-eastwards, your direction of travel all the way to Hawes. It is appropriate that, as you head towards the 1,800 ft contour, this stretch should be known as Cam High Road. This section also forms part of the Dales Way, a pleasant walk of some 95 miles from Leeds to the Lake District but far less challenging or rewarding than the Pennine Way or Coast to Coast, with much pounding along the flat. There are superb views from here on a good day, including the Three Peaks and the Dent Head viaduct on the Settle–Carlisle line. The Dales Way goes off to the right but the Pennine Way, passing the 100-mile mark, continues to a farm road, turning left on to it and then, in around half a mile, left off it to proceed along West Cam Road, a wide grass path or 'green road'. You soon contour the west slopes of Dodd Fell, remaining at just under 1,900 ft throughout. The going is straightforward and, in good visibility, quite delightful, but in poor conditions, it can be anything but.

Beyond Dodd Fell you head for Ten End Peat Ground, forking right at a junction of paths here (left provides a more direct route for Hawes which may be preferred in bad weather). Now you begin to descend, slowly at first, then more rapidly, with the beautiful prospect of Wensleydale opening out before you. The path becomes less distinct as you follow first the left side, then the right side, of a wall, in due course reaching Gaudy House and joining Gaudy Lane. When this ends at a junction of lanes, you cross over and follow field paths to a housing estate at the western edge of the village of Gayle. You pass through the estate, turn briefly left on to the Gayle–Hawes road, then bear right along a path, which shortly arrives in the little town of Hawes itself (103.1). Hawes is an obvious stopping-place on the Way, with an excellent range of amenities and a chance to stock up on supplies and enjoy a few creature comforts. It has many visitor attractions, including the Dales Countryside Museum, a traditional ropemaker's, and a creamery that offers a fine range of home-produced Wensleydale cheeses for sale. Pennine Way walkers who feel able to take a couple of days out, or feel they have done enough, may wish to use Hawes as a base for exploring the lovely Wensleydale countryside with its pretty villages among the lush green meadows, and impressive hills towering behind. Hawes is one of only very few tourist traps visited by the Pennine Way, and while some may dislike the place for that, it is undoubtedly useful for the purchase of postcards and presents.

Hawes to Keld (12.3 miles) via Thwaite

ENJOY: Hardraw, Great Shunner Fell, Thwaite, Swaledale, Kisdon Force

You leave Hawes by following the road heading northwards off the A684, signposted to Hardraw. Some maps say Hardrow, some say Hardraw, but let's not call the whole thing off – this is one of the best bits! You could simply walk to Hardraw along this road, but the Way uses a path to cut a corner, then soon turns left off the road and wanders north-westwards through the pastures to arrive in the village. You turn left on to the road to cross the bridge over the

The Pennine Way

stream, but by entering the Green Dragon Inn beside the bridge, and paying an entrance fee, you can walk out to the magnificent Hardraw Force. Seen at its best after heavy rainfall, this is England's highest waterfall above ground, and a quite incredible spectacle, the water cascading 100 ft over a tree-clad limestone ledge. Although notices forbid it, many cannot resist the temptation to walk round immediately behind the fall, in the tiny space between the cascade and the cliff face. All I can say is that you do so at your own risk!

Back on the Way, having crossed the bridge by the pub, you turn right and proceed north-westwards along a walled lane on to Bluebell Hill, effectively the start of the long, laborious climb to the summit of Great Shunner Fell. At Bluebell Hill you lose the walls but continue on a clear track. The going is excellent as far as Little Fell, but here you leave the track, bearing right to head just west of north and then swinging northwards on a much more indistinct path. As with Fountains Fell, the going gets rougher and peatier as you gain more height, but the reward on a clear day is a fantastic view back to Wensleydale and beyond. Finally you swing north-eastwards to reach the 2,340 ft summit of the fell, the highest ground reached so far. On days of good visibility this is one of the highlights of the walk; we reached the summit in pouring rain with no views to speak of. Great care is needed to identify the correct route as you begin descending, heading north-eastwards through an unpleasant sea of peat, although flagstones mitigate the worst sections. Some two miles after leaving the summit, you swing south-eastwards, and reach a walled lane, which makes for firmer going as you drop down to the B6270, turning right to little village of Thwaite. It was here that my companions and I found sustenance – as well as the opportunity to dry out – at the Kearton Restaurant; named after Richard and Cherry Kearton, well-known naturalists and pioneers in wildlife photography who came from the village.

The next section is quite magnificent. Leaving Thwaite, you head north-eastwards, uphill, to reach the hamlet of Kisdon, then just before Kisdon Cottage you bear left and begin a tremendous walk, initially just east of north and then swinging north-westwards, towards Keld. You proceed along a limestone shelf amongst trees, bracken and grass, while to your right is a steep slope leading down to the river Swale. A little less than half a mile short of Keld and just beyond Birk Hill, a detour to the right takes you to the beautiful Kisdon Force. The Way does not go quite as far as the centre of Keld, but turns right and drops steeply to cross the Swale and then climb, again steeply, up the other side with the spectacular falls of East Gill Force to your right. For the drop down to the Swale and the climb back up again, you will be overlapping with Wainwright's Coast to Coast Walk, described elsewhere in this book. Many walkers will, however, wish to detour to Keld (115.4).

Originally, Keld was a Viking settlement, and its name comes from an old Norse word for a well or a spring; it is not only a picturesque place, its sturdy cottages of grey stone blending beautifully with the surrounding hills and woodland, but it has a timeless and enduring quality which is somehow reassuring. Accommodation is available, although with no 'night life' to speak of in the village, the best entertainment may be the exchange of experiences with other walkers. Indeed, one of the pleasures of walking the Pennine Way is the fellowship amongst those attempting it, and from casual meetings along the Way can come friendships and possibly even romance. The unattached traveller, having taken a shine to a similarly eligible walker met whilst walking the Way, may repair contentedly to a hostel bed that night to enjoy dreams of a true walkers' wedding, followed by a honeymoon spent bagging a few dozen Munros together. Sadly, they may well find conversation that flowed so naturally on the magnificent heights of Pen-y-Ghent or by the sparkling cascade of Hardraw rather harder to come by in the British Home Stores cafeteria in Reading.

Keld to Baldersdale (14.2 miles by direct route – 3 miles extra for Bowes loop) via Tan Hill

ENJOY: Tan Hill Inn, God's Bridge, Bowes

Having passed East Gill Force, you wave goodbye to Coast to Coast walkers, who turn right to cross the stream just above the Force, while you turn left and proceed north-westwards past the buildings of East Stonesdale, then heading just west of north, you gradually climb out of the dale on to the moors. For a while the going is excellent, and there are lovely views back to Keld and its surrounds. Having crossed Lad Gill you swing north-eastwards, still gradually climbing, and although the Way hereabouts is sometimes unclear and a little juicy underfoot, you will be spurred on by the thought of reaching the Tan Hill Inn. At length it comes into view, and your pace will surely increase as you head towards it; although you may only have walked four miles from Keld, you will surely want to halt awhile at this Way-side pub, which is also the highest pub in England, at 1,732 ft. Historically it has served as an important centre of industrial and commercial activity, being the meeting of four trade routes, as well as an obvious place of rest and refreshment for moorland travellers. Many of the patrons would have come from the numerous collieries nearby, all of which are now abandoned, with derelict airshafts the only surviving evidence of the mining activity. Having refreshed yourself at the Tan Hill Inn – we spent a full two hours chatting by its roaring open fire – you turn briefly right on to a road, then almost immediately left to proceed north-eastwards and gradually downhill across Sleightholme Moor. You follow alongside Coal Gill Sike for a short while, then are joined by Frumming Beck and later Sleightholme Beck to your left, eventually reaching Sleightholme Moor road and turning left on to it, following it to the buildings of Sleightholme. The walk across Sleightholme Moor is boggy and unpleasant, and you may in fact be tempted to stick to the road all the way, using the Arkengarthdale road as far as

Cocker, then picking up Sleightholme Moor road. This is a logical bad weather alternative, although Wainwright severely reminds us that 'strictly this isn't doing the Pennine Way'.

Having passed the buildings of Sleightholme, the Way shortly forks left on to a path that proceeds north-eastwards to Trough Heads Farm, crossing Sleightholme Beck at Intake Bridge. At Trough Heads Farm you have a choice between the main route and the Bowes loop, the latter involving two extra miles but a chance to visit the village of Bowes.

The *main* route forks left to turn north-westwards and proceeds in that direction over heather and grass towards the A66, passing over the river Greta by means of a natural limestone bridge, known as God's Bridge. A tunnel is used to pass under the A66 – in bygone years, walkers had to walk across this very busy trans-Pennine road – and you then embark on a singularly uninspiring four-mile trudge across open moorland, still heading north-westwards. You begin by crossing Bowes Moor and passing the ruins of Ravock Castle, then having gone over Deepdale Beck you rise gently to the 1,402 ft Race Yate, before descending over Cotherstone Moor to reach a road just south of Clove Lodge. You turn left on to the road and follow it past the lodge.

The *Bowes loop* route forks right at Trough Heads to proceed northwards then eastwards, passing the farms of East Mellwaters, West Charity Pasture and Lady Mires, proceeding roughly parallel with the Greta. At Lady Mires you briefly join a road which you could follow all the way to Bowes, but the loop route soon turns left on to a path that goes forward to cross the Greta and head north-eastwards to Swinholme (if, owing to high water, the Greta is impassable, you will have to follow the road all the way to Bowes). You briefly join a lane here, but soon turn right and proceed eastwards through the fields to reach Bowes. Bowes has two features of interest; it is dominated by its huge Norman castle keep, and is also the site of a Roman fort, of which some of the ditches are still visible. There is also the possibility of refreshment and accommodation in the village. You leave Bowes by following the main street westwards then turning sharp right over the A66 by a footbridge, following the metalled road north-westwards across the moors as far as West Stoney Keld. The loop route goes forward on a track to the ruined farmhouse of Levy Pool then continues north-westwards across drab moorland, passing the 1,274 ft millstone outcrop of Goldsborough, and shortly afterwards reaching the Cotherstone–Clove Lodge road. You could just turn left on to that and be reunited with the main route at Clove Lodge in less than a mile, but the official loop route crosses the road and proceeds to East Friar House, turning left and following fiddly paths to reach the road and join up with the main route a little further north of Clove Lodge.

You now proceed down the road to Blackton Bridge in Baldersdale (129.6 via *direct* route, all subsequent mileages based on direct route), knowing that you have reached roughly the halfway point on the Pennine Way.

Baldersdale to Langdon Beck (13.7 miles) via Middleton-in-Teesdale

ENJOY: Middleton-in-Teesdale, Low Force, High Force

Having crossed Blackton Bridge over the river Balder, with Blackton Reservoir immediately to your right, you swing just north of east to go forward to Birk Hat Farm. You then swing just west of north, passing High Birk Hat Farm, and having crossed a metalled road linking Balder Head with Romaldkirk, you proceed on to Mickleton Moor. The Way swings more northwards to reach the farm at How, then proceeds down to Grassholme reservoir in Lunedale, turning left onto a metalled road to cross the water and continue north-westwards along the road to the hamlet of Grassholme. Shortly you turn right and proceed over pastures, just west of north, to the

B6276 Brough–Middleton-in-Teesdale road. You cross straight over on to a track that starts out north-westwards, then climbs north-eastwards, your direction now all the way to Middleton-in-Teesdale. Beyond the buildings of Wythes Hill the track disappears and you strike out over open fields, continuing to climb; the fields give way to heather and bracken and as you reach the top of the rise, you are treated to a lovely view across Teesdale, which is ample reward for the tedious miles tramped since Tan Hill. To the right is the walled and reputedly haunted plantation of Kirkcarrion, the site of a large tumulus. It is all downhill now, and you can enjoy a quite delightful walk on springy turf to reach the valley at the village of Middleton-in-Teesdale. The Way turns left on to a cart-track just before the bridge over the Tees, but most travellers will wish to detour into the village which lies across the bridge (135.6).

Middleton-in-Teesdale, which boasts an excellent range of amenities, is a pretty village of sandstone houses and whitewashed cottages. Standing amongst tall trees that overlook the village is Middleton House, one of the village's more imposing buildings and former headquarters of the Quaker-owned London Lead Company. The building is now a shooting lodge, but a memorial to the London Lead Company remains in the village in the form of a blue and white memorial fountain, which was erected in 1877. Another feature of interest is the sixteenth-century detached belfry just to the north of the parish church; the belfry retains one of its three original bells, which is rung by using both hands and a foot!

The next eight miles are sheer joy. Navigation is easy and uncomplicated as the Way proceeds chiefly north-westwards beside the Tees, following it upstream. The early walking is not so much spectacular as pleasant, as the Way proceeds through the meadows beside the tree-lined river, passing Scoberry Bridge and Wynch Bridge, soon after which you meet Low Force, a succession of splendid mini-waterfalls. The river bed between Scoberry Bridge and Low Force is wide, with numerous rocky islands and platforms, many carpeted with flowers, while columns of dolerite rock – formed as a result of seismic activity some 300 million years ago – guard the riverbanks. Beyond Low Force, as you pass Holwick Head Bridge, the surroundings get even better. The trees around the river become more profuse, with junipers attractively clothing the slopes, and the noise of the river is noticeably louder. Then comes the magnificent cascade of High Force. Although it is not the highest waterfall in the country, its thunderous surge of water makes it the biggest, as the Tees, after proceeding from its source on Cross Fell (which you will visit some 30 miles further on), suddenly crashes over a band of shale down a 70 ft drop into a wooded gorge surrounded by deep foliage and dolerite rock. It is a truly awesome sight, and, like Hardraw, is seen at its best after wet weather. So there is something to be said for all the Pennine Way rain after all.

The final three miles from here to Langdon Beck are somewhat anticlimactic; you deviate away from the Tees a little at Bracken Rigg and climb on to High Crag, then join a farm road at Cronkley Farm and return to the river at Cronkley Bridge. You cross the bridge and turn left, proceeding alongside the Tees to the point where it is met by its tributary, Langdon Beck. The Way then simply continues along the riverbank, but this time the bank of Langdon Beck, keeping it to the left as far as Saur Hill Bridge. The route crosses the bridge, but by detouring right here you soon reach Langdon Beck Youth Hostel (143.3). This is a useful stopping-place for those covering the Middleton to Dufton section in two days, since only the strongest walkers can hope to manage it in one day. We arrived at the hostel in excellent shape, knowing that Dufton was well within our capabilities next day, and such was our relaxed mood that we enjoyed some keenly-contested games of chess that evening. No self-respecting bed and breakfast or youth hostel should be without a stock of games and puzzles to while away a long evening and to keep one's mental as well as physical faculties exercised. Naturally enough, they will not be at the top of the owner's list of maintenance priorities, and users should not be surprised to find papier mâché models masquerading as rooks and bishops, or a jigsaw representation of the Arc de Triomphe which is missing 200 square metres of blue sky and the front half of a green 1968 Citroën saloon.

Langdon Beck to Dufton (12.6 miles) via Maize Beck

ENJOY: Cronkley Scar, Cauldron Snout, High Cup, Dufton

Remarkably, your general direction of travel for this section is south-westwards, effectively taking you further away from your ultimate objective. A straightforward walk over grassland from Saur Hill Bridge brings you back to the Tees, which you now follow upstream for some two and a half miles, keeping the river to your left. Almost at once you pass the farm at Widdybanks, and can look across the river at this point to Cronkley Scar, a hill of jagged rock rising majestically beyond the fast-flowing waters. The riverside walk which follows will pose no navigation problems but does require some scrambling over boulders and scree around Falcon Clints. We stopped at one point along this part of the walk to admire a remarkably docile grouse; this bird, with its distinctive 'go back' call, is a common sight on the Pennine moors, and with many of these moors being used for grouse-shooting during the season, there are sometimes path diversions.

The riverside walk comes to a dramatic climax with Cauldron Snout, a magnificent cataract crashing down through the rocks on a channel of dolerite. You clamber through the boulders that border the cataract until you reach and cross a bridge high above the cascades, although before making the crossing you may wish to detour further upstream to inspect the infamous Cow Green reservoir, the construction of which in the 1960's caused huge controversy. Its stark concrete dam wall, which can be seen from the Pennine Way, sits most uncomfortably with the natural surroundings. Having crossed the bridge, the Way leaves the Tees and follows a farm road as far as the farms of Birkdale, running parallel with Maize Beck, a tributary of the Tees. Having left Birkdale you ford Grain Beck and embark on a section of nondescript peaty moorland; this used to be one of the more infamous sections of the Way, but in recent years it has been improved and you should have few problems. Two miles from Birkdale you find yourself right beside the beck which you follow just south of west.

Your labours will soon be rewarded by your arrival at High Cupgill Head and what is perhaps the greatest moment on the whole walk. Suddenly, with no warning, the featureless moorland comes to an end, and the ground falls spectacularly away in front of you to reveal a fabulous view of the Vale of Eden with the mountains of Lakeland towering up behind. This is High Cup, consisting of a sweep of sheer whinstone cliffs to the right and the left, and, immediately ahead, a huge basin of grass and scree through which High Cup Gill flows. Some refer to this whole scene as High Cup Nick, but do so incorrectly, as the Nick is merely a cleft in the escarpment. The Way follows the right-hand sweep of cliffs, passing a pillar of basalt known as Nichol Chair and making a magnificent descent along a cairned route that arrives just below Peeping Hill. The views are stupendous, and on a good day you can see the Galloway hills in southern Scotland as well as Lakeland peaks. As you pass the old quarries and profusion of holes and pots you may be reminded of the descent from Pen-y-Ghent to Horton.

You turn briefly north-west, then join a lane which swings just south of west and proceeds past Bow Hall Farm into the lovely village of Dufton (155.9), whose squat sandstone cottages, set round a spacious green, make a delightful sight. With refreshment and accommodation available, it is an obvious stopping-place for Pennine Way walkers, as there is nothing now on offer for nearly 20 miles, but despite the attractions of the village, an early night is advisable as you now have a very long and tiring day ahead. One piece of trivia that walkers may swap as they enjoy their evening drink in the village is that Dufton was the home of the cobbler who gave his name to Nichol Chair. He is reputed to have mended a pair of boots on the top of the slender basalt pillar, despite the apparent lack of room for both his tools and his backside. Work must have been more fun before the advent of Health and Safety inspectors.

Dufton to Alston (19.4 miles) via Garrigill

ENJOY: Dufton Pike, Knock Fell, Little/Great Dun Fell, Cross Fell, Garrigill

Having arrived in Dufton further from your ultimate objective than you were at Langdon Beck, you waste little time making up the 'lost' ground, heading resolutely north-eastwards all the way to Knock Fell. Inevitably, it is also uphill all the way. After leaving Dufton you head initially for Coatsike, then continue along a lane to the old farmhouse of Halsteads and having crossed Great Rundale Beck, you proceed along a walled track, climbing steadily. The climb is enlivened however by lovely views to the Eden valley as well as to the very distinctive summit of Dufton Pike. Gradually the gradient becomes stiffer, as you ford Swindale Beck and continue roughly parallel with it, passing Knock Hush, one of a number of watercourses created artificially to scour vegetation and see what minerals lay in the subsoil. Coast to Coast veterans may remember seeing some hushes in the moors above Swaledale. You leave Swindale Beck and haul yourself past the distinctive cairn known as Knock Old Man and up to the 2,604 ft summit of Knock Fell, comfortably higher than any ground covered so far. The views make the effort well worthwhile, and there is even better to come.

You swing north-westwards, your direction of travel all the way to Cross Fell, and now are faced with three further peaks in succession, each preceded by a slight dip and then a brisk ascent. The walking is generally extremely good underfoot, and as most of the hard climbing has now been done, the lungs will not be greatly tested any further. The main problem is likely to be bad weather; these very lofty summits attract violent air currents, the source of a local meteorological phenomenon known as the Helm Wind. When low cloud or mist come down, navigation could be a serious problem. The first of the three peaks is the 2,780 ft Great Dun Fell, easily identified even in bad weather by its radar and weather stations and its very conspicuous 'golf ball' which is visible from as far away as Helvellyn in the Lake District. The 2,761 ft Little Dun Fell, which follows, is quite uncluttered, and you may wish to pause on the summit before tackling the final peak, Cross Fell, which at 2,930 ft is the summit of the Pennine Way and provides tremendous views to Lakeland. If you are blessed with good weather you may feel your walk to reach this point, particularly in the final stages, has been almost too easy, but when the mist or rain have closed in you will have a real struggle to locate the path to the summit in what is a huge featureless grassland area.

No less difficult, but crucially important, is locating the route off the summit; this heads north-westwards and steeply downhill to meet a cairned path, actually an old corpse road (used to transport bodies for burial), on to which you turn right and which you follow north-eastwards all the way to Garrigill, nearly eight miles away. You will notice the profusion of old mineworkings as you proceed on your way, and you should look out also for the bothy or shelter known as Greg's Hut. The going is now straightforward on an excellent track through the heather, although the lovely views to the Eden valley have been left behind. One interesting feature of this section is the accumulation of blue crystals of fluorspar, a non-metallic mineral which, although regarded as waste material in lead mining, has been used in steel manufacture. At length the corpse road becomes a walled lane, still descending, and drops down to the South Tyne valley, arriving at the village of Garrigill (171.4), a pretty village, and a welcome one too, being the first settlement since Dufton to offer accommodation and refreshment.

However, some walkers may still prefer to press on to Alston. The Way turns north-westwards at Garrigill, joining a road that proceeds through the village and out the other side, going roughly parallel with the South Tyne. Soon, however, you turn right onto a path that follows the riverbank, keeping the river to your right. After just over a mile of delightful riverside walking you switch to the opposite bank, briefly leaving the river and heading across a number of fields past the farms of Sillyhall and Bleagate, the gentle pastoral landscape quite a contrast to the wilds of Cross Fell. You then return to the river and, keeping it to your left, go forward into Alston (175.3) which, built along a steep cobbled street with side streets of stone houses, is claimed to be the highest market town in England. The town has all the amenities a walker could want, including not only ample refreshment and accommodation facilities, but banks and, at the time of my visit, a laundrette. There's also the famous Alston bottle shop, boasting a collection of many thousand bottles, although the man principally responsible for accumulating this extraordinary collection, Arthur Roland, claimed not to drink anything except tea.

Alston to Greenhead (16.5 miles) via Slaggyford

ENJOY: South Tyne Railway, Lambley Viaduct, Maiden Way

This section is arguably the most tedious on the whole route, with no great scenic rewards and plenty of opportunity to lose yourself. You proceed out of Alston pleasantly enough, on a path that keeps the South Tyne close to your right, but then branch off north-westwards, away from the river, passing Harbut Lodge and proceeding across fields, over the A689 and forward to Gilderdale Burn. Beyond Gilderdale Burn you join a cart-track, continuing north-west then swinging north-eastwards past the grassy ramparts of the old Roman fort at Whitley Castle, and arrive at the farm at Castle Nook, where you are reunited with the A689. You cross the road and swing north-westwards again, proceeding through a number of fields and passing the little hamlet of Kirkhaugh. The path is often indistinct on the ground but you can be guided by the course of the old Haltwhistle–Alston railway which you keep to your right. As the A689 comes in from your left, you again eschew tarmac to swing under the old railway, by means of a viaduct picturesquely bathed in woodland, and proceed alongside Thornhope Burn. Now the South Tyne comes in from the right, and, having passed the meeting of Thornhope Burn with it, you briefly follow the South Tyne upstream until you reach your friend the A689 again. At last you are allowed the privilege of a walk alongside it, soon reaching the pretty but amenity-less village of Slaggyford (180.9).

You leave the A689 by turning right up a lane that proceeds parallel with the old railway, then having crossed Knar Burn, pass underneath the railway once more and head uphill slightly away from it, still heading north-westwards. The Way passes the buildings of Merry Know then swings north-eastwards and downhill, crossing the A689 again and arriving at the hamlet of Burnstones. The walk from Slaggyford to Burnstones is fiddly and can get very muddy, and it may be possible to follow the old railway track as an alternative, as we did. We turned right on to the road at Burnstones and found refreshment at the Kirkstile Inn at Knarsdale a short way down the road. However, the Way bears left at Burnstones, and there then follows the fastest walking of this 17-mile slog, as you proceed first northwards, then slightly west of north, along the Maiden Way for two and a half miles. This is an old Roman road linking Kirkby Thore in the old county of Westmorland with a fort near Hadrian's Wall. It is a pleasant moorland march, the route being very easy to follow and largely clear on the ground, with a parallel wall or fence to guide you. Having proceeded in a straight line along the Maiden

Way, crossing Lambley Common, the Pennine Way then swings north-westwards to reach the disused Lambley Colliery and enjoys one final meeting with the A689.

Wainwright calls this next section 'uninteresting' and I think he was being kind! From Lambley Colliery you proceed just west of north across featureless pasture, reaching the barn of High House and briefly swinging north-eastwards to cross Hartley Burn by a footbridge. This is a pleasant enough spot, but beyond, as you proceed north-westwards, there is a dismal section of fiddly field walking, passing the buildings of three farms, some of them ruinous. Beyond the third farm, Greenriggs, you cross over the twin moors of Round Hill and Wain Rigg, passing just to the east of the triangulation point on Black Hill; this is rather less dire than its namesake further south, but no lovelier. There is no path as such, and a compass is essential in mist. Continuing north-westwards you arrive at Gap Shields, swinging north-east, and with some relief you pick up a track here, bearing right on to it and following it slightly south of east, then a little north of east. Looking at the map you appear to have covered two sides of a triangle since escaping from Wain Rigg, but near some old clay pits you swing north-westwards and then decisively north-eastwards, following a good cart-track to cross the A69. Crossing over, you continue north-eastwards to reach what is called the vallum, a broad ditch which served as an old military boundary, then turn right to walk by the vallum as far as a road linking Gilsland with Greenhead (191.8). Most walkers who have come from Alston today will have had enough and will be ready for a bed at Greenhead, which lies just a quarter of a mile away and offers refreshment and accommodation. There is cause for triple celebration here. You have the worst section of the route behind you, you have reached one of the best sections of the route (namely the walk along a section of Hadrian's Wall), and you have now reached the end of the Pennine Range.

Greenhead to Steel Rigg for Once Brewed (6.6 miles) via Aesica

ENJOY: Thirlwall Castle, Walltown Crags, Aesica, Windshields Crags

This section is very short, but enables you to really enjoy Hadrian's Wall. It is a tremendous journey, and certainly makes up for the sad tramping you have experienced since Lambley Colliery. Beyond the Gilsland–Greenhead road, you swing north-eastwards, immediately reaching Thirlwall Castle, a fortified tower-house almost 700 years old but ruinous for at least the last 300 years. Now overlapping with another national trail, Hadrian's Wall Path, you heading eastwards – your principal direction of travel all the way to Rapishaw Gap – and follow a section of Roman ditch to reach Walltown Quarry, then join a road heading for the farm at Walltown. After half a mile or so of road walking, you bear sharply left, uphill, to reach Hadrian's Wall at Walltown Crags. The Wall was a Roman frontier system built under the direction of the emperor Hadrian between 122 and 126 AD to mark England's northern boundary and to prevent tribes such as the Scots and the Picts from launching raids into northern England. It was skilfully built to take advantage of the lie of the land. Some of it, including the section that you will walk, was constructed on serrated dolerite crags of the Whin Sill (a seam of igneous dolerite that runs across northern England), providing a barrier that was partly natural and partly man-made. The Pennine Way follows the Wall for eight miles, and they are eight tough miles, faithfully following the ridge with its ups and downs, and occasional rocky scrambles; the irregular formations of dolerite have little sympathy for tired legs! The reward, however, is a grandstand view of the north Pennines and Cheviots, and the thrill of having the Wall itself immediately beside you.

Just under two miles from Walltown Crags you reach the remains of a fort known as Aesica, then continue past Burnhead, briefly joining a road before proceeding on to Cawfield Crags. You descend to a road at Caw Gap then rise again on to Windshields Crags, at 1,230 ft the highest point on the Wall. This is all superb walking, with glorious panoramic views stretching as far back as the Solway Firth, and no difficulties underfoot or with navigation. Shortly beyond Windshields Crags you reach the B6318 (198.4) where a right turn leads you to the Twice Brewed Inn and the Once Brewed Youth Hostel. The inn got its name from the belief that the ale supplied there was fermented twice to give it added strength, while the hostel owes its name to a remark made upon its opening to the effect that it was hoped nothing stronger than tea, brewed only *once*, would be consumed there! Tea is of course a life-saver for weary walkers. A huge pot of piping hot tea, accompanied by a plate of cakes, is an answer to every hiker's prayer. Less welcome is the hotel room where the guest is forced to confront the intricacies of a jug kettle with a somewhat temperamental element meaning that after waiting 10 minutes from switching on the device he still can't be certain if the water therein is actually getting any warmer at all.

Steel Rigg to Bellingham (14.8 miles) via Wark Forest

ENJOY: Peel Crags, Hotbanks Crags, Warks Burn

From the Once/Twice Brewed turning you continue along the Wall over Peel Crags and past Crag Lough, then climb on to Hotbank Crags. Just beyond these crags is Rapishaw Gap, where you leave the Wall. The view from Rapishaw Gap towards Cuddy's Crags and Housesteads Crags is superb and worth photographing before you leave the Wall for the last time. Now you turn left at Rapishaw Gap to head in a vaguely northerly direction, sometimes just east and sometimes just west of north, across a rather nondescript landscape of open grassland and heather. To your right is Broomlee Lough, and ahead is Wark Forest. Having passed just to the east of the farm at East Stonefolds you plunge into the forest, where you stay for most of the next five miles. This is generally acknowledged as an unwelcome interlude, the dreary conifers of Sitka and Norway spruce packed tightly together so as to ensure minimum light and maximum claustrophobia. Fortunately progress is fast and straightforward on a wide well-defined track, and there are two interludes of open country as you proceed north-eastwards. There is also a standing stone called Comyns Cross towards the end of the first break in the woodland. Having emerged from the final tranche of forest, you continue north-eastwards across grass moorland and arrive at Warks Burn, which is extremely picturesque. Beyond, there is a fiddly and rather unexciting walk across pasture dotted with old farmsteads. At Low Stead you join a road and follow it north-eastwards to a T-junction of roads, crossing straight over and following a path north-eastwards to Houxty Burn. You cross the burn and ascend north-eastwards on to Ealingham Rigg, passing the unfortunately named buildings of Shitlington Hall and then proceeding over Shitlington Crags.

Shortly you reach a walled cart-track, turning right to follow it, and head briefly just south of east, enjoying good views to Bellingham and the valley of the North Tyne from here. After barely half a mile you turn left off the cart-track and proceed across some rather boggy pasture, initially going north-eastwards then swinging north-westwards, descending into the North Tyne valley. At length you arrive at the B6320, turning left on to the road and following it over the river into Bellingham, pronounced 'Bellin-jam' (213.2).

Bellingham

The little town has a wide main street and marketplace flanked by sturdy buildings of grey stone, and there are many places available for refreshment and accommodation; you may permit yourself some celebration having broken through the 200-mile barrier using Countryside Commission measurements although according to Wainwright 200 miles were clocked up back at Greenhead. Bellingham is the last place on the whole route where provisions are readily obtainable, and there are still over 40 miles to go. Although most of the buildings are nineteenth-century, the parish church of St Cuthbert dates from the twelfth century, and its stone roof was to guard against marauding bands of sixteenth-century cattle thieves known as Border Reivers.

Bellingham to Byrness (14.7 miles) via Padon Hill and Redesdale Forest

ENJOY: Hareshaw Linn, Deer Play, Padon Hill

This section is not one of the best on the Pennine Way. However, you can get it off to a good start by detouring from Bellingham to a superb waterfall called Hareshaw Linn, a 30 ft cascade into a rocky chasm surrounded by towering cliffs and woodland, situated a couple of miles north of the centre of the town. Annoyingly, it is necessary for you to retrace your steps to Bellingham before continuing. The start of the walk towards Byrness is easy enough, consisting of a straightforward walk along the West Woodburn road and then a farm road, heading north-eastwards and uphill to the farm at Blakelaw. You then swing in a more northerly direction and proceed across grass and heather moorland, gradually gaining height and veering to the north-west to pass Hareshaw House and Abbey Rigg, where there is an old colliery. The Way crosses the B6320 Bellingham–Otterburn road and you now begin one of the least inspiring sections on the northern half of the route, consisting of a walk across marshy grass and heather through featureless moorland terrain. In bad weather you will almost certainly need a compass to steer you along, as there are virtually no landmarks. Initially you proceed uphill just east of north on to Lough Shaw, then swing west of north to pass the 1,183 ft summit of Deer Play, where on a good day there is a fine view to the Cheviots, and beyond Deer Play you proceed north-westwards to the 1,167 ft summit of Lord's Shaw. Beyond Lord's Shaw there is a descent to the Gib Shiel–Troughend road, and now things get easier. Having crossed the road, the Way once again strikes out north-westwards over the moors, but beyond Whitley Pike and Padon Hill there is the reassurance of a fence to your right, and this stays with you all the way to Redesdale Forest where you will join a road. Although you skirt the western edge of Padon Hill it is worth detouring to enjoy the tremendous views from the 1,240 ft summit with its pepperbox monument commemorating Alexander Padon, a Scottish Covenanter who held open-air services here.

The Way loses height beyond Padon Hill but then climbs to the 1,191 ft Brownrigg Head; this can be quite an arduous ascent, especially in bad weather. Your moorland tramp is almost over however, and after a squelchy descent off Brownrigg Head you enter the massive Redesdale Forest, turning right at Rookengate on to a metalled road and pounding north-westwards along it for three and a half miles as far as the hamlet of Blakehopeburnhaugh. The road walking temporarily ends just beyond Blakehopeburnhaugh, at the bridge crossing of the river Rede. Immediately beyond the bridge you turn left on to a path that proceeds quite delightfully along the riverbank north-westwards as far as the farm at Cottonshopeburnfoot. Continuing north-westwards, the Way crosses the Rede again and follows a forest trail towards Byrness, crossing the river one more time to enter the village (227.9), originally established to accommodate construction workers building a nearby reservoir, and then adopted as a Forestry Commission village to facilitate the management of Redesdale Forest. In recent years it has become a useful place of refreshment for road travellers on the busy A68, which passes right through the village. It is also an almost mandatory stopping-place for Pennine Way walkers, being the very last settlement on the route where amenities of any description are available. Ahead is a very tough 27-mile march across the Cheviots to Kirk Yetholm with no shelter or refreshment available, and although it is possible to detour off the route to obtain accommodation, the detour is necessarily a long one. Many walkers will hope to do the whole walk to Kirk Yetholm in one go, starting as early as five or six in the morning. With the excitement of the long walk ahead, it is unlikely either that sleep will come easily that night, or that even the most competitive Scrabble player in the party will that evening quibble unduly about a deviation from the rules that has somehow enabled both 'Blakehopeburnhaugh' and 'Cottonshopeburnfoot' to mysteriously appear on the board.

Byrness to Kirk Yetholm (27 miles, 24.7 miles omitting The Cheviot) via Windy Gyle

ENJOY: Chew Green, Lamb Hill, Windy Gyle, Hen Hole, The Schil, White Law

This section begins with an awkward and steep ascent out of the village through the trees, heading north-eastwards on a forest path which when we walked it was by no means obvious. With some relief you emerge on to the 1,358 ft Byrness Hill, swinging north-westwards past Saughy Crag and then northwards to Windy Crag. Heading just east of north and continuing to gain height, the Way then continues across the open moor, but navigation is assisted by a fence running alongside you to the left. You proceed past Ravens Knowe then, descending, swing west of north and go forward on to Ogre Hill where you cross the border into Scotland. The Way crosses the border fence and heads northwards away from it, then swings eastwards, passes over Coquet Head and crosses back over the border fence to Chew Green, the site of Roman camps; these camps were a stopover on Dere Street which was an old Roman road linking York with Scotland. The Way then swings north-westwards and proceeds just east of north to follow Dere Street, passing just to the east of the 1,664 ft summit of Brownhart Law. You then stay alongside the border fence for a little under a mile, passing the site of a Roman signal station. This is tremendous walking with no navigational problems and sweeping views across some of the loneliest countryside in the British Isles. The Way then leaves the security of the fence, striking out north-eastwards for two miles through trackless, albeit cairned moorland terrain; becoming reunited with the fence just south-west of Lamb Hill. The ground can be very wet underfoot, although beyond Lamb Hill the going improves.

Now things get easier as you proceed confidently beside the fence for just over two miles, heading north-eastwards past the 1,677 ft Lamb Hill, uphill to the 1,842 ft Beefstand Hill and forward to the 1,812 ft Mozie Law. The Way then moves a little away from the fence but stays parallel with it and continues eastwards to pass Foul Step, then, proceeding a little south of east, rejoins the fence. You continue alongside the fence, heading just south of east, then cross the fence and swing eastwards to climb to the 2,034 ft Russell's Cairn, which unless you are detouring to The Cheviot is the halfway point between Byrness and Kirk Yetholm. Russell's Cairn consists of a mound of stones that are of Bronze Age origin; the hill on which it stands is called Windy Gyle, an appropriate name if ever there was one, because the wind can blow ferociously hard on this exposed Cheviot summit. The views are magnificent, from what is the highest point on the ridge so far. Beyond Windy Gyle you continue north-eastwards beside the border fence for over four miles, keeping the fence to your right on your descent to Clennell Street and thereafter keeping it to your left. At Clennell Street (241.6) you have the opportunity to break your journey by detouring to the left to Cocklawfoot (two miles) or to the right to Uswayford (one mile); you may be fortunate enough to obtain accommodation at either, although this can't be guaranteed. It is the logical place to leave the route if you have decided to split the Byrness–Kirk Yetholm walk into two days, especially as there are no further convenient opportunities to leave the ridge. It's for situations like these that one contemplates the possibility of camping, and the peculiar joys it brings. Freedom. Flexibility. Seeing nature at first hand. Being at one with the mysteries of the night. Missing tent pegs. Thunderstorms at 3.30am. Attacks of midges with more tenacity and deadly accuracy than a Luftwaffe dive-bomber squadron. And improvised heating equipment providing lukewarm beakers of tea and pieces of meat that are burnt down one side and resemble mobile salmonella factories down the other.

Beyond Clennell Street the walking is tough, and although there are no navigational difficulties thanks to the fence, there is a lot of climbing on surfaces which can be atrocious. You pass Butt Roads (certainly no roads) at 1,718 ft, continue to Kings Seat (again, neither king nor seat) at 1,743 ft, then climb to Score Head at 1,910 ft where the going does become extremely difficult. Peat-hags, or peat-bogs, bring back unpleasant memories of Bleaklow and Black Hill, but added to that is a climb of almost inhuman severity to the 2,419 ft west top of Cairn Hill. The relief at reaching this summit is quite indescribable, particularly for walkers who are missing out The Cheviot and who can now begin marching north-westwards towards Auchope Cairn and downhill to Hen Hole. However, for the sake of completeness if nothing else, many hikers will wish, as we did, to make the detour to The Cheviot, up and back on the same path, involving a return trip of just under three miles north-eastwards via the 2,545 ft top of Cairn Hill. This used to be one of the most fiendish parts of the whole Pennine Way, consisting of a trudge along a wide whaleback ridge on an appalling peaty surface with peat-hags just waiting to engulf the walker. Despite the fact that we had all entrusted our rucksacks to the baggage-carrier for this section, and were thus carrying less weight, two of us sank majestically into the peat en route for the summit; one of these unfortunates was in it up to his waist and required the assistance of two people to help him out. We literally had to crawl our way to the summit column, at 2,676 ft the highest ground since leaving Cross Fell, and found an extraordinarily disappointing view. We fought our way back to the main route, our consciences squeaky clean but our clothes precisely the opposite. Things have now changed for the better, and walkers who detour to the Cheviot can enjoy proceeding along a proper flag path.

On return to the main route, you now proceed north-westwards across very squelchy terrain as far as the 2,382 ft Auchope Cairn, an important moment on the walk, for not only does the surface underfoot greatly improve but there is no higher ground to come, and the worst of the walk from Byrness is behind you. The Way proceeds north-westwards – the direction of travel all the way to the end – and, still keeping immediately to the right of the border fence, moves confidently downhill on a good track passing just to the south of the impressive Hen Hole, a narrow ravine and waterfall flanked by huge cliffs, the unusual formations resulting from glacial retreat 10,000 years ago. There is then a tough climb to the Schil, the last major summit on the Way at 1,985 ft; this ascent seems particularly cruel after what has gone before, but there is a splendid view from the summit and if you opt for the low-level route from Black Hag there is now no more serious climbing to be done. From the summit, the Way descends rapidly, crossing the border fence and pulling away from it, proceeding round the western edge of the 1,801 ft Black Hag.

Here you have a choice of routes. You may either turn left off the ridge and descend along a far from obvious path that takes you past the ruin of Old Halterburnhead to the farm at Halterburnhead, joining a road here that takes you safely to the end of the national trail at Kirk Yetholm. This used to be the official way but is now more of a bad weather alternative to a higher-level path that is now designated as the main route. This continues along the ridge, maintaining a height of well over 1,000 ft and returning to the border fence as it proceeds by way of Steer Rigg and climbs to White Law, the last really good viewpoint on the Way with views to the Lammermuir Hills – a preview of the joys of the Southern Upland Way! Beyond this summit, you remain beside the border fence, passing the Iron Age hill fort of Great Hetha, but now begin to lose height and soon bear left, away from the fence, descending more quickly. At length you reach the road that has come up from Halterburnhead and are reunited with the alternative route, a simple mile of road walking now taking you to journey's end at Kirk Yetholm. The last mile is always the hardest of all, especially for those who have walked all the way from Byrness in a single day, but as the houses of Kirk Yetholm and its nineteenth-century village kirk come closer, tiredness is forgotten and replaced by great excitement and a real sense of achievement. Reaching the Border Hotel in the village (254.9 via The Cheviot and main route from Black Hag) is a really marvellous moment for even the most hardened hiker, and following congratulations all round, there can be few better ways of celebrating successful completion of the walk than a few drinks and perhaps a meal in the hotel. We obtained a free drink here courtesy of Wainwright, having presented our *Pennine Way Companions* as evidence that we had done the complete walk, though I cannot say if that tradition will persist by the time you read this. What is certain, however, is that as you linger in the charming village and then catch a bus from nearby Town Yetholm back to civilisation, you will bask in the satisfaction of having risen to a formidable challenge, that of walking not only the most famous but also the toughest long-distance route in Great Britain, which may well rank as one of your greatest life experiences. But don't expect staff at local inns or hotels to be the least bit interested in your exploits – unless you happen to have left a trail of them on the carpet as you came in.

The Pennine Bridleway

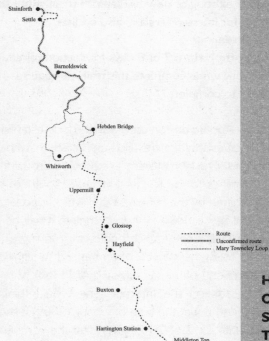

Designation: National trail.
Length: 130 miles so far including Settle
Loop (projected total length 350 miles)
Start: Middleton Top or Hartington,
Derbyshire.
Finish: At the time of writing, the
continuous open section of the Pennine
Bridleway ends with the Mary Towneley

**HIGHLIGHTS
OF THE OPEN
SECTIONS OF
THIS WALK:**
- **Chee Dale**
- **Roych Clough**
- **Cown Edge**
- **Rooley Moor
  Road**
- **Top of Leach**
- **Mary Towneley
  Memorial**
- **Stoodley Pike**

Loop which straddles Yorkshire and Lancashire. However, by the time this book appears it is expected that the linear section will have extended to Wycoller in Lancashire and the projected end of the trail is Byrness in Northumberland.

Nature: A traverse of the Pennines, the so-called backbone of England, using either existing or new bridlepaths throughout thus rendering it suitable for horse riders and also cyclists.

Difficulty rating: Strenuous.

Average time of completion: 7 or 8 days for sections already open and available, but when complete this trail will require around three weeks to complete.

The Pennine Bridleway – not to be confused with the long-established Pennine Way – is the newest national trail. So new, in fact, that it hasn't actually been finished yet. The ultimate aim is to provide a route from the bottom of the Pennines to the top (including the southern part of the Peak District, omitted by the Pennine Way) which is accessible by walkers, cyclists and horse-riders. When complete it will be the country's first purpose-built long-distance bridleway, running all the way from Derbyshire to Byrness in Northumberland (a significant staging post towards the end of the Pennine Way). To look at some of the optimistic forecasts on the Internet, one would think its completion was imminent, but at the time of writing (2009) it seems likely that it won't be until 2012 or 2013; given that the completion date depends on the availability of funding, for which there are so many competing priorities, it could be longer still.

The Pennine Bridleway certainly will not be, and does not pretend to be, as daunting as the actual Pennine Way. While it stays quite close to that route, and occasionally overlaps with it, it is more of a benign younger brother or sister, albeit it will be a rather lankier one when the route is complete. The sections of route that have been opened so far follow well-defined paths, tracks, packhorse trails, lanes and quiet roads, pass through a number of settlements offering food, accommodation and public transport links, and tend to go round the side of the tallest hills rather than over their summits. That said, much of the terrain is still quite wild and remote, amenities aren't always readily available and, when complete, the route as a whole will be the second longest of the national trails, beaten only by the South West Coast Path. So it deserves to be treated with respect rather than indulgence. It's currently a rather strange beast. What is available so far is a linear walk from near Wirksworth to Summit near Todmorden which opened in 2004, linking into a circular route known as the Mary Towneley Loop, which was the first section to open in 2002. Then there's an entirely separate section further north, the Settle Loop, which was opened in 2005. Since then things have gone rather quiet, despite promising murmurings on the Pennine Bridleway website. However, it's anticipated that a further linear section, from the Mary Towneley Loop to Wycoller, will have opened by the time this book appears. This chapter gives a full description of what is available as far as the Mary Towneley Loop; in the closing paragraphs there's some brief information about the Settle Loop, the walk on to Wycoller and the projected route to Byrness. While future reprints of this book will hopefully be able to announce that more has been opened and provide a full description of what has become available, the best source of up-to-date information in the meantime is the internet or telephone enquiry of local tourist information offices.

Middleton Top to Chelmorton (17 miles from Middleton Top, 9.5 miles from Hartington) via Longcliffe

ENJOY: Middleton Top, Harboro Rocks, Tissington Trail.

There are two possible starts to the Pennine Bridleway, Middleton Top and Hartington. The longer route, from Middleton Top, is described first.

Middleton Top isn't the centre of the universe but does provide parking and refreshment facilities and is within easy reach of the Peak District town of Wirksworth, once a hub of the lead-mining industry. The good news is that most of your first day's walk is very straightforward, as for nearly all of it you will follow the High Peak Trail using the course of the old Cromford & High Peak Railway, a line which dates back to 1830 linking the Cromford Canal and High Peak Canal. On leaving Middleton Top with its (at the time of writing) excellent visitor centre, you are almost immediately reminded of the area's industrial past with a disused quarry to your right. Ironically your first three quarters of a mile or so from Middleton Top is south-westwards, away from your ultimate objective, and indeed as far as Longcliffe, nearly four miles in, you make very little significant progress northwards. Initially you head south-westwards parallel with Manystones Lane rising up the Horton incline, a steep climb for railway stock but not so bad for walkers, then strike out north-westwards passing just to the south of the 1,200 ft high limestone outcrops known as Harboro Rocks. You pass just to the north of the village of Brassington, crossing a minor road, then round the edge of the little village of Longcliffe, crossing the B5056 Fenny Bentley–Grangemill Road. Now you do head more decisively north-westwards, passing to the left of the beech-topped Minninglow Hill, where there's a Neolithic tomb. You're given a further reminder of earlier times as you continue over Gallowlow Lane, which is believed to go back to the Roman age, and then there are shades of Batman as you pass Gotham and its granges – post-medieval farmsteads – before crossing the A5012 Cromford–Hartington road just west of Pikehall. You proceed past the brick works of Friden near the little village of Newhaven and, maintaining a north-westerly course, you go forward to pass under the A515 Buxton–Ashbourne road.

Shortly beyond the tunnel under the road, the Tissington Trail comes in from the left; this follows another old railway line which has come up from Hartington, two miles to the south. This is actually an official alternative route to Middleton Top as a start to the Pennine Bridleway, consisting of a very pleasant stroll up the Tissington Trail from the old Hartington Station just over a mile east of the pretty Peak village of Hartington. It's also nine and a half miles shorter than the route from Middleton Top.

The two routes having reunited, you proceed north-westwards past the picturesquely named hamlet of Parsley Hay – it sounds like the venue for an Enid Blyton story – with the A515 never far away to the right. You're now embarking on 'White Peak' country, the high-level carboniferous limestone plateau of the southern Peak District, and looking at a large-scale map of the area you get the impression of a spider's web with the huge numbers of walled fields. The White Peak attracts many varieties of birds, plants and insects; plants include kidney vetch, bloody crane's-bill, wild strawberry, white campion and wood sorrel, while among wildlife to look out for is the bank vole, brown hare, kestrel, chaffinch, sparrowhawk, nuthatch and a little butterfly called the northern brown argus. Beyond Parsley Hay you pass several disused mineshafts round the hamlet of Sparklow, where maps show a welcome pub. Mining used to be a significant aspect of the local economy, and has been from Roman times; at one time it was estimated that 10,000 miners were at work in the lead rakes and veins of the White Peak. Keeping a parallel course with the A515, you now go forward beyond Sparklow to Dow Low passing to the right of Cronkston Low, which is capped by a tumulus. At Dow Low the High Peak Trail ends, and you veer sharp right to head north-eastwards to the A515; having stayed close to this road for so long you now turn right to follow it briefly eastwards, then turn left, north-eastwards, along the pleasant Highstool Lane. It makes a change NOT to be on an old railway line! At the end of the lane you turn left then shortly right, north-eastwards again, along another lane to come within spitting distance of Chelmorton (17) which offers a good range of amenities and is an obvious stopping point after a good day's walk. If you are doing the Pennine Bridleway or indeed any 'big walk' in day stages, availability of public transport will often dictate your start and finish points. One possible answer is to drive two cars to the end of your planned day's walk, drive one back to the start, and get walking with the certainty of having transport waiting for you at the other end. It's safe, flexible and relieves you of some major logistical problems when planning your walking adventure. Doesn't work quite so well, of course, if you're on your own.

Chelmorton to Hayfield (19 miles) via Peak Forest

ENJOY: Five Wells, Chee Dale, Monk's Dale, Tideswell, South Head, Roych Clough, Mount Famine.

From Chelmorton you continue northwards along Pillwell Lane, passing very close to the Five Wells Neolithic chambered cairn, one of the most impressive of its kind in Great Britain. You cross the very busy A6, then go briefly north along a lane before veering north-westwards down into the beautiful wooded Chee Dale, a real highlight of this section. Chee Dale is an example of one of the loveliest aspects of the White Peak, namely the precipitous dales formed by the erosive action of meltwater at the end of the last Ice Age, which split the limestone plateau. The steep rocky sides of the dales enjoy a wealth of plant, bird and insect life including national rarities like the blue-flowered Jacob's-ladder, small copper butterflies and migrant pied flycatchers and wheatears. You cross the river Wye and the course of an old railway which used to run from London (St Pancras) to Manchester and is now enjoying a new lease of life as the very popular Monsal Trail, which goes through some of the loveliest scenery in the Peak District. You pay for your steep descent with a very steep climb out of Chee Dale heading just east of north, then veer north-westwards round the edge of Tunstead Quarry, an enormous limestone works. You proceed

The Pennine Bridleway

away from the workings northwards towards Tunstead, then veer sharply eastwards, downhill, to arrive at the village of Wormhill. Beyond Wormhill you veer in a more northerly direction and reach another fine wooded dale, Monk's Dale, part of the Derbyshire Dales National Nature Reserve with a magnificent variety of wildlife and plant life including the early purple orchid. Your stay in the Dale is all too short, the trail heading away from it eastwards along a lane to Monksdale House and a crossroads. The Pennine Bridleway turns left, north-westwards, up a lane, but by going straight over the crossroads you can easily reach the lovely village of Tideswell, famous for its well-dressing ceremony and superb fourteenth-century church. The mapping in the official national trail guide doesn't cover the village.

Maps

The easy availability of guides to the individual Big Walks, complete with mapping, means that theoretically you shouldn't need to buy separate maps for your journey. That said, you may wish to take maps anyway, to put the path you are walking into some kind of context, enable you to locate and access places of interest off-route, and provide a rudder should an official route be unexpectedly closed or diverted and there is no signposted alternative. And of course you may be quite happy just to use maps without recourse to guide books. Happy, that is, providing the first gust of wind of the day does not blow your map inside out and make it impossible to refold it properly, the first shower of the day does not reduce it to pulp and leaves you wishing you'd invested in the weatherproof edition and you don't find that the various maps you've pulled out of your bookcase two days before you set off leaves a small section of route uncovered and you're faced with the choice of making further inroads into your children's inheritance by buying yet another map you know you'll never need again, or spending half your lunch hour queuing to use the notoriously temperamental library photocopier with a disconcerting propensity for jamming the moment it sees you walking in through the front entrance.

You follow the lane from Monksdale House to Wheston, keeping another steep-sided wooded valley called Peter Dale to your left. Beyond Wheston you follow a walled lane north-westwards, then turn sharply left, south-westwards, down to Hay Dale, sharing your walk with the Limestone Way at this point; you emerge from the dale and head westwards briefly, then at the next road junction bear right for a road walk. Initially the walking is unexciting but as you continue on the road up to the A623 Baslow to Chapel-en-le-Frith road at the village of Peak Forest there is a tremendous view ahead to the Dark Peak, a much more formidable proposition than the White Peak. From Peak Forest you head north-eastwards, initially on a lane, then veer north-westwards along a lane through Perry Dale. You're now beginning to leave the White Peak country behind and are entering the Dark Peak country, forsaking the limestone for the darker gritstone and the tightly-enclosed fields for broad expanses of moorland. The Dark Peak is indeed an apposite name, because the impression is of a dark, peaty heather-clad wilderness above valleys dotted with reservoirs. The landscape was effectively the result of the activities of Stone Age and Bronze Age man, whose deforestation left the soil exposed to nature; the huge areas of peat bog result from the waterlogging of exposed soil and consequent steady decay of vegetation. Yet these harsh surroundings have, perhaps paradoxically, generated a rich variety of bird life and plant life. The grouse is the bird most associated with the bleak moors, but others you may encounter include the hen harrier, peregrine, curlew, snipe, ring ouzel, merlin, crossbill and golden plover, while the bogs and peaty pools may host such plants as bogbean and marsh cinquefoil. Beyond Perryfoot you continue north-westwards, gaining height all the time, to pass Rushop Hall and cross another road. Now enjoying excellent views to South Head, you continue along the moorland edge to go round the top of Bolehill Clough (a clough being a deep stream valley). The going gets even more spectacular as you plunge down into Roych

The Pennine Bridleway

Clough, with the imposing peaks of Brown Knoll and Horsehill Tor to your right, the former not far shy of 1,900 ft. Looking up towards Brown Knoll, Pennine Way veterans will get a real sense of déjà vu as they gaze at this barren unforgiving landscape. Those who do recall the Pennine Way in the bad old days before the era of flagstone paths may wallow in a few moments of nostalgia as they recall sinking slowly into the mire, desperately trying to obtain a compass bearing in one hand whilst clutching a mud-stained Alfred Wainwright Pennine Way Companion with the other.

The going just gets better and better as you rise out of Roych Clough, continuing in a north-westerly direction on a clear walled track with the lofty South Head immediately to your left. This is some of the highest walking on the linear section of the national trail and on a clear day the views to the Kinder plateau are breathtaking. Almost immediately after passing South Head, you proceed below and just to the left of the biblical-sounding Mount Famine; there follows lovely open walking, with views now to the hill known as Chinley Churn to your left, and you descend steadily, the A624 Chapel-en-le-Frith–Hayfield road now not far away to the left. An excellent path brings you sweeping down into the valley, with the enticing prospect of Hayfield – the biggest settlement on the path so far – just ahead. There's some pleasant woodland walking before you reach the River Kinder and keep it close by as you enter the village, as far north as Edale where the actual Pennine Way begins. Hayfield (36) is a very popular base for visitors to the Kinder Scout area of the Peak, so book early in holiday periods. And not just your accommodation: these days if you are travelling to your 'big walk' by train, unless you live close by you will inevitably pay far less if you book your journey in advance than if you simply turn up and buy a ticket on the day. It will certainly get your walking holiday off to a bad start if you find you've paid possibly ten times more than the person sitting next to you for exactly the same standard of comfort, same wait for the buffet trolley, same annoyance at the buzz of the personal stereo of the student opposite, and same 90-minute delay at Crewe. So it will pay you to book ahead either online or at your local railway station ticket office. But if you go for the latter do not expect to be too popular after taking 30 minutes arranging a reserved journey from Wokingham to Manchester and back whilst the ticket machine's broken and 26 shoppers are queuing behind you for cheap day returns to Bracknell.

Hayfield to Uppermill (19 miles) via Hollingworth

Enjoy: Lantern Pike, Cown Edge, 'Pots & Pans' Obelisk

You begin with a walk out of Hayfield on the Sett Valley Trail, following the course of an old railway – shades of your endeavours on day one! You then leave this trail in just under a mile, cross the Sett and veer north-eastwards, heading uphill along a lane and going forward to Lantern Pike from which there are magnificent views to Kinder and back to Hayfield. Now veering just west of north, you descend along a walled track past Matleymoor Farm, arriving at a road. You turn right to follow it briefly, then bear left, westwards, the surroundings here becoming noticeably more remote. Shortly you bear right to follow a splendid ridge path alongside Coombes Rocks and Cown Edge Rocks. You turn north-westwards and descend across fields, crossing two roads leading into the village of Charlesworth (just down to your left) then joining a lane and a path taking you to the A626 Glossop road just above Charlesworth. You cross the road then head roughly westwards along field-edge paths – something of an anticlimax after the exhilaration of Lantern Hill and the ridge. You pass under a railway and through the village of Broadbottom, then veer right, north-eastwards, along Hague Road and continue through comparatively low-lying farmland using a path known as the Valley Way. You arrive at the A57 at Hollingworth, cross over it and go on to shortly cross the A628.

The Pennine Bridleway

You emerge from Hollingworth along a road, then pull away from the built-up area, heading in a generally northerly direction through Hollingworth Nature Reserve along a path which takes you to Lees Hill. You swing sharply left to walk beside Higher Swineshaw Reservoir then veer again sharply south-westwards beside Lower Swineshaw Reservoir and head westwards through Stalybridge Country Park, passing to the right of two more reservoirs, Brushes and Walkerwood. There are in fact some 50 reservoirs in the valleys of the Dark Peak. With Manchester staring at you ahead, you now veer north-eastwards, keeping Harridge Pike and Slatepit Moor to your right and the houses of Carrbrook to your left. You join a lane round a housing estate and proceed along Moor Edge Road, passing the town of Mossley to your left and overlapping here with the Tameside Trail. The Pennine Bridleway certainly meets a lot of named paths! You pass round the left-hand edge of Noon Sun Hill, although the rather loftier Alphin Pike is not far beyond to the east, and Alderman's Hill, with its distinctive 'pots and pans' obelisk war memorial, can be observed to the north-east. The lane becomes a proper tarmac surface and continues just east of north to hit the A635, close to Saddleworth Moor with its infamous 'Moors murders' associations. Then, having passed beyond the A635 between the villages of Friezland and Greenfield, you'll find the walking becomes temporarily more urban in nature. You join the Tame Valley Way which comes in from the left, and soon cross the A669, now following not only the Tame Valley Way but the course of another old railway; you pass along the eastern fringes of Lower Arthurs and into Uppermill, the river Tame not far away to your left. Uppermill (55), a bustling little town with ample refreshment opportunities, is well served by amenities and if you fancy a night on the town the centre of Manchester is remarkably close. In fact looking at the map of the walk from Hayfield to Summit, at the end of the next section, there's more than a hint of the M25 about the path, providing what looks like part of an orbital route round a great city. Don't expect to find quite so many traffic cones on your route, though.

Uppermill to Summit (17 miles) via M62

ENJOY: Hollingworth Lake, Syke Moor, Rochdale Canal

Your day's walk starts innocuously enough, with a tramp away from the fleshpots of Uppermill along the course of the old railway, veering north-eastwards along lanes to the next settlement, Diggle. You join yet another named path, the Standedge Trail, and now head resolutely north-eastwards from the Tame valley up into the moors, climbing steadily on to Diggle Edge and alongside the Standedge Railway Tunnel. You then veer away from the Standedge Trail to go forward to cross the A62 at Standedge Cutting and very briefly meet the Pennine Way. However, your acquaintance is fleeting, as your route dips south-westwards on a lane that leads to another Blytonesque-sounding spot, Bleak Hey Nook, before veering north-westwards, briefly joining Dirty Lane. To your left here is the site of the Castleshaw Roman fort, dating back to around 80 AD and marking the line of an old military road. From Dirty Lane you go on along the top of the dam between the two Castleshaw Reservoirs. Continuing to Low Gate lane you climb steeply then veer right, north-eastwards, up Moor Lane, now enjoying some open moorland walking. Take care to bear left (north-westwards) shortly, walking to the A640 Denshaw-Huddersfield road, crossing it and passing the edge of Dowry Reservoir. You follow Dowry Road uphill then, continuing to ascend, veer right, north-eastwards, along a gorgeous track with Rape Hill ahead of you, to meet the so-called Station to Station Walk.

You bear left now, downhill, to walk past the Readycon Dean Reservoir. Continue westwards, again descending, to arrive at the A672 Ripponden Road, bearing left to follow alongside it briefly. You then bear right onto a track that takes you north-westwards past the

The Pennine Bridleway

right-hand edge of Piethorne Reservoir, then climb, keeping Binns Pasture to your right, before descending along Tunshill Lane. You're now sharing your path with the Rochdale Way. Just before Dick Hill you bear right and now begin your approach to the M62, the noise of which you'll have been aware of for a while. You bear north-eastwards on a track round Nicholas Pike then veer dramatically south-westwards and swing more gently north-westwards to pass under the M62 motorway. Beyond the M62 you continue past the houses of Rakewood to arrive at Hollingworth Lake, another reservoir, which was as popular a recreational facility in the nineteenth century as it is now; it was here that Captain Webb practised before becoming the first person to swim the English Channel. Don't be tempted into following the reservoir all the way round (well, you can if you like, but you'll have to backtrack) but turn right and eastwards, away from the Station to Station Walk and the Rochdale Way, and proceed uphill. You pass Hollingworth Hill to your left, beyond which to your right is the wonderfully named Benny Hill – the only location on a national trail to share its name with a television personality. Unless, of course, you can think of any others as you attempt to get off to sleep at the end of your day's exertions. Makes a change from counting Pennine sheep anyway…

Having raised a dutiful smile at the name, you now veer northwards over Syke Moor, onto a tarmac road then along a walled lane past Draught Hill. This is all delightful walking, enhanced by the views to Blackstone Edge to the right. You arrive at a road at Lydgate then soon leave it to continue on a path round the left-hand edge of Stormer Hill to reach the A58. Cross the road and head north-eastwards to Castle Clough, then veer north-westwards above Higher Chelburn Reservoir to cross Leach Hill. It's now downhill to the Lower Chelburn Reservoir and on to the Rochdale Canal at the very pretty Summit Lock; you cross the bridge and ascend to the A6033 at the north end of the village of Summit (72). This is a key point on your route for two reasons – firstly you have finally got past the sprawl of Manchester, and secondly you've reached the Mary Towneley Loop. This is a novel concept on a national trail – part of a trail which actually creates a 'round robin' walk in itself. It is named after the late Lady Mary Towneley who campaigned for a long-distance route that was suitable for horses, and indeed in 1986 she rode all the way from Derbyshire to Northumberland to highlight the state of the country's bridle routes and launch the idea for the Pennine Bridleway.

Summit to Lumb (17 miles) via Broadley

ENJOY: Watergrove, Healey Dell, Prickshaw, Rooley Moor Road, Top of Leach

Joining the Mary Towneley Loop at Summit you may feel a little like someone jumping onto a carousel at a fairground – a sense of joining something dynamic and just that little bit different, bearing in mind that none of the other national trails boast loop routes as such. From the main road crossing at Summit you head briefly north-westwards then sharp left to follow round the north-west edge of Calderbrook before striking out westwards between Blackbow Hill and Long Hill. You go forward to Grimes and descend to Turn Slack Clough then ascend again onto Ratcliff Hill and veer north-westwards, bending round High Lee Slack and passing to the north-east of East Hill. Things level out for a while although the views remain splendid. You veer south-westwards to the edge of Watergrove Reservoir which holds over 700 million gallons of water and is a haven of bird and plant life. From the reservoir you head up Ramsden Road, passing the site of the original Watergrove Village where there was a population of about 200 towards the end of the nineteenth century; they were evacuated during the construction of the reservoir in order to maintain water purity. You drop down to Longshoot Clough along a track, with Middle Hill away to your right, then pulling away from Watergrove Valley you veer south-westwards, renewing your acquaintance with the Rochdale Way and keeping Brown Wardle Hill to your right. Past Brown Wardle Hill to your right is the town of Whitworth, and having passed Manchester on the linear route you're now moving closer back down to Rochdale at the top end of the Manchester sprawl. Continuing south-westwards you pass Lobden golf course and Rushy Hill, both of which are just to your left, and come down to the village of Broadley, sandwiched between Whitworth and Rochdale. In fact the Pennine Bridleway swings sharp right up a lane parallel with the main road through the village, passing along Highgate Lane close to the hamlet of Healey Stones, once renowned for nude kicking competitions!

At Tonacliffe you reach and go over the A671 then having crossed the pretty river Spodden and enjoyed the lovely Healey Dell Nature Reserve you pass close to Spring Mill Reservoir and swing south-westwards via Prickshaw Lane to the beautifully restored hamlet at Prickshaw. You go forward to Knacks Lane, reaching here what is the southernmost point on the Loop, then bear right onto Rooley Moor Road, an ancient route linking Manchester and Burnley. The character of the route changes again, as you leave the valley behind and rise up into moorland, which, although bleak, does offer superb views on a good day. You now head resolutely north-westwards along Rooley Moor Road past Prickshaw Slack and Hamer Hill to the right, and Warm Slack Hill to your left, to arrive just to the north-east of Top of Leach. Just beyond the Top of Leach, well over 1,500 ft above sea level, you leave Rooley Moor Road and bear left onto another track; you pass well above Cowpe Reservoir which is to your right, and north-westwards along the course of the Rossendale Way via Cragg Quarry. You reach Black Hill and now, at what is the western-most point on the Loop, you veer sharply right, north-eastwards, enjoying splendid views to Rossendale. The going gets quite steep for a time as you drop down to Cowpe Road, having reached which you follow close to it down to the A681 Rawtenstall-Bacup road at Waterfoot, now in Rossendale.

Urban walking now takes over, providing quite a contrast to the bleak moorland you've left behind; you follow roads north-eastwards away from the A681 past Boothfold then veer slightly west of north to pass Edgeside. Eventually you pull away from the houses, along a path that goes roughly parallel with the B6238 at Whitewell Bottom then crosses this road just north of the little village of Lumb (89). As you sit in your B & B that night, whether in Lumb or some other town or village in Rossendale, you will particularly hope for a good weather forecast for next day in view of the terrain to be walked. Those who wake up to bucketing rain on the day of a planned walk, whether on the Pennine Bridleway or elsewhere have a straight choice: do the walk anyway, and miss the 'unforgettable', 'stunning', 'superb' and 'magnificent' views their path guide tantalisingly says they will enjoy 'on a clear day'; or take a day off, possibly putting carefully planned schedules out of kilter and resorting to indoor attractions. Which may range from simply sitting grumpily in pubs and cafes to (in popular walking centres) traipsing round outdoor goods shops commiserating with fellow sufferers, drooling over state-of-the-art clothing and footwear, and topping up supplies of walking socks complete with packaging depicting infuriatingly happy-faced ramblers frolicking under cloudless blue skies.

Lumb to Blackshaw Head (18 miles) via Holme Chapel

ENJOY: Mary Towneley Memorial, Cliviger Valley, Shedden Clough

From the B6238 crossing just above Lumb you proceed in an essentially northerly direction along lanes through rough farmland and grassland with fine views. Just beyond Clough Bottom Reservoir over the B6238 to the right, you meet the Rossendale Way and turn right to follow this briefly, leaving it and heading now predominantly

north-eastwards. You follow a track along the southern fringe of
Red Moss, a very enjoyable walk, then proceed parallel with and in
fact immediately beside the B6238 to its junction with the A671. (In
very bad weather you could just stick to the B6238 all the way from
Lumb!) You cross the A671 – the actual route provides a crossing
point a little south-east of the B6238 junction – then continue east/
north-east along the east side of Easden Clough to bring you to
the memorial of Mary Towneley herself. From beside the memorial
there are good views to Burnley and also the mass of Pendle Hill,
over 1,800 ft high. The memorial is a good reminder that not
even Alfred Wainwright succeeded in having the Coast to Coast
or indeed a part of any national trail named after him, so she has
achieved something he didn't!

Alfred Wainwright
Most keen walkers, particularly those who enjoy walking in
Northern England, will be familiar with the life and work of Alfred
Wainwright (AW). Born in Blackburn, not a million miles from the
projected course of the Pennine Bridleway, in 1907, he became
Borough Treasurer at Kendal in 1948 and whilst working there
produced his legendary Pictorial Guides to the Lakeland Fells.
However, he wrote many other books about walking, including
guides to the Pennine Way and his very own creation, the Coast To
Coast, covered elsewhere in this book. His work is revered not only
for his beautifully written descriptions and line drawings but his
outspoken views and bon mots which, delivered in the obligatory
lugubrious Lancashire drawl, can be guaranteed to feature in the
many television programmes of his walks – the availability of DVDs,
video recorders and iPlayers meaning schedulers can get away with
restricting showings of them to 11 p.m. on Sunday nights or 7 a.m.
on Boxing Day mornings.

You drop down quite steeply then swing sharply right, south-
eastwards, passing to the north of Stone House Edge and arriving
at a railway line. You go under it then parallel with it before swinging

sharply left to arrive at the little village of Holme Chapel on the A646 in the Cliviger Valley; Holme Chapel has a pretty church, and in the churchyard is buried Henry Wood, who was Clerk of Works during the rebuilding of St Paul's Cathedral following the Great Fire of London. From the A646 you now head predominantly north-eastwards, enjoying fine views to the Cliviger Valley and sandstone crags known as the Thieveley Scout Crags, back over the A646 across the valley. You pass above Green Clough and arrive at another road, bearing right onto it then shortly left into open moorland. You now proceed to Shedden Clough, once a significant source of limestone; the grassy hillocks you see here are called 'hushings', which came about as part of the excavation process. The landscape hereabouts is extremely picturesque, with mixed woodland, including oak and beech, to enjoy. Continue in a predominantly northerly direction to pass over the dam of Cant Clough Reservoir, from which a track takes you to, and along the east side of, Hurstwood Reservoir. At Gorple Road, just beyond this reservoir, you have reached the north-west end of the Loop. Now you swing eastwards along Gorple Road (actually a track), climbing all the time through a remote gritstone moorland landscape, rising to Spring Head and maintaining the height over Shuttleworth Moor. You descend steeply to the Widdop Reservoir and walk alongside its south-eastern end; at the far corner, the northernmost point of the Loop, bear right onto Halifax Lane, then leave it and follow an access lane to Gorple Lower Reservoir. Cross the dam of the reservoir at its eastern end and in fact arrive at the Pennine Way, with which you overlap briefly as you head southwards. The Pennine Way has, meantime, come up from Colden on its way to Heptonstall Moor and Bronte country, with views here not only towards Heptonstall Church tower but one of the classic local landmarks, Stoodley Pike. The Pennine Bridleway leaves the Pennine Way and heads southwards then south-eastwards along Edge Lane round the west side of Standing Stone Hill; it then veers sharply right, south-westwards, along School Land Lane and then sharply left, eastwards, along Brown Hill Lane. This brings you to a road along which you go forward to Jack Bridge. You follow a lane briefly eastwards beyond Jack Bridge, then climb very steeply up just west of south, crossing the Calderdale Way and arriving at another road just east of Blackshaw Head (107).

Blackshaw Head to Summit (10.7 miles) via Mankinholes

ENJOY: Stoodley Pike, Mankinholes, Bottomley Lock

This is a short section bringing you back to Summit. You head initially downhill, enjoying superb views to Stoodley Pike, erected in 1856 and standing 120 ft high; you then continue on a lane which zigzags downhill to arrive at the Calder Valley, the railway and the A646 once more. Having crossed the A646 you head uphill and again meet and indeed overlap with the Pennine Way as you pass through Callis Wood. However the Pennine Bridleway forsakes its elder brother to turn sharp left along the edge of the woodland, reaching a road at Horsehold; you bear right to follow the road then right again along Kilnshaw Lane, and now head south-westwards to meet the Pennine Way again. You simply cross it this time, and despite the allure of Stoodley Pike ahead of you, you actually contour the slopes below it, heading westwards then veering south-westwards along London Road, an old packhorse trail. If you fancy a detour to the monument, from which on a clear day the views will be fantastic, there are paths available for the purpose including the course of the Pennine Way itself. You go forward to arrive at the pretty village of Mankinholes, joining the Calderdale Way. Bear right to pass through the little village, which boasts a youth hostel, then bear left along a path to Lumbutts which is dominated by a water tower the height of which almost matches that of Stoodley Pike. From Lumbutts you follow a lane uphill, getting to within a mile of the town of Todmorden; however, you leave the lane and strike out on a track, first south-westwards to Rake Head then southwards. There are excellent views westwards to the sprawl of housing south of Todmorden together with the canal, railway and road, while eastwards to your left is a much wilder landscape. You begin to descend, dropping quite steeply then rising to arrive at Bottomley; another sharp descent follows bringing you to the Rochdale Canal which you cross at the most attractive Bottomley Lock, and from there you climb to the A6033. You cross the road and also a tunnel over the Manchester to Leeds railway after which, keeping the A6033 to your left, you climb steeply up a zigzag path. Now you proceed fractionally east of south along a good track with views across the A6033 to the Lower Chelburn Reservoir which you'll recall from your walk from Uppermill (see above) – a sign that the Mary Towneley Loop is now pretty much complete (117.7). Indeed as your path curves in a more south-easterly direction to reach Calderbrook Road you meet the linear route coming in from your left, ending your walk on the Loop route – closing the Loop, if you like.

Now you've completed the Loop, what happens? This is, at the time of writing, the extent of the available continuous walking on the Pennine Bridleway. The ten-mile Settle Loop, further north, is available, offering some splendid walking in the beautiful limestone country between Settle and Malham, but this can hardly be said to be part of the national trail at present as it isn't connected to the rest of the route. For that reason, I have chosen to omit a full route description from this edition of the book, but provide just a summary instead. The Settle Loop exits Settle by heading north-eastwards towards the neighbouring town of Stainforth, before veering in a more easterly direction and then just south of east across a limestone upland landscape with views to Malham Tarn, which lies just over a mile to the north-east of the Settle Loop at its nearest point. The Settle Loop then veers south-westwards, skirting Kirkby Fell with an easy detour possible hereabouts to Malham Cove and Malham which lie a little to the south-east. The Settle Loop, however, heads westwards and then south-westwards beneath Rye Loaf Hill and then via Stockdale Lane and Lambert Lane to return to the start.

As far as the linear aspect of the Pennine Bridleway is concerned, an extension of the path as far as Wycoller should be open by the time you read this, and that will be a big step towards linking the existing route with Settle. The linear route overlaps with the Mary Towneley Loop to the section of the Loop between Hurstwood Reservoir and Widdop Reservoir, then will proceed round Boulsworth Hill to the Forest of Trawden, east of the settlements of Burnley, Brierfield, Nelson and Colne, and arrive at Wycoller. It will of course be for each individual walker planning a linear walk from Middleton Top (or Hartington) to Byrness to decide how much of the loop routes to incorporate into the journey. Technically you'll be able to walk clockwise round the Mary Towneley Loop, as described above, to pick up the new linear route to Wycoller thus missing out the eastern section of the Mary Towneley Loop; or having followed the existing linear route to Summit you could walk anticlockwise round the Mary Towneley Loop via the Calder Valley to Widdop Reservoir and continue the new linear walk from there, omitting the western part of the Loop. Of course to say you've 'done' all of the Pennine Bridleway and keep your conscience squeaky clean will require you to complete the whole Mary Towneley Loop then find your way from Summit to the moors where the linear route leaves the Mary Towneley Loop. Then, of course, you'll need to consider factoring in the ten-mile Settle Loop to your itinerary. A demanding logistical exercise indeed. Extravagant things, consciences...

From Wycoller the projected route would then appear to head for Barnoldswick, skirting Colne, veering south-westwards and easing round the north-east side of Pendle Hill before heading more resolutely northwards, skirting the Forest of Bowland. It will pass through or close to Long Preston before reaching Settle, where the Settle Loop begins; skirting the east flanks of Ingleborough Hill and Great Whernside, two of the Three Peaks, the route then will go forward to cross the A684 Hawes-Sedbergh road. The route will apparently veer eastwards through the western part of Wensleydale, one of the best-loved of all the Yorkshire Dales, before veering north, close to the B6259 just east of Wild Boar Fell to reach Kirkby Stephen – a significant staging post on the Coast to Coast walk. Passing the amusingly named Fat Lamb Inn, the Pennine Bridleway will then proceed north-westwards to the east of Appleby-in-Westmorland to reach Dufton; here the Pennine Way is met, and the two routes will never be too far away from each other from then on. However instead of scaling the heights of Cross Fell, as the Pennine Way does, the Bridleway heads for Melmerby then veers north-eastwards, crossing the Pennine Way and the A689 Alston-Brampton road and going forward to meet the A69 in the vicinity of Haltwhistle. The new national trail will head eastwards parallel with the A69 and the nearby Hadrian's Wall but not actually on the Wall itself; having veered northwards the Pennine Bridleway will cross the Wall and continue to Wark and north-westwards to Bellingham. Which just leaves one more day's walking, Bellingham to Byrness. However, although they mirror the start and finish points of the traditional penultimate day on the Pennine Way, the Bridleway route is set to be somewhat less taxing, skirting (and appearing to offer a spur route to) Kielder Water and passing through extensive forestry to the north and east of Kielder Water. The Pennine Bridleway then will stay very close to the Pennine Way for the last couple of miles. Then at Byrness your work is done. Pennine Way walkers still have the trifling matter of a twenty-nine mile stroll to Kirk Yetholm.

The Southern Upland Way

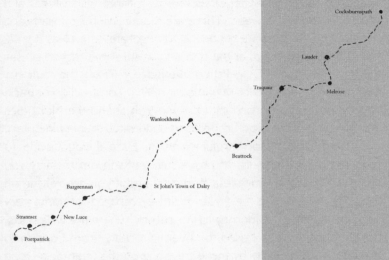

Designation: Scottish National Long Distance Walking Route.
Length: 212 miles.
Start: Portpatrick, Dumfries & Galloway.
Finish: Cockburnspath, Scottish Borders.
Nature: A coast to coast walk across high-level and often remote terrain of Southern Scotland.
Difficulty rating: Strenuous, severe in places.
Average time of completion: 12–14 days.

HIGHLIGHTS OF THIS WALK:
- **Portpatrick**
- **Loch Trool**
- **Benbrack**
- **Sanquhar Castle**
- **Wanlockhead**
- **Lowther Hill**
- **Ettrick Head**
- **Three Brethren**
- **Melrose Abbey**

The Southern Upland Way, opened in 1984, was the first official national coast to coast route, running from Portpatrick on Scotland's west coast to Cockburnspath on its east coast. While at 212 miles it may not be the longest of the paths in this book, it is certainly one of the toughest, proceeding through the uncompromising and often exceedingly remote terrain of southern Scotland, with villages and towns few and far between. There are mountains, huge forests and long stretches of desolate moorland to negotiate, as well as a great deal of hill-climbing and, at the start and finish, some rugged coastal walking. Unlike Offa's Dyke Path or the Ridgeway Path, the route has not been designed to follow a particular historic construction or track; the satisfaction lies in marching from the Irish Sea to the North Sea through some of the most unspoilt and underrated scenery in Britain.

Logistically it calls for careful planning. Even if you decide to camp you need to ensure you have sufficient supplies to carry you through the long amenity-less stretches, and if you are relying on a 'proper' bed for the night you must be prepared for some very long days indeed. The journey to Portpatrick, where the walk starts, is not straightforward; I used the overnight coach from London to Stranraer – used chiefly by those travelling on the Stranraer–Larne ferry – and found myself being decanted from the vehicle at 4.15 a.m. Deciding to walk to Portpatrick via the Southern Upland Way itself, and then catch a bus back to Stranraer, I began tramping through the streets of the town, the deathly silence around me suddenly being broken on a street corner by the sounds of an all-night party that even at 4.40 a.m. was still in full swing.

Portpatrick to A77 for Stranraer (8 miles) via Knockquhassen

ENJOY: Portpatrick, Dunskey Castle, Irish Sea coast

Portpatrick, reachable by bus from Stranraer, is a lovely place to begin the walk. At one time it was the terminus of the main ferry route between Scotland and Northern Ireland, although this has since been transferred to Stranraer. It is now a peaceful holiday centre with attractive stone houses and cottages, while half a mile south are the ruins of the sixteenth-century Dunskey Castle. In the heart of the village are the preserved ruins of a seventeenth-century parish church in which runaway marriages – often between couples eloping from Ireland – were performed at a fee of £10 for the officiating minister, before the ceremonies were stopped by the Church in 1826. It is with some reluctance that you will set off from this pretty place and begin the long walk across Scotland. As with Wainwright's Coast to Coast Walk, the journey begins with a coastal walk slightly west of north, effectively taking you further away from your ultimate objective. It is a splendid walk, firstly rounding the tiny coves of Port Mora and Port Kale, and then climbing steeply to pass the little headlands of Catebraid and Stronie, continuing on to the bigger headland of Black Head and Killantringan lighthouse. You turn right on to the lighthouse road and follow it away from the coast, as far as the B738; you turn left along this road then right up a narrow metalled road past the intriguingly-named settlement of Knock and Maize.

At a T-junction of roads you bear right, then shortly right again onto a lane which peters out after a turning to High Auchenree, and you continue just north of east across Broad Moor. The route, which can be quite juicy underfoot, is very indistinct on the ground and you should follow the waymarks carefully. However, this is an attractive section, with the Knockquhassen reservoir immediately to your left and, beyond that, views to Stranraer, Loch Ryan and the distinctive summit of Ailsa Craig. You reach a metalled road, turning right to follow it, and navigation is very easy for a while as the Way makes use of a succession of metalled roads, with just one small intervening stretch of path, to head south-eastwards past Ochtrelure and arrive at the A77 (8). This is as near as the route gets to Stranraer, which is not only a ferry terminal but a pleasant town with good facilities for walkers and holidaymakers. Its sixteenth-century Castle of St John became the town jail and in the late seventeenth century held Covenanters (about which more below) during campaigns of religious persecution by Graham of Claverhouse. Nowadays, however, it has to be said most people, particularly south of the Border, associate Stranraer predominantly not with its history and beauty but with lower league Scottish football, the result of their match often the last before the all-important pools news.

A77 to New Luce (15 miles) via Castle Kennedy

ENJOY: Castle Kennedy, Water of Luce

Much of this section is very easy going, with little indication of the rigours ahead. You follow another succession of lanes north-eastwards across land lying just a few feet above sea level; this is the 'neck' of the Rhins, a thin peninsula that stretches right down to the Mull of Galloway. Having passed under the railway bridge, you turn right through a strip of woodland running parallel with the railway to reach Castle Kennedy, a pleasant village with a mixture of modern housing and some cottages dating back to 1860. You arrive at the A75 Stranraer–Newton Stewart road, and cross to head north-eastwards through the grounds of the original Castle Kennedy.

Castle Kennedy

Built around 1600 for John Kennedy, fifth earl of Cassilis, it was gutted by fire in 1716 and is now roofless. However, a new mansion house, Lochinch, was built in the grounds between 1864 and 1868, and the two buildings – the ruined original and Lochinch – stand at either end of an isthmus created by two large lochs in the ground, Black Loch and White Loch. The gardens are particularly noteworthy for their outstanding display of plants.

The Way does not take in much of the grounds but soon returns to the Castle Kennedy–New Luce road, turning left to follow it to Chlenry, where you turn right and follow a path quite steeply uphill north-eastwards through a mixture of woods and open land. You keep the road quite close to your left, and shortly return to it, enjoying magnificent views to the surrounding hills and moors. Having turned right to follow it again, you soon forsake it once more, turning right onto a track and then following the northern fringe of a large area of forest. Heading north-eastwards, you pass to the north of Craig Fell and cross the Glasgow-Stranraer Railway and the delightful Water of Luce, shortly beyond which you hit the Glenluce–New Luce road. Although you could follow this road northwards to New Luce, where food and accommodation are available, you may wish to get a few more miles under your belt, as New Luce is easily reachable again a little further on. The Way, having arrived at the road, turns left onto it then shortly bears right to proceed north-eastwards along a track towards Kilhern, gently gaining height. After the easy miles of lowland road bashing, it is quite a contrast to be proceeding across a remote, albeit comparatively low-lying stretch of moorland, with a sense that civilisation is now left behind and the real work has begun. The track, though well-defined on the map, can be exceedingly boggy and progress may be especially slow in bad weather. At the ruined buildings of Kilhern, quite a sad but at the same time dramatic sight in the formidable surroundings, you swing left and head north-westwards, passing just to the left of the Caves of Kilhern, a ruin of a chambered cairn dating back to the third millennium BC.

You pass along the right-hand edge of a patch of woodland and gently drop to a metalled road. The Way turns right on to the road, but by detouring left you will soon reach New Luce (23), an attractive village with some eighteenth-century buildings, although much of the village, including its church and bridges, is nineteenth-century.

New Luce to Bargrennan (17.5 miles) via Knowe

ENJOY: Laggangarn, Craig Airie Fell, Hill of Ochiltree

Having joined the metalled road, you soon pass a waterfall, keeping the Cross Water of Luce to the left. Where a road fork is reached, you turn left and proceed uphill north-eastwards, keeping to the lane, climbing steadily past the settlement of Balmurrie. Beyond Balmurrie the lane swings north-westwards towards Kilmacfadzean, but before reaching this house you turn right off the lane and strike out north-eastwards across the moors, keeping Closs Hill to your left and Balmurrie Fell to your right. More immediately to the right is Cairn-na-Gath, a long cairn which again is of the third millennium BC. The path is somewhat unclear on the ground; in good visibility you will be guided by the excellent marker posts but in bad weather you may need a compass to steer you safely across the moors and into the forest. You then proceed north-eastwards along a wide path through the thick woodland, which in wet weather can seem like a treadmill. A clearing in the forest heralds the remarkable standing stones of Laggangarn; the sandstone slabs, each bearing a cross with arms broadening outwards, were probably erected during the second millennium BC.

The Way continues north-eastwards through the forest, along the lower slopes of Craig Airie Fell. At certain times tree felling may be in progress, so care is needed to follow temporary signposting. Shortly after passing just to the right of the fell summit, marked by a triangulation point well over 1,000 ft above sea level, you arrive at a clearly defined forest track. Route-finding difficulties cease for the moment, as you turn right on to the track which eventually turns into a metalled road, and you keep on it for some four miles, heading just south of east, passing the little settlements of Derry, Polbael and Waterside. Although the forest relents a little as you pass to the south of Loch Derry, it soon returns and dominates the walk on to the B7027 Barrhill–Newton Stewart road. In wet weather it is at least good to have a firm surface underfoot, and the surrounding scenery, though hardly hospitable, is an impressive mixture of forest and moorland. You turn right on to the B7027 and soon arrive at the little village of Knowe (an appropriate name because in answer to any question about amenities, the answer is likely to be negative) where you turn left and head north-eastwards through an extremely juicy area of forest, emerging at a metalled road by Glenruther Lodge. You turn left on to the metalled road, still going north-eastwards, climbing steadily. If the weather is bad, you could simply remain on this road as far as the house at Garchew, but the Way opts for a more direct route across country to reach that point.

Turning right as the road bends slightly left, you take a path that climbs to the triangulation point at the Hill of Ochiltree, then head north-eastwards over Glenvernoch Fell, descending through a small clump of woodland to reach Garchew. It is imperative to follow the marker posts as the path here is unclear, but there is always the escape route provided by the road to the left. The views are awesome; the prospect to the north is a massive area of coniferous forest, and trees – lots of them – are visible in every direction. Just to the east of Garchew you bear left off the metalled road and head north-eastwards across open moorland, dropping gently to reach the A714 at Bargrennan (40.5). There is little of historic interest here save for a pretty nineteenth-century church, built as a chapel of ease, but the main significance of this village is that it is the last settlement of any consequence for 25 miles and thus an almost obligatory staging post for the walker. There is hotel accommodation here at the House o' Hill. Though this hotel is used to catering for footsloggers, many hotels are not. Having hauled himself and his saturated equipment into the immaculate reception area, the rain-soaked walker's discomfiture will redouble when he has to take his place in the queue behind guests sporting the latest designer wear and without a hair out of place. When his turn comes, the proprietor may endeavour to reduce his unease with such hideous understatements as, 'Bit damp out there today' or encouraging remarks like, 'Forecast's even worse for tomorrow'. Hence a panicky evening watching every local weather forecast on all 300 available channels in the hope of finding one that promises it will stay dry.

Bargrennan to St John's Town of Dalry (25.5 miles) via Loch Trool

ENJOY: Water of Trool, Loch Trool, Clatteringshaws Loch, Shield Rig

Immediately after leaving Bargrennan, and having crossed the A714, you plunge into Glentrool Forest. You head initially south-eastwards along the banks of the Cree, before veering north-eastwards beside the delightful Water of Minnoch. When the Water of Minnoch meets the Water of Trool, you simply continue alongside the latter river, proceeding just north of east. This is lovely walking on a clear path. There is a temporary and somewhat unwelcome brush with civilisation as you find yourself passing through the Glen Trool caravan park, but after leaving this behind you can enjoy a superb walk along the southern shore of Loch Trool, still heading just north of east. Dominating the scene across the loch is the Fell of Eschoncan, comfortably over 1,000 ft high, and a bit further to the north-east is Buchan Hill, more than 1,600 ft high. Though the going is undulating, the path is clearly defined and nothing like as hard as the tramp up the side of Loch Lomond which West Highland Way walkers will recall. Having reached the east end of the loch, you swing south-eastwards past Glenhead and climb through the woods to join a forest track, turning left on to this track to begin eight miles of forest track walking. At first you climb, then having obtained your first view of Loch Dee, keep this to your left as you continue south-eastwards to Black Laggan, swinging north-eastwards towards the River Dee, also known as Black Water of

Dee. To your right, beyond the forest, there are views to the 1,800 ft summit of Cairngarroch.

As the track swings eastwards there is a left-hand turn that you miss at your peril; a moment's inattention might result in your carrying on literally miles out of your way. Having made the necessary left turn on to another track, you cross the Dee and soon reach a T-junction of tracks, turning right. Off you go again, heading just south of east. The surroundings are so thickly forested that the going is uninteresting, but at least it is fast, with no route-finding problems. At length you reach Clatteringshaws Loch, a welcome oasis amidst so much woodland, and boasting a wildlife centre on its eastern side. You proceed along the north side of the loch, but then the track swings north-eastwards, away from the waterside, and soon after crossing Pulcagrie Burn, reaches a narrow metalled road and the end of the long forest track walk. By turning right on to the metalled road you can get to the A712 which proceeds down to the wildlife centre (it *is* a long way) but your route bears left on to the metalled road, following it briefly. You then bear right and begin to climb, swinging just east of north, along a path which seems quite rough after the firm forest tracks. The landscape is again primarily woodland, but at length you emerge at the summit of Shield Rig. Though little more than 950 ft up, and dwarfed by the Rig of Clenrie and Meikle Millyea to the west, this is an excellent viewpoint in the heart of the Galloway Hills, with superb views to the surrounding moorland, mountains and hills, and a real sense of isolation. You continue north-eastwards but begin descending, picking up a stony track at Clenrie and going forward to a small car park, then swinging south-eastwards along the track which turns into a metalled road.

Heading in a generally easterly direction, you then keep walking along the road, eventually being joined by Garroch Burn which runs parallel with it. There is the feeling of returning to civilisation, with a number of houses and farms dotted about the surrounding rolling landscape. It seems quite a long tramp along tarmac, but as the road moves more decisively south-eastwards again, you turn left on to a path that crosses the burn and climbs eastwards up on to Waterside Hill. Walkers who have come all the way from Bargrennan in one day may resent this last stiff climb, but the reward is a fine view down to the Water of Ken and the welcome sight of the village of St John's Town of Dalry. There is a sharp descent to the A762 and then, after crossing this road, there is a curious end to the day's work, consisting of a peaceful walk over the meadows beside then across the Water of Ken into St John's Town of Dalry, usually shortened to Dalry (66). A stop here is virtually obligatory, as there are no more amenities for the next 26 miles – and they are very tough miles.

St John's Town of Dalry

The most interesting historical feature in the village is an ancient block of stone in the rough shape of a chair, and known as St John's Chair which, according to local legend, John the Baptist rested on during his supposed travels through Britain. St John was the patron saint of the medieval religious order known as the Knights Hospitallers who once owned the land on which the village lies. This is how the village got its rather lengthy full name. Dalry boasts attractive cottages and an early nineteenth-century church, the churchyard of which has a Covenanter's Stone marking the grave of two murdered Covenanters (see below). On a more prosaic note, it has some useful shops and accommodation, and a welcome bar in the Lochinvar Hotel, its name doubtless inspired by a small loch three miles to the north-east with the ruins of an island castle that is said to have been home to the eponymous hero of a romantic ballad by Sir Walter Scott.

St John's Town of Dalry to Sanquhar (26 miles) via Stroanpatrick

ENJOY: Manquhill Hill, Benbrack, Sanquhar

This next section is one of the most challenging on any route described in this book. There are sections elsewhere that are more technically demanding, but they can be shortened. On this section of 26 miles however, you will see but a handful of buildings, no accommodation except a single bothy, and no places of refreshment (nor any easy detours to find them), and although there are roads, no public transport serves them. Furthermore the terrain, although posing no particular terrors, is rough, and careful navigation is essential. Having proceeded along Dalry village street along the A702 you turn left to head just east of north – your direction of travel for the first three miles or so – and proceed up an obvious track. This peters out and you proceed across undulating open grass moorland, going by the house at Ardoch and passing to the east of Ardoch Hill, approaching an area of forest. You keep to the west of this woodland, enjoying a pleasant walk beside Earlstoun Burn but taking great care to follow the marker posts. Having followed quite close to the edge of the woodland, which is bordered by Lochinvar to its east, you then swing left to head northwards and reach a metalled road. You join it, proceeding in the same direction, swinging marginally east of north and crossing Black Water at Butterhole Bridge. Already, Dalry seems a very long way away.

After crossing the bridge, the road swings more clearly north-eastwards, and as it does so, you leave the comforting tarmac and climb steadily northwards on to Culmark Hill, dropping down to the house at Culmark. The path is by no means obvious on the ground but if you lose the route you can simply aim for the house – possibly with the help of a compass if visibility is poor – and there pick up a track that proceeds north-westwards to the B729. On your approach to the B729 you cross the Stroanfreggan Burn, a tributary of the Water of Ken, while nearby is a prehistoric burial mound named Stroanfreggan Cairn, and a hillside named Stroanfreggan Craig. Walkers who have not yet suffered a sense of humour failure by tramping the remote and publess moors and forests of Galloway might see the potential for the name Stroanfreggan, particularly if delivered with a certain virulence, to be employed as a peculiarly Scottish expletive.

The Way turns right on to the B729, then just short of the tiny hamlet of Stroanpatrick, turns left to begin the most gruelling part of this long section, consisting of a climb north-eastwards to Benbrack. Following a path, you head across an area of moorland, and into a large forest plantation. The trees are well spaced and it is a lovely open walk on to Manquhill Hill, just under 1,400 ft high. The extremely well-defined path skirts the summit, and looking back there are tremendous views to some of the wildest scenery in southern Scotland. It is now good fast walking downhill on an excellent path, before an uncompromisingly steep climb to the summit of Benbrack, the highest point yet reached on the Way at just over 1,900 ft. As you pause every so often to catch your breath and stop at the summit, it is essential to look back and enjoy the increasingly spectacular views. Rough peaty walking follows as you proceed northwards across open moorland between two large areas of forestry to reach Cairn Hill, then turn eastwards on to Black Hill.

Now things get easier. Swinging northwards you begin to descend, skirting the western edge of the forest then turning north-eastwards into it as far as Allan's Cairn.

Allan's Cairn and the Covenanters

This pillar of red sandstone commemorates two Covenanters, Scottish Presbyterians subscribing to various bonds or covenants for the security and advancement of their cause. One of the most celebrated covenants was that directed against the Laudian Prayer Book imposed by Charles I, while in 1643 a further covenant pledged the Scots to preserve Presbyterianism in Scotland and extend it to England and Ireland. Covenants were declared unlawful in 1662 and Covenanters were brutally persecuted for the next 25 years by troops of the Episcopalian government of the Stuart king Charles II. The Covenanters put up a brave resistance; in 1666 they actually mounted an uprising in Dalry, but many who were involved were subsequently tortured and hanged.

The Southern Upland Way

The Way swings north-westwards at Allan's Cairn and soon turns left, briefly heads south-westwards on to a forest track, then shortly bears right on to another forest path that heads downhill. It makes a wide loop, briefly swinging south-westwards again to reach the Chalk Memorial Bothy. This is the only chance of shelter between Dalry and Sanquhar; although facilities are basic, in extreme weather it may be a virtual life-saver, and if you are carrying any surplus food, it may be a nice gesture to leave some for any benighted walkers coming along after you. That said, one should perhaps check the best before date on the packet; a party of bedraggled hikers, collapsing into the bothy after battling over Benbrack in a blizzard, may be less than grateful for your offering of three stale custard creams and four paper-wrapped slices of wafer-thin ham that are no longer simply on the turn but are now locked in mortal combat with each other to see which can get out of the door first.

Soon after passing the bothy, you reach a junction of tracks where you turn right and proceed just north of east. Having passed the settlement of Polskeoch, the track turns into a metalled road which you follow as far as Polgown, about two miles further on, where you turn left on to a path that climbs again, heading north-eastwards. This is a tough climb, not only because it comes towards the end of a long day, but also because the going underfoot is rough and often very muddy. Again, it is essential to follow the marker posts. There are tremendous views to the surrounding moors and hills, but the most satisfying moment comes when, having hauled yourself to the hill crest just to the north-west of Welltrees Hill at well over 1,500 ft high, you see Nithsdale and the town of Sanquhar below you, with nothing to separate you from the town but a steady downhill march. The spirits rise as you proceed confidently north-eastwards down an excellent path, your objective now gloriously clear. However, it will almost certainly take you longer than you think, with several stiles guarded by electric fences to negotiate as you drop down. At length you pick up a track running north-eastwards from Euchan

Cottage and follow it to Ulzieside, where, having reached the valley bottom, you turn left on to a metalled road and follow this north-westwards past a golf course to a T-junction.

At the junction you turn right to cross the river Nith by means of Blackaddie Bridge, then make your way directly to the centre of Sanquhar (92). You have just completed the hardest part of the Way. Sanquhar has all the amenities a tired, hungry walker could wish for, as well as a station with rail links to Dumfries and Glasgow, and is an interesting little town in its own right. The town's most historic feature is its castle, most of which dates back to the sixteenth century, although there is some earlier work. As well as the castle there is a granite monument marking the spot where Covenanters formulated declarations in 1680 and 1685 in their fight to defend Presbyterianism against the Stuarts. The town also has a post office that has apparently been in business since 1738. One trusts the first customers are somewhere near the head of the queue by now.

Sanquhar to Wanlockhead (8 miles) via Cogshead

ENJOY: Coupland Knowe, High Mill Knowe, Wanlockhead

The next settlement of any size, Wanlockhead, is just eight miles away, giving weary walkers the opportunity of a lighter day, although this section, proceeding into the Lowther Hills, is no pushover. Turning right off the A76, you leave Sanquhar by a path that heads north-eastwards, gently uphill. A lane is briefly joined and then forsaken for another path which strikes out across pleasant open countryside with one short wooded interlude, soon after which you cross a burn, and just beyond that you join the lane leading to Brandleys. Before reaching Brandleys Cottage, however, you bear left, and still heading north-eastwards, you begin a climb which increases in severity the further you get from the lane. The views are spectacular, particularly as you traverse the shoulder of Coupland Knowe and look left to the equally impressive Conrig

Hill. It is a pity to have to descend steeply to Cogshead, keeping an area of forest to your left, but having reached the foot of the hill you bear right and ascend again, on to Highmill Knowe, from where the views are magnificent.

It is then a steep but clearly defined descent to a wide track where you turn right. (During the shooting season, it is necessary to follow an alternative route to this point from Cogshead, following a winding track northwards through frankly rather uninspiring areas of forest, eventually emerging and heading south-eastwards alongside Wanlock Water along the wide track at which the main route arrives after descending from Highmill Knowe.) You then proceed south-eastwards along the wide track into the village of Wanlockhead (100), an attractive place with many cottages of bright colours, some dating back to the middle of the eighteenth century. What may surprise some visitors is that, standing 1,380 ft above sea level, it is the highest village in Scotland; one might have expected that honour to go to a village in the Highlands. The most interesting aspect of the village, however, is that it is effectively a vast museum of lead-mining, its principal industry until 1934 and again briefly in 1957–58. Many of the mine-shafts, smelters and wagonways can be seen in and around the village, while also on show is a nineteenth-century beam engine, a water-wheel pit and ruined miners' cottages. Gold and silver have also been mined in the area, and gold from near the village was used in the Crown of Scotland.

Wanlockhead to Beattock (20 miles) via Daer Water

ENJOY: Lowther Hill, Hods Hill

The start of the next section is impressive indeed. Having passed through the village, you cross over the B797 and follow a track past the pub, joining a path that climbs dramatically, heading south-eastwards. In due course you reach a metalled road and, still proceeding south-eastwards, alternate between road and path to climb to the summit of Lowther Hill, marked by what looks like a giant golf ball, but which is actually part of a civil aviation radar system. At just under 2,400 ft, it is the highest point on the route and the views are absolutely magnificent – ample reward not only for the climb but for the long miles of forest walking earlier in the journey. If you have good weather, the walk from here to the A702 – south-eastwards via Cold Moss and Comb Head as far as Laght Hill, then swinging just north of east – is the most exciting and rewarding on the whole route. It is a great rollercoaster of a walk, involving some unbelievably steep descents and climbs, but with a tremendous sense of space and openness, glorious views and a well-defined path with no route-finding problems. I was fortunate to see a mountain hare on this section, jumping up a hillside with remarkable agility.

From Laght Hill it is a steady descent to the A702; you turn left along the road, then right on to a path which first crosses then runs beside Potrenick Burn, before crossing Portrail Water. Swinging south-eastwards, you enter an area of forest and shortly pick up a forest track that heads firstly south-eastwards then in a more easterly direction, emerging into more open countryside before diving back into the forest again. You arrive at a metalled road and turn left on to it, dropping down to Daer Water. You cross over the water then leave the road, bearing right on to a track, then left on to a path which skirts the edge of Daer Reservoir and its associated works, heading initially north-eastwards then south-eastwards. Having passed the end of the strip of woodland separating the works from the path, you turn left and begin climbing very steeply away from the reservoir on to Sweetshaw Brae, just north of east. The going, on rough grass moorland, can be squelchy underfoot. Beyond the summit of Sweetshaw Brae, just under 1,500 ft, the gradient relaxes and it is easier going, still just north of east, on to Hods Hill, just over 1,850 ft. The views are quite stupendous; the

The Southern Upland Way

Lowther Hill golf ball is an obvious landmark, but further away you can see Solway Firth and the Lakeland fells.

From the top of Hods Hill you swing south-eastwards and then, turning just west of south, descend dramatically before rising again to the summit of Beld Knowe. You have reached the edge of another large area of conifer forest which, as you climb to Beld Knowe, you keep close to your left. Then, swinging south-eastwards again, you plunge into the forest and embark on a long march south-eastwards through the middle of it, beginning with a long descent, then a climb to Craig Hill, then another drop. The walking is not too claustrophobic; the Way follows a wide avenue through the trees, and there are breaks, including one very pleasant open interlude during which you cross over Garpol Water. It is fast, easy walking on clear paths, and it is only near the end that your way appreciably narrows. Eventually you emerge at a metalled road, turning left and following it initially uphill through woodland and then out into more open country, before descending into Annandale. You cross over the London–Glasgow railway and swing from south-eastwards to north-eastwards to reach a T-junction at the long, straggly village of Beattock (120), spread out along the road you have just reached. The Way is left, over Evan Water (a tributary of the river Annan), and then almost immediately right.

Beattock is the first habitation of any size since Wanlockhead, and offers some amenities, but the town of Moffat is only a mile and a half away to the north-east via the A701, and has the full range of creature comforts. The statue of a ram in Moffat's wide high street emphasises that this is an important sheep-farming area, while its popularity as a holiday resort grew from the discovery, in the middle of the seventeenth century, that the water from the wells of the town had medicinal qualities. Robert Burns was one of those who came to take the waters and was inspired to compose the drinking song 'O Willie brew'd a peck of Maut'. Beattock is reckoned to be just past the halfway point on the Southern Upland Way, although it is not certain how much a comfort that would be to the walker who, after glancing at his map and realising that a line drawn due south from the village would still pass well to the west of the Irish Sea-facing towns of Morecambe and Blackpool, might well feel his peck of Maut turning more than a little sour in his throat.

Beattock to St Mary's Loch (21 miles) via Ettrick Head

ENJOY: Craigmichen Scar, Peniestone Knowe, Crosscleuch Burn

Having turned right off the metalled road running through Beattock, you pass underneath the A701 and A74(M). This is a very busy road and the traffic noise stays with you for some time; it can seem very intrusive after the quiet unspoilt walking you have enjoyed. Immediately beyond the motorway you join a metalled road, heading eastwards to a T-junction and just before this junction you pass over the river Annan. At the T-junction you cross straight over on to a path, climbing steeply then dropping just as quickly to reach another road. You turn left on to this, but shortly you reach a junction and here turn right across Moffat Water then immediately left to head north-eastwards, following a delightful path that passes through woodland and then beside the river. It is a surprising but charming interlude amidst so much rugged scenery; the meadows and hedgerows are a delight, and you can refresh yourself with wild raspberries in summer.

Shortly after crossing a metalled road, the spell is broken as you leave the riverbank and turn right to head initially south-eastwards, proceeding uphill. The Way, now an obvious track, swings to the left to head just north of east and continue uphill into another large area of forest. It is quite a slog, but before you get into the forest there are magnificent views back to Moffat and Lowther Hill. Continue through the forest in a generally easterly direction, then emerge onto Gateshaw Rig and enjoy a magnificent high-level march up to Croft Head, well over 2000 ft high, and forward to the crags of

Craigmichen Scar. You find yourself faced with a stunning panorama of big fells, steep gullies, streams, forestry and moorland; I walked this section under cloudless blue skies, and considered it the highlight of the whole route. Still climbing, you continue north-east across the watershed which, like the watershed crossings experienced on the Coast to Coast and on the Pennine Way, is a boggy wilderness, and the sense of isolation is quite palpable.

Beyond the watershed you reach Ettrick Head, a crucial landmark in the walk. Not only is this the source of Ettrick Water, a tributary of the Tweed which flows into the North Sea (your ultimate objective), but generally speaking the walking from now on, whilst still challenging, lacks the formidable qualities and logistical headaches of the western half of the route. At Ettrick Head the Way picks up a clear track which drops down north-eastwards through forest and then more open country to the houses of Over Phawhope and Potburn. Beyond Potburn, still heading north-eastwards, the track turns into a narrow metalled road which you follow for five miles, beside Ettrick Water, past a number of isolated settlements. This area is associated with James Hogg, the so-called Ettrick Shepherd who became a prolific poet; he was particularly well known for his composition of romantic ballads in the early nineteenth century. The road walk is not unpleasant, and though tarmac crunching is not the best sort of walking, the surroundings are delightful and it is very fast going.

Finally, at Scabcleuch you leave the tarmac (the birthplace monument of James Hogg at Ettrickhill lies a mile or so further along it) and turn left to head first just west, then just east of north, uphill on a path that at over 1,600 ft contours the hillside of Peniestone Knowe and goes forward to Pikestone Rig. This is glorious ridge walking on springy turf with wonderful views across lofty green hills and neat patches of forest, and the enticing prospect of Loch of the Lowes to the north-west. It is important not to be sidetracked on to the path that drops down to this loch; you do indeed drop down, but north-eastwards, keeping the loch well to your left. Descending steeply past Riskinhope Hope you cross the delightfully refreshing Crosscleuch Burn, then gird up the loins and climb again, passing along the west fringe of another area of forest and just to the east of the summit of Earl's Hill. The path arrives at a clear track, and the Way turns left on to this track to head north-westwards and descend to St Mary's Loch (141). It is a long, long descent, but the views to the loch are magnificent and the walker who has tramped here from Beattock – there being no amenities at all en route – will feel a real sense of achievement. Accommodation and food are available at the Tibbie Shiels Inn by the lochside. Tibbie was the wife of a mole-catcher and, having opened the inn when her husband died in 1824, continued to run it until her death in 1878 at the age of 96!

St Mary's Loch to Traquair (12 miles) via Blackhouse

ENJOY: St Mary's Loch, Ward Law, Blackhouse, Traquair House

Turning right at the loch, you enjoy a lovely loch-side walk north-eastwards along a good path, which widens into a track, then just beyond the loch you turn right on to a path which swings north-westwards to meet the A708 Moffat–Selkirk road. Crossing straight over, you continue in the same direction, climbing somewhat laboriously to Dryhope Tower. At a T-junction of paths you turn right and head north-eastwards again – your direction of travel virtually all the way to Traquair. There follows a lovely moorland walk along a fine path which initially passes to the west of the 1,380 ft Ward Law and the east of South Hawkshaw Rig, the ground thereabouts rising well over 1,600 ft. A number of hills in southern Scotland are given the name 'Law', and the walker with a penchant for playing on words might think back on his last frustrating walking expedition and reflect that Sod's Law the ideal description of a hill which is totally shrouded in mist whilst the land beneath it is completely cloudless – the mist of course having lifted completely once you've got down the other side.

The Way then descends to the attractive little hamlet of Blackhouse, in a quite idyllic setting, nestling as it does in the valley of Douglas Burn with a beautiful woodland backcloth. The Way briefly picks up a track to pass by Blackhouse and its tower, then enters the wood immediately behind and ascends once more, on a lovely grassy path which is kind to aching feet. In hot weather this woodland walking is delightfully refreshing and it lacks the hemmed-in feel of some other forest sections on the route, with a marvellous view back to St Mary's Loch as you gain height.

Emerging from the woodland you find yourself on open moorland just east of Deuchar Law, and keeping a steady elevation of around 1,500 ft as you proceed past Blake Muir, you can enjoy a glorious ridge-top promenade with views across miles of wonderful scenery including mountains, heather-clad hills, forests and the town of Innerleithen. All good things must sadly come to an end, and there follows a rather slow anticlimactical descent into the Tweed valley. Eventually you arrive at the B709 and turn left on to it, following it for a mile to reach Traquair (153). With its neat cottages and gardens, and eighteenth-century church, it is a pleasant place to linger, but walkers who have reached the village in good time and have a couple of hours to spare should continue beyond the village centre (virtually no amenities) to visit Traquair House, one of Scotland's oldest inhabited mansions. Built in the tenth century, and virtually unaltered in the last 300 years, it has been visited by 27 Scottish and English monarchs and has many interesting features, including embroidery by Mary, Queen of Scots, an eighteenth-century library, and a Brew House which is equipped as it was two centuries ago and is licensed to sell its own beer. A mile to the south-west of the village there is a knoll which is the site of St Bryde's Church, believed to have existed since before the twelfth century. The Way turns right off the B709 in Traquair, but by continuing along it you can reach Innerleithen, which contains an excellent range of amenities, and after a reasonably easy day it's a good place to rest, be pampered, and look not only back on some great walking but look ahead to just as enjoyable and somewhat more hospitable surroundings.

Traquair to Galashiels (13 miles) via Yair

ENJOY: Minch Moor, Brown Knowe, Broomy Law, Three Brethren

Beyond the B709 at Traquair, the Way follows a course slightly south of east. You begin by following a track, which proceeds clearly but quite steeply uphill, and indeed in less than three miles you will rise from 500 ft to well over 1,600 ft. You enter an area of forest and proceed along a clear path through the woods on to Pipers Knowe. A path leading off to the right hereabouts provides an uphill detour to the spectacular viewpoint of Minch Moor, well over 1,850 ft above sea level and offering a fine panorama. The Way itself steers a steady high-level course along a small strip of open land between the thickly-planted conifers, before emerging into open country. It is an exhilarating march along an old drove road, crossing over Brown Knowe and skirting Broomy Law before climbing to one of the undoubted highlights of the whole route, the Three Brethren. The Brethren are in fact tall neat cairns, and from this vantage point you will enjoy another tremendous view in all directions, encompassing heather-clad moorland, rolling green hills and large patches of forest. The eye is drawn particularly to the Eildon Hills, the very distinct volcanic hills behind Melrose, which, rising to 1,476 ft, will be a feature of the landscape for many more miles.

The Way turns sharply right here and drops steeply, but rather than continuing uphill to Peat Law, turns abruptly left, enters woodland and proceeds in a north-easterly direction that will be maintained virtually all the way to Galashiels. The descent through the woodland is undoubtedly anticlimactical, and indeed the walking now assumes a less remote feel which persists all the way to Lauder, some 16 miles further on. Having descended, you continue along a woodland track to the hamlet of Yair, turning right along a lane that leads to the A707, meeting it at the attractive triple-arched Yair Bridge across the Tweed. You go over the bridge, turning left at the T-junction and then immediately right on to a track. It is galling, after losing so much height since the Three Brethren, to have to haul yourself up again, but you must proceed over Hog Hill and forward on a path which is not wonderfully clear. The reward for your efforts is a good view to Galashiels, now immediately ahead of you, and of course the Eildons. Having dropped to just 350 ft or so at Yair Bridge, and climbed back to nearly 1,000 ft, you drop down again to pick up a path that snakes round the edge of the largish town of Galashiels (166). It has derived much prosperity from tweed, and its Scottish College of Textiles is the headquarters of the Scottish tweed manufacturing industry. The town's motto 'Sour Plums', which can be seen on the municipal buildings, refers to a Border foray in the fourteenth century when a party of English raiders were slain whilst they picked wild plums.

Galashiels to Lauder (13 miles) via Melrose

ENJOY: Abbotsford House, Melrose, Lauder

From Galashiels the Way swings south-eastwards past the eastern fringe of Gala Hill, climbing and then dropping down to meet a track, turning left and following it to meet the A7. You cross this busy road and continue downhill to be reunited with the river Tweed, turning left to follow alongside it, now heading north-east. There is quite a contrast hereabouts; across the river is the serenely beautiful Abbotsford House, the home of Walter Scott, but ahead is a rather dreary combination of industrial estate, modern housing and busy road. Having passed underneath the road bridge over the Tweed, you join a road which takes you past a sewage works, then turn right on to the course of an old railway (now a footpath) and proceed south-eastwards. This is tame stuff after what has gone before, but soon you bear left off the old track and having crossed a metalled road, follow a pleasant path south-eastwards along the south bank of the Tweed. Tweeddale is noted for its great variety of wildlife, including otters, herons and kingfishers, and you may be fortunate enough to observe some of these creatures as you pass along the bank and through the meadows to reach Melrose.

Melrose

The highlight of this attractive town, sheltered by the Eildon Hills and the resting place of the heart of Robert the Bruce, is the ruin of Melrose Abbey, a Cistercian abbey founded by David I in 1136, partially destroyed two centuries later, and wrecked in 1545. Commemorated in verse by Walter Scott, it has elaborately carved stonework and fine traceried windows, and contains the tombs of Alexander II and the wizard Michael Scot, who legend says caused the Eildon Hills to split into three. Like Galashiels, the town has plenty of amenities including several excellent eating places.

The Way crosses the Tweed by means of a footbridge just to the north of the town centre, then turns left and doubles back on itself, following the north riverbank westwards to reach the B6360 just west of Gattonside. There is then a right turn and for a while the Way heads north then just east of north, initially on a path, then a lane, then another stretch of path. Gradually you gain height, from just over 330 ft in the valley to over 800 ft and, swinging west of north, you continue on a path that widens into a lane. This is very fast, easy walking, and it is really enjoyable as well, with extensive views across a most attractive rolling landscape. You reach a crossroads of lanes and go straight over, heading initially just east of north along a metalled road, but then turn left and join a path heading north-westwards across a stretch of grassy open land. You cross a metalled road and suddenly the surroundings become dramatic, as you quickly lose height, then swing north-eastwards, keeping a deep grassy gorge to your left. On your right is a golf course and ahead are the Lammermuir Hills, your last real challenge on the Way. Before that though, you drop down into the little town of Lauder (179).

The Way skirts the edge of the town, meeting the A697 at the town's south-east end, but most walkers will want to detour into the centre as it is the last place on the route where supplies can be obtained. It is a very pretty town; its most interesting features are its tollbooth where dues were once extracted from stallholders at street fairs, and a sixteenth-century church with an octagonal spire. The town's name may remind walkers of the singer Harry Lauder, himself a Scotsman although not from these parts. One of his song titles, 'Keep Right On to the End of the Road', could not be more apt for a hiker who is now less than 35 miles from the end of this long journey, but with the far from hospitable Lammermuirs looming ahead, and the obvious danger of being benighted somewhere amongst them, there may be more than a hint of the prophetic in his composition 'Roamin' in the Gloamin'!'

Lauder to Longformacus (15 miles) via Blythe Water and Twin Law

ENJOY: Thirlestane Castle, Twin Law

The Way turns briefly right on to the A697, then left on to a path which enters the grounds of Thirlestane Castle, and uses a footbridge to cross Leader Water before heading north-eastwards through a pleasant area of woodland beside Earnscleugh Water. You turn right at Drummonds-hall on to a track which leads to and crosses another arm of the A697, joining a path that leads to the curiously-named settlement Wanton Walls. Here you branch left to head decisively north-eastwards – your direction of travel almost all of the way to Twin Law, the climax of this section. You proceed uphill to enter an area of woodland, and in the wood turn right on to a track, soon emerging at the south-eastern tip of the woods, then turning left to proceed uphill along the fringe of the woodland. As the fringe begins to swing from north-east to north-west, you leave the woodland altogether, and there is a dramatic change to the character of the walk as you find yourself pitched from pleasant rolling farmland and woodland into remote moorland terrain. When I walked the route I chose this very moment to go off course; it is extremely important to follow the waymarks or, if bad weather precludes this, to take a compass bearing. The path is very indistinct on the ground as, from the edge of the woods, you strike out north-eastwards across the moors into the heart of the Lammermuir Hills, shortly crossing Shawdon Burn then continuing through an extraordinarily barren, almost eerie landscape. You begin to lose height, and turn right on to a path that drops down to cross Blythe Water at its confluence with Wheel Burn, then climb back up on a far from obvious path to reach the southern tip of a patch of woodland on Scoured Rig.

Now the going is a lot more straightforward. You follow the south-east-facing fringe of the wood, arriving at a clear wide track on to which you turn left, the track soon leaving the wood behind and dropping down to the buildings of Braidshawrig. Ignoring the left turn over Easter Burn, you swing round eastwards to climb uphill, and then follow this trusty track slowly but surely higher and higher into heather moorland which seems to become more formidable and inhospitable with each step. Finally you turn sharply south-eastwards and proceed triumphantly to Twin Law, over 1,360 ft above sea level. This is the Lammermuirs' answer to the Three Brethren – two huge and beautifully constructed cairns in a fantastic setting, with wonderfully extensive views including the Eildons and, on a clear day, your first glimpse of the North Sea.

Now heading just north of east, you drop quickly downhill to a track, turning left on to it and then shortly right on to another track which in due course turns into a proper metalled road. You follow this all the way to Longformacus, initially maintaining a north-easterly direction, then swinging south-eastwards to pass the eastern edge of Watch Water Reservoir, before turning north-eastwards through much less formidable woodland scenery and proceeding downhill into the village (194). Most walkers without camping gear will wish to call it a day here, having tramped 15 weary miles from Lauder, but accommodation and amenities are severely limited and those who have been foolish enough to leave such matters to chance may have to resort to a taxi to Duns, the nearest town and the best part of ten miles away.

Longformacus to Cockburnspath (18 miles) via Abbey St Bathans

ENJOY: Whiteadder Water, Abbey St Bathans, North Sea coast

The Way turns right on to the main street of Longformacus then shortly left on to a road which heads north-eastwards away from the village. As the road curves a little to the left towards Dye Water, you turn right off the road, climbing initially south-eastwards, then swinging north-eastwards to pass along the edge of Owl Wood and dropping down through Lodge Wood to reach the B6355. You turn left on to it then shortly right, climbing again before descending steeply and picking up a track that proceeds northwards then north-eastwards through woodland. It is lovely woodland walking, never far from the very attractive Whiteadder Water to your left, and culminates in the lovely village of Abbey St Bathans where refreshment may be available. You cross the water then turn left to follow alongside it before climbing out of the valley and proceeding uphill across fields along rather poor paths, heading northwards to join a track leading to the hilltop hamlet of Whiteburn. You cross a minor road and continue northwards on a track, then turn eastwards on a field path to a road, turning left along it and shortly bearing right to follow a lane that heads north-eastwards past the buildings of Blackburn. The lane becomes a proper metalled road and having swung briefly south-eastwards, turns north-eastwards again and descends to the A1. All this is desperately anticlimactical walking, aggravated by the fact that you will probably be extremely tired by now. You cross over the A1 then turn left to proceed northwards on a path that is sandwiched between this highway and the London–Edinburgh railway, which you soon cross. You continue north-westwards through the attractive Penmanshiel Wood with its pines, gorse, ash, elm and sycamore, initially remaining on the valley floor, then climbing quite steeply. It is a cruel ascent with the end so near, but you are rewarded by your first really impressive view of the North Sea and the coastline as it stretches towards Dunbar.

You descend to the A1107 which you cross, then drop very steeply along a path downhill, north-eastwards towards the sea, until after crossing a metalled road, you reach a caravan park. Swinging left, you pass round the caravan park, and climb again on to the clifftops. This is a magnificent moment, for you can now justly claim that you have walked from coast to coast, and the trudge from Abbey St Bathans is quite forgotten as you enjoy a wonderful cliff walk north-westwards. In just a short piece of coastal marching you negotiate a rugged headland and pass above the lovely Cove Harbour with its twin jetties, then shortly afterwards you turn left and head southwards back to the metalled road you crossed just before gaining the cliffs. You cross back over it, then follow a path westwards, back under the railway and A1, into Cockburnspath (212), reaching the official end of the route at the market cross in the pleasant village centre. At the time of writing, direct buses run from here to Dunbar and Edinburgh; expecting a conventional bus, I was somewhat nonplussed when the 3.50 p.m. Edinburgh service on a July Friday afternoon turned out to be more of a van, which would certainly not have been big enough to accommodate any more than a select few triumphant coast to coast walkers. As you speed away towards Scotland's capital – assuming there was room for you in the vehicle – you will be bound to reflect back on what has been an astonishing walk, whatever the prevailing conditions. You may have enjoyed it so much, and be so captivated by Britain's coast as a basis for long-distance walking, that you will soon be annoying your family by planning another coast to coast pilgrimage or a coastal walk. Or the whole experience may have been so unpleasant that you will be only too pleased to consign the rucksack to the loft, and confine any more mention of Stranraer to your football pools coupons.

The West Highland Way

Designation: Scottish National Long Distance Walking Route.
Length: 93 miles.
Start: Milngavie, East Dunbartonshire.
Finish: Fort William, Highland.
Nature: A walk through fine Scottish Highland scenery using well-signposted and well-defined paths and tracks.

HIGHLIGHTS OF THIS WALK:

- **Craigallian**
- **Dumgoyach**
- **Conic Hill**
- **Loch Lomond**
- **Rob Roy's Cave**
- **Falls of Falloch**
- **St Fillan's Priory**
- **Beinn Dorain**
- **Rannoch Moor**
- **Ba Bridge**
- **Buachaille Etive M**
- **Devil's Staircase**
- **Kinlochleven**
- **Dun Deardail**
- **Ben Nevis**

The West Highland Way

Difficulty rating: Moderate, strenuous in places.
Average time of completion: 6–7 days.

The West Highland Way provides a splendid snapshot of the Scottish Highlands and an excellent introduction to the particular joys and challenges of walking in Scotland. It was opened in 1980 with the aim of providing a safe and uncomplicated route through the glorious West Highland countryside, using a number of historic routes including drovers' roads, old railway lines, and military roads that were masterminded in the eighteenth century by General Wade and Major Caulfield. There is no particular historic significance in the chosen start and finish points of the route. The start of the journey, on the fringes of the Glaswegian suburbs, is Scottish walking at its most benign and as much suited to Sunday strollers as to long-distance walkers. By the end however, the foot-traveller will be within easy reach of some of the most challenging walks that the country has to offer. The Way is not especially technically difficult, as the route is so well waymarked and the tracks are usually very obvious, even in bad weather. It is therefore not surprising that thousands of walkers attempt it each year. The surroundings certainly are magnificent. No walker can fail to be seduced by the wildness and remoteness of the heather moorlands, the peace and mystery of the lochs, the panoramic views, and, of course, the high mountains. With this scenery comes a huge variety of wildlife, from wildcats and otters to ptarmigans and golden eagles.

Sadly, however, not all of those who start off from Milngavie full of optimism and enthusiasm will complete the journey. The reasons for failure will vary. Some walkers will have underestimated the degree of patience needed to negotiate the walk beside Loch Lomond. Some will be surprised by the lack of amenities on certain parts of the journey. Some will have quite inappropriate footwear for the negotiation of muddy or flooded sections of the route, or the long hours of pounding the old stony military roads and drovers' tracks.

Some will simply be beaten back by the most fickle adversary of all – the weather. A lengthy downpour can transform what would be a painless and exhilarating day's march into a thoroughly demoralising and unhappy experience, prompting the hardiest adventurers to think twice before proceeding any further. Advance planning, proper equipment and awareness of the facilities that exist – or do not, as the case may be – are all essential.

Milngavie to Drymen (12.25 miles) via Carbeth, Dumgoyne and Killearn

ENJOY: Craigallian Loch, Dumgoyach

Milngavie (pronounced 'Mull-guy') makes a pleasant start to the Way. A wall-plaque in the town square announces the official start of the route. The Way turns off the square to leave the town in a direction slightly west of north, along the course of an old railway. It then proceeds beside a stream, Allander Water, before turning right into Allander Park and joining a well-defined track which proceeds north-westwards through Mugdock Wood. Mugdock was gifted to the people of Glasgow in 1980 by Sir Hugh Fraser and is now one of some 40 country parks in Scotland. Continuing along an excellent track, you reach Craigallian Bridge and cross a road, then proceeding close to Allander Water, you carry on in a north-westerly direction to reach Craigallian Loch. The loch is very pleasantly situated amongst trees with the fine backdrop of Craigallian House. The route swings gently north-eastwards as it passes to the left of the loch, then goes forward to pass just to the right of Carbeth Loch. There are good views ahead to the imposing tops of the Campsie Hills, of which Dumgoyne, at around 1,500 ft, is the most impressive, whilst the Kilpatrick Hills lie to the west.

Having passed Carbeth Loch you continue to the B821. A right turn here would take you to the village of Strathblane, but the Way goes left along the road before soon turning right. Now the character of the walk changes, turning from a gentle woodland and loch-side ramble to a more exciting march through wilder and more open countryside, as excellent views open out across the farmland of Strath Blane to the mountains around Loch Lomond. You proceed along a good path heading just east of north to pass the buildings of Arlehaven, then swing north-westwards to pass just to the west of the huge wooded hill of Dumgoyach and nearby standing stones which date back to the New Stone Age. You arrive at Dumgoyach Farm where you join a farm road that heads north-eastwards, descending to Dumgoyach Bridge. Here the character of the route changes again, as it turns left (north-westwards) and for the next four or five miles follows the course of an old railway – the Blane valley line. To the right are splendid views to the summit of Dumgoyne, but much nearer at hand, and one suspects more pleasing to the visitor, is the Glengoyne Distillery, reached by a short detour to the right less than a mile beyond Dumgoyach Bridge. When the connoisseur of fine liquor learns that Glengoyne has been producing malt whisky since 1833 and its shop offers supplies of it all the year round, he may decide to terminate the walk there and then on the basis that the remaining 84 miles would only be an anticlimax.

Stronger-willed West Highland Wayfarers will continue along the old railway line, crossing the A81 at Dumgoyne village and continuing virtually parallel to it as far as a crossing of the B834. The walking can be muddy and becomes uninspiring for a while – a sewage works has to be passed just beyond Dumgoyne village, and the surrounding trees and nearby houses tend to blot out the wider views – but better things lie ahead. After crossing the B834 the route, continuing to follow the old railway line, stays to the right of the A81 but then crosses it and continues north-westwards to reach a minor road. You turn left on to it, leaving the old railway, and soon arrive at the hamlet of Gartness where there is a fast-flowing river, the Endrick, and some modest but charming waterfalls. The

Endrick is a fine salmon stream and herons are commonly seen in its waters. Having crossed the river, you follow the road for two miles or so, heading confidently towards Drymen. However, soon after a sharp left-hand bend, with Drymen straight ahead, the route turns right on to a path which leads to the A811. Many walkers will wish to detour to Drymen (12.25), either continuing along the minor road or turning left at the A811. The half-mile detour alongside this busy road can be trying, but Drymen (pronounced 'Drimmen' and meaning 'little ridge') contains a pretty village green and many attractive buildings of red sandstone, and offers a good range of amenities. There will be precious few of those now for the next thirty miles, and none between here and Balmaha, another seven miles distant, and even at Balmaha amenities are very limited. Hoping for a pleasant loch-side cafe there to welcome me after the long trek from Drymen, I had to make do with a polystyrene beaker of tea and a greasy ring doughnut, consumed at a sodden table provided on the patio outside.

Drymen to Rowardennan (13.5 miles) via Balmaha

ENJOY: Conic Hill, Loch Lomond

The route, having reached the A811, turns right on to it and proceeds beside it as far as the hamlet of Blarnavaid, then turns left. A steady climb takes you into the extensive woodland of Garadhban Forest. Through the woods there are excellent views not only of the Campsie Fells and the low-lying terrain that has been crossed since Milngavie, but also of Loch Lomond, which will become the dominant feature of the walk for many miles. The forest, dominated by larch and spruce, is home to many woodland birds including finches and crossbills. The Way follows an excellent track through the forest, heading north-westwards. With the western fringe of the woodland in sight, two possible routes are signposted. The main route heads right, continuing north-westwards through the forest.

The West Highland Way

For a month in spring, during the lambing season, you must turn left (south-westwards), initially through the forest and then into open country along a track leading to Milton of Buchanan, then turn right for a rather tedious road walk to Balmaha, where at the car park you meet the main route. Meanwhile the main route emerges from the wood, and strikes out westwards across the bracken-clad moor, with panoramic views to the southern end of Loch Lomond. After crossing the Burn of Mar there is a big climb up to Conic Hill, which means 'hill above the bog' and is on the line of a great geological fault covering Scotland. This is the first serious test of the lungs of the West Highland Way pilgrim; the ascent is not especially steep but it is long and tiring. It actually goes round the edge of the summit and a detour is needed to reach the very top, at comfortably over 1,000 ft. Even if the detour is not made, the surrounding views are magnificent.

A very steep descent south-westwards follows on a slippery cobbled surface towards Balmaha on the eastern shore of Loch Lomond. You then proceed on a rather easier track through woodland known as the Balmaha Plantation, the gradient easing as you make further progress, and soon you arrive at the huge car park at Balmaha (19). From Balmaha onwards, the Way follows the eastern shores of Loch Lomond, up to its northern tip. It is an extremely tough walk, immediately beginning with a stiff climb to Craigie Fort which sets the scene for the next 20 miles or so. The next mile, round Arrochymore Point, is innocuous enough as you proceed through pleasant woodland on a good path, and then briefly join a road. The road goes all the way to Rowardennan, which lies on the route, and you might feel tempted to stick to it if pushed for time. The route, however, soon leaves it for a rather circuitous wander through the forest to the left of it, rejoins it near Cashell Farm, forsakes it again for a forest walk to the right, briefly returns to it and then leaves by turning left into the forest again. The Way stays close to the shore of the loch for a while, but then cuts off the headland of Ross Point to proceed more directly north-westwards, eventually reaching the road once more but immediately leaving it to continue near the loch edge as far as Rowardennan (25.75). Here the road option ends.

Rowardennan offers modest amenities but its setting is splendid, with views across the loch and also to the summit of Ben Lomond. This is the most southerly of the Munros (Scottish mountains over 3,000 ft high). Beyond Rowardennan you will for a while stick to a forest track but at Ptarmigan Lodge, a short way north of the village, you have the choice of turning left up a rougher path (note that this has in recent times been closed owing to subsidence; check before you set out), giving closer views to the loch and the chance to visit a crag known as Rob Roy's Prison.

Rob Roy

Born in 1671, Rob Roy became a protection racketeer following the collapse of his cattle-droving business. He gained the reputation of the Robin Hood of Scotland following a feud with the Duke of Montrose, and it is believed that it may have been in this rocky den on the shores of Loch Lomond where he held Montrose's men to ransom.

Neither the Prison, nor Rob Roy's Cave some miles further up the route, are easy to locate, but there is a joy in the unspoilt and remote nature of the surroundings and you might reflect on the consequences of exploitative entrepreneurs invading the area: wide access roads, capacious car parks and shops selling everything from Rob Roy sew-on rucksack badges to Rob Roy assorted caramel fudge.

Rowardennan to Inverarnan (13.25 miles) via Inversnaid

ENJOY: Rob Roy's Prison/Cave, Island I Vow, Glen Falloch

The main route proceeds along the obvious forest track – watch for the alternative route via Rob Roy's Prison at Ptarmigan Lodge, but see note above – and progress is fast for the next three miles. Then, however, the firm track gives way to a much more challenging path through the woods. Although the line of the path is clear, there are numerous small obstructions in the form of tree roots and rocks, as well as subtle undulations on often muddy surfaces which make the going exceedingly awkward. It is up to you to decide how best to negotiate the obstructions, but you must take care because a single slip could mean a nasty fall and the end of the West Highland Way adventure. There are numerous crossings of streams, some of which take you over bridges, but others require some energetic fording. After rain, which comes frequently to the loch, the path can be extremely boggy. There is one brief respite from the woodland walking as you pass the charming house at Cailness, but forestry remains the primary theme as you struggle on to Inversnaid (33). The reward for reaching this oasis is a very impressive waterfall and a hotel offering welcome refreshment. Inversnaid is not without historic interest either; a garrison was established here in 1713 in an attempt to control the MacGregor clan.

Beyond Inversnaid, the going – still alongside the eastern shore of the loch – is deceptively easy for a while, but beyond the boathouse the gentle wide track narrows to provide several miles' more awkward walking through the woods. The trickiest section is around Rob Roy's Cave. The cave is somewhat less dramatic than it sounds, being merely a crack in the rock, although the view at the almost sheer outcrops of rock in the midst of the thick woodland is impressive. The walk continues through the woods up the eastern side of the loch, the going marginally easier than it was south of

Inversnaid, but still slow and awkward at times. Ironically, cars can be seen heading effortlessly along the A82 on the western shore of the loch. Now you can appreciate the contrast between the two ends of the loch: at its southern end, a wide lake set in gentle rolling countryside, and at the northern end, a much narrower and deeper trench of water with a more formidable background of mountains and hills, formed by earlier glacial activity. At its deepest point the loch is 630 ft and at its widest it is five miles. It contains 30 islands, some of which were populated by Irish missionaries from the fifth century who hoped that the island setting would protect their monasteries and convents from marauders.

The loch, and the woodland on its banks, is home to a stunning array of bird life. Peregrines, merlins, red harriers, willow warblers, tree pipits, tufted ducks, green wagtails, chaffinches, jays, woodpeckers, redstarts, pine martens, nesting pied flycatchers and dippers can all be seen on this section of the Way. Foxes and deer are not uncommon and if you are very fortunate you may see a wildcat or an otter; otters have often been seen on the burns and rivers that feed the loch. Continuing towards the northern end of the loch, you will pass one of the loveliest of the islands, named Island I Vow, which contains a sixteenth-century castle ruin. In the spring the island is awash with daffodils. Half a mile after leaving I Vow behind, the path turns slightly away from the loch to give an easier walk, before passing the hamlet of Doune and descending back to the lochside. Across the loch is the village of Ardlui, reachable at certain times by means of a ferry. At the ferry 'terminal', the route turns away from the loch, heading still north-westwards past the buildings of Ardleish. Here you reach the head of the loch and can sigh with relief, knowing that the most difficult section of the route is behind you.

The Way, now heading north, climbs up to a superb vantage point just to the east of the modest summit of Cnap Mor, and from here the view down Loch Lomond is staggering. Looking at the way in which the wooded east bank slopes so steeply, it is quite impossible to see how a path could have been forged through it! A good path initially across moorland, past the tiny Dubh Lochan, and then downhill through woodland brings you to the hamlet of Beinglas and its unusual assembly of wooden wigwams, which at the time of writing were offering accommodation. There is a fine waterfall just to the east of the route, as Ben Glas Burn tumbles down to meet the river Falloch. Nearby is the slightly larger settlement of Inverarnan (39), reached by a walk across a field, over a footbridge across Glen Falloch, and alongside the busy A82. The Drovers at Inverarnan offered one of the more bizarre night's stays that I experienced on my walk up the Way, its more memorable characteristics being a prodigious array of stuffed animals and a TV offering access only to an obscure satellite channel.

Inverarnan to Bridge of Orchy (18.25 miles) via Tyndrum

ENJOY: Falls of Falloch, St Fillan's Priory, Beinn Dorain

With Loch Lomond left behind, the Way now proceeds initially northwards and then north-eastwards along the east bank of the River Falloch, which flows into the loch. The A82 is now a much closer companion, immediately beyond the west bank of the river, and beyond the A82 is the railway. This is the famous West Highland Railway linking Glasgow with Oban, Fort William and Mallaig. Opened in 1894, it is a remarkable feat of engineering and one of the most scenic lines in Great Britain. For a few miles the path, river, road and railway proceed together up Glen Falloch, all four thoroughfares sandwiched between massive inhospitable mountain wildernesses. The going is clear and excellent, and also exciting, contrasting happily with the closed claustrophobic walking in the woodlands by Loch Lomond. Two miles or so beyond Beinglas are the Falls of Falloch. These are at their best after heavy rains, when they become a quite breathtaking spectacle. There are numerous sets of falls, with vast volumes of white water being hurled through the narrowest and rockiest of gorges, all with the fine backcloth of the hills and mountains beyond Glen Falloch. The river becomes more subdued beyond the falls, but here heavy rainfall can be a distinct disadvantage, for the path hereabouts is liable to flood and even the provision of planks may not prevent boots, socks and feet taking an unscheduled soaking.

At the pretty farm of Derrydaroch, you cross the Falloch and proceed immediately adjacent to it; at one point a massive waterfall careers down to hit the ground barely a yard from the course of the path. Shortly afterwards you cross both the road and railway in close succession, and continue along an old military road, climbing steadily away from Glen Falloch although still proceeding north-eastwards. In just about a mile, however, the route abruptly changes direction, swinging north-westwards into an extensive area of woodland. By continuing north-eastwards you may detour to visit Crianlarich. This village contains the best range of amenities since Drymen, and also has a railway station on the West Highland Railway, although trains are infrequent. Alfred Wainwright, the famous fellwalker, relates how, having planned to catch the 8.30 a.m. train from Crianlarich to Fort William, he set off from his hotel to the station and, to his horror, saw his train leaving, having been timed to depart at 8 a.m., with no more trains to Fort William until the evening. Even great men can make mistakes...

The Way proceeds north-westwards through the forest. Unlike the Loch Lomond walk, the path here is much wider and clearer, and there are frequent views to the valley of Strath Fillan to the right, as well as the huge 3,843 ft summit of Ben More. There are numerous other Munros nearby, including Ben Lui, Ben Oss, Beinn Dubhchraig and Ben Challum. Deer are common hereabouts, and you should look out for buzzards and even eagles. Always well-marked, the route snakes its way north-westwards; it is the best sort of walking, being comfortable and easily navigable but in surroundings that are quite magnificent. Having gained some height since the crossing of the A82 beyond Derrydaroch, the Way now drops down into Strath Fillan to cross both the railway and the A82 again. You turn left to proceed alongside the A82 then turn right to cross the wide River Fillan. Just like Glen Falloch, Strath Fillan nestles cosily between formidable mountains, and manages to accommodate road, river, railway and West Highland Way. The Way remains in Strath Fillan as far as Tyndrum. After crossing the river, it heads briefly north-eastwards on an obvious track, soon passing the remains of St Fillan's Priory. St Fillan was an Irish monk who brought Christianity to many Highlanders twelve centuries ago.

Near Kirton Farm the Way swings north-westwards on a metalled track, gaining a little height, then at Auchtertyre swings south-westwards to return to and cross over the A82 at Tomna Croiche. Here there are excellent views to Ben Lui and Beinn Dubhchraig. The route proceeds in a roughly westerly direction alongside the river through a moorland landscape, crossing a narrower tributary stream and entering an area of woodland on a wide track. Shortly, however, the Way leaves this track, turning right to head north-westwards on a path through the woods. This path can get very muddy and in wet weather you may be forgiven for wishing you had stuck to the A82 which proceeds more directly to Tyndrum (51). The Way reaches a metalled minor road by Tyndrum (Lower) Station, and turns right to reach the A82 and the village centre. Just the other side of the A82 is Tyndrum (Upper) Station, giving Tyndrum arguably more railway stations per head of the population than any other village in Great Britain and possibly much of Europe. The village enjoys a good range of amenities including, at the time of writing, a self-service restaurant that is a favoured stopping-place for A82 drivers. The wet and weary walker approaching the village in search of refreshment can only pray that his visit is not immediately preceded by that of a coach party which quickly forms a queue that snakes halfway round the room, leaving him to tag miserably on the end and shuffle wretchedly food-hatchwards for the next 20 minutes whilst octogenarians ahead of him debate earnestly with the serving staff the relative merits of mushroom-filled jacket potatoes or beef and onion hotpot.

The next six miles to Bridge of Orchy must rank as one of the fastest and easiest sections on the whole route. Since it follows an old military road for much of the way, the surface is firm and the track so wide that only a genius could get lost. Moreover, after an initial climb there is a steady descent and then comparatively level walking all the way. Initially the route squeezes neatly between A82 and railway climbing steadily northwards. While the A82 strikes out in a more north-westerly direction, the Way continues northwards, dropping down gradually and proceeding beside a river named Allt Coire Chailein, with the railway maintaining a somewhat higher elevation to the right. As you approach the valley bottom, you have the quite magnificent spectacle of the 3,530 ft Beinn Dorain straight ahead of you, the starkness of its summit perhaps underlined by the flatness of the river valley immediately to hand. At length you arrive on the valley bottom and, having crossed the river of Allt Kinglass, swing north-westwards on a wide track that heads unerringly on to Bridge of Orchy. Progress is extremely easy and the walking remains both interesting and enjoyable; the broad flat valley gives fine views to some of the most dramatic Highland scenery, with bleak craggy slopes and thickly forested hills. On reaching the village (57.25), you cross the railway – this is the last you will see of the West Highland Railway until Fort William – and join a metalled road that goes forward to reach the A82. Bridge of Orchy has for a long time served walkers' needs well, the station providing trains to Glasgow and the hotel offering both luxury and budget accommodation. Its bar is a popular meeting place for West Highland Way walkers, who are now far enough up the route to compare copious notes about their experiences. I will not easily forget the man in his late twenties who, never having done any long-distance walking before, flew from London to Glasgow and set forth in a pair of brand new boots that he had never worn before, let alone broken in. They were giving him so much pain that he was now virtually immobile and was making plans to fly home the next day!

Bridge of Orchy to Kinlochleven (21.25 miles) via Kingshouse

ENJOY: Rannoch Moor, Ba Bridge, Buachaille Etiv Mor, Devil's Staircase

After crossing straight over the A82 and the River Orchy on a bridge that dates back to 1750, the route resumes innocuously enough along a metalled road, but as this bends to the right the Way goes straight ahead, following a track north-westwards through an area of forest and climbing steeply. Emerging from the forest the track continues to climb round the edge of the mini summit of Mam Carraigh. There are fine views from here, most notably ahead to Loch Tulla, its shores bedecked with mature Scots pine. Then, almost at once, you descend in a westerly direction to reach a metalled road by the Inveroran Hotel (60). You turn left on to the road, and make easy progress briefly south-west, then north, along the tarmac. As you go, you cross the Victoria Bridge over the river known as Abhainn Shira which flows into Loch Tulla, clearly visible to the right. Beyond Victoria Bridge you go forward to Forest Lodge. This is a crucial moment on the journey, for here the metalled road gives way to the track that will take you over Rannoch Moor. For the next six miles, until civilisation is reached in the form of the next A82 crossing, the Way proceeds northwards over the immense wilderness of the moor. The track, a drovers' road, is well-defined and firm, proceeding confidently over the moor with no difficulties of navigation or negotiation even in bad weather, although after heavy rain there can be some flooding on the path itself. Despite its firm surface, the track remains but a slender lifeline amidst surroundings that are terrifying in their bleakness. There are acres upon acres of peat and long, reedy grass, concealing expanses of water and bog that would engulf the walker in an instant; desultory patches of pine forest; streams that curl round the accumulations of peat and broaden into lochs or lochans; and frowning down on the scene are the summits of Meall Beag, Beinn Chaorach and their neighbours, forming a natural barrier to what lies beyond the moor and adding to the sense of total isolation. There are a few isolated patches of forest which serve as useful landmarks for the walker. Near to one of these, just north-west of Meall Beag, is Ba Bridge, underneath which flows the Ba, one of the many watercourses on Rannoch Moor. On a fine day it is the perfect place to stop and take in the surroundings. A mile or so beyond Ba Bridge the track climbs slightly, and the A82 comes into view. As the A82 is approached, the track becomes rougher and you must pick your way carefully along the boulder-strewn path to reach the path that leads to the White Corries ski lift. You go forward to cross the A82 and join a well-surfaced track on the opposite side. Half a mile down this track, proceeding north-westwards, you reach the Kingshouse Hotel (69.5), surely one of the most isolated hotels in Britain. It gets its name from the fact that the building was used after the Battle of Culloden as barracks for the King's troops.

From Kingshouse Hotel the West Highland Way joins a metalled road heading north and then west, and shortly before the road reaches the A82 it branches off and heads along a track heading north-west. The track is in fact an old military road that is as well-defined as the drovers' road across Rannoch Moor, but follows a somewhat erratic course north-westwards, never far from the A82. In due course you return to the A82 and proceed right alongside it, finally joining it at Altnafeadh. On a fine day, the walk from Kingshouse to Altnafeadh is magnificent, with views to the nearby Buachaille Etive Mor whose very distinctive and imposing peak resembles a massive pyramid. It is an extremely difficult mountain to climb; Alfred Wainwright says that it is a mountain he can look at for hours without any thought of trying to climb it. It is known as the gateway to Glencoe, and indeed that remarkable glen, full of romantic and historical significance, is just a few minutes' drive away.

At Altnafeadh the route turns right away from the A82, following a track which passes through a patch of woodland and then into an open and much more exciting rugged landscape. A testing climb now ensues. This ascent to the saddle between the peaks of Stob Mhic Mhartuin and Beinn Bheag is known as the Devil's Staircase, and the summit of the pass, at 1,800 ft, is the highest point of the route. Though long and lung-testing, the Devil's Staircase is not actually as bad as it sounds, with no difficulties of navigation even in bad weather as the path is so clear. The view from the top certainly gives ample reward for the hard work, with magnificent mountain vistas back to Buachaille Etive Mor and forward towards Ben Nevis. As the long descent begins, you will catch your first tantalising glimpse of Kinlochleven, the first settlement of any size on the Way since Drymen. However, this is still six miles away and you may wish to pause before continuing in order to gird up your loins for the descent. You can also enjoy the magnificent scenery around you – there is nothing quite as good as this to come – and perhaps amuse yourself by looking at the astonishing names given to streams and mountains nearby. As you proceed, you will need to ford the streams of Allt a Choire Odhair-bhig and Allt a Choire Odhair-mhoir, and to the left are the hills of Sron a Choire Odhair-bhig and Meall Ruigh a Bhricleathaid. Try getting your tongue round those after a few well-earned jars at the Kingshouse.

The descent to Kinlochleven is long and sometimes arduous, and may take a lot longer than you perhaps think it should. However, the route, although initially rough underfoot, is clearly defined; the obvious path follows an old military road which winds its way north-westwards, widens to negotiate a zigzag section that passes a dam and a reservoir, and then continues downhill at a more gentle gradient. The more height is lost, the less barren and more wooded the surroundings become, and buildings become more dominant, although there are good views to the Mamore hills beyond. In due course you arrive in the valley of the river Leven, passing round the edge of the aluminium works that dominate the village. There is no doubt that the works, powered by the Blackwater Reservoir and connected to it by a huge pipeline coming off the hills, are something of an eyesore, but they are an integral part of the local economy. The route actually runs alongside the pipeline as it nears the works. Then, just before the aluminium works, you swing to the right to cross the pipeline and then the Leven, swing left to join a metalled road past some suburban housing, then go left again along a riverside path which arrives at a road. The route turns right on to the road, although most of the amenities of the village (78.5) can be found by turning left. After the wilderness of Rannoch Moor and the noble grandeur of Buachaille Etive Mor, it seems somewhat incongruous that just a few hours later you should be marching through a sprawling industrial village, which, it has to be said, is rather lacking in charm. The setting, however, is magnificent, with delightful views across Loch Leven, on the eastern shores of which the village is situated. Before the ferry across Loch Leven was replaced by a bridge at North Ballachulish, this road through Kinlochleven was the only through road link between Fort William and Glencoe. Walkers can, however, be grateful for the amenities which this formerly important road link, as well as the A82, have spawned; it is in fact the last point on the Way before Fort William that supplies are available.

Kinlochleven to Fort William (14.25 miles) via Glen Nevis

ENJOY: Ben Nevis

There is a long uphill slog out of the village, but the views provide more than ample reward for your efforts, particularly those across Loch Leven to Sgorr na Ciche, a mountain better known as the Pap of Glencoe. Ahead are the Mamore hills, with numerous Munros all around (mountains over 3,000 ft). As with the peaks around the Devil's Staircase, they seem to be a challenge to pronounce, let alone climb! The West Highland Way avoids these lofty summits but even so you certainly need a pause for breath as the path levels out and Kinlochleven and its industrial paraphernalia disappear from view. An extraordinary section of the route follows, as you take a steady level course westwards through a giant mountain pass, using the lower slopes of Stob Coire na h-Eirghe. Views are restricted to the barren rocky summits on either side, although in fine weather the surroundings will not seem intimidating, and you can enjoy a straightforward walk, keeping your eyes out for short-eared owls, kestrels and ravens. There is a good firm path in the midst of a remote wilderness offering little or no shelter. Two ruined farmhouses are testimony to the harsh reality of the surroundings. Eventually, the path swings from west to north-west and, dropping fairly gently, heads towards an area of forest. Indeed, forest walking is to dominate the remainder of the walk.

Proceeding on a good path, an easy but nondescript march northwards through the woods brings you to Blar a'Chaorainn with nothing of note except a metalled road and a signboard giving the heartening news that Fort William is just six and a half miles away. In bad weather you could simply follow the metalled road to Fort William. However, the official route, eschewing tarmac, swings in a more decisive north-easterly direction, emerging from the forest, and the summit of Ben Nevis is now clearly visible as you embark on a pleasant section of more open walking. Soon the Way enters woodland again, emerges briefly and then plunges into the trees once more, following a narrower and more undulating track. The track, heading north-eastwards through Nevis Forest, is easy enough to follow, and there is some dramatic scenery; at one point the path drops steeply to cross a magnificent rocky gorge before rising again. The conifers are tightly packed and there is an almost surreal blackness and stillness amongst them, with the track itself passing narrowly between them and inducing understandable feelings of claustrophobia. As the path rises, you can make a detour to the right to visit the Iron Age hill fort of Dun Deardail, in a magnificent open setting away from the forest. Soon after Dun Deardail you reach a clearing that gives the first really good view to Glen Nevis and the outskirts of Fort William. The end is now truly in sight. Nonetheless, the descent is lengthy and tiring, like the drop to Kinlochleven. You meet a forest track and turn left on to it, making fast progress northwards, although the pounding on the hard surface provides more punishment for the feet which, at this late stage in the walk, may have been protesting for some time.

Having turned right off the track, you follow a narrower path quite steeply down to a metalled road, passing the graveyard. The metalled road in fact links Glen Nevis Youth Hostel, a significant landmark for reasons as stated below, and Fort William. The route turns left on to the road and simply follows it for roughly a mile and a half until Nevis Bridge (92.75) on the outskirts of Fort William. Here, as the A82 is reached again, you will be welcomed by a prominent 'End of West Highland Way' sign erected by the nearby Ben Nevis Woollen Mill store, which I understand offers souvenirs for those who successfully complete the path. It is certainly reassuring to have it confirmed that the walk has ended and that you can, with a perfectly clear conscience, secure more comfortable transport to take you into the centre of Fort William, reached by turning left along the A82. Fort William derives its name from a fort that, having been built of earth and wattle in 1655 by General Monk, was rebuilt in stone in 1690 by order of William III. The Jacobites failed to capture it both in 1715 and 1745 and it continued to be garrisoned until 1855 when it was demolished. Nowadays it is a very busy tourist centre, the principal shopping centre in the west of Scotland north of Glasgow, and a useful base for exploring the areas of Lochaber and the Great Glen, providing some of the loveliest and most spectacular scenery in Great Britain. You could continue your walk by following the Great Glen Way, another Scottish National Long Distance Walking Route described elsewhere in this book, all the way to Inverness, and/or tackle Ben Nevis, Britain's highest mountain. Its base is easily accessible from the town, and the climb itself, although lengthy, will pose no problems in fine weather. Wainwright rather condescendingly describes it as a 'friendly giant, accepting geriatrics and infants with open arms'. But then, how can one really trust the word of one who doesn't even know the time of the first morning train out of Crianlarich?

The Speyside Way

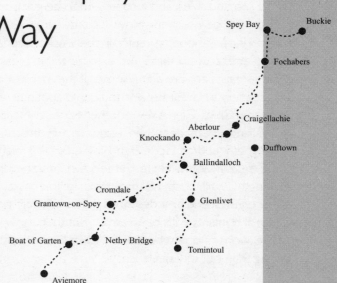

Designation: Scottish National Long
Distance Walking Route.
Length: 80 miles.
Start: Buckie, Moray.
Finish: Aviemore, Highland.
Nature: A delightful walk close to the
course of the River Spey, the whisky centre
of Great Britain.
Difficulty rating: Easy.
Average time of completion: 6 days.

The Speyside Way is one of the gentler official
long-distance routes of Great Britain, aiming to

HIGHLIGHTS OF THIS WALK:

- **Buckpool Harbo**
- **Tugnet Ice Hous**
- **Earth Pillars**
- **Craigellachie Bridge**
- **Aberlour**
- **Ballindalloch Castle**
- **Glenlivet Distille**
- **Carn Daimh**
- **Grantown-on-Spey**
- **Loch Garten**

provide a journey through one of the loveliest parts of northern Scotland. It goes from Buckie, on the Moray Firth, to Aviemore, the well-known ski resort in the Cairngorms, and boasts a splendid combination of natural beauty, variety of wildlife and historical features of great interest. As the name of the route implies, the River Spey is a frequent companion on the walk, but there is in fact very little riverside strolling. There's plenty of old railway walking, some enjoyable woodland rambling, a little coastal tramping and a foray into higher ground, hugging the spectacular Cairngorm mountain range. The route as a whole is a paradise for nature lovers: as well as the great variety of trees lining the Spey, such as silver birch, hazel, rowan, willow and alder, there is a tremendous diversity of bird life including the eagle, woodpecker, capercaillie and osprey, and in the beautiful woodlands you should look out for red squirrel and wildcat. There are some fine man-made features on or very near the route, such as Ballindalloch Castle, the Ice House at Tugnet, Arndilly House and Craigellachie Bridge, and those with a sweet tooth may be drawn to the home of Baxters, the jam producers, at Fochabers, and Walkers the bakers at Aberlour. Arguably the region's principal claim to fame is that it's the home of the Scottish malt whisky industry with many distilleries on or near the route. The walking is generally easy and not logistically challenging, with plenty of towns and villages en route and no huge distances between any of them; much of the walking is on firm paths and tracks, and the way is exceedingly well signed using the Scottish National Long Distance Walking Route emblem. Although it's no pushover, and there are some tough sections, it is a walk to be enjoyed, and indeed Sandy Anton points out in the official route guide that 'it is not primarily a test of physical endurance.' Which is perhaps a polite way of saying that if you're seeking to raise money for a worthy cause, the Pennine Way or Southern Upland Way might be seen as a rather more laudable challenge walk.

Buckie to Fochabers (10 miles) via Portgordon and Spey Bay

ENJOY: Buckie, Tugnet Ice House, Moray Firth Wildlife Visitor Centre, Fochabers

The first part of your walk isn't by the Spey at all but along the North Sea coast by the Moray Firth alongside Spey Bay, beginning at the former harbour of Buckpool, now part of the little town of Buckie. Buckie is in fact an amalgam of several fishing villages; it is well known today for its white fishing and catching and preparing shellfish, while the town's Heritage centre has an exhibition devoted to the life of the herring. From Buckie you head westwards for what will be a short coastal walk, initially by a roadside then along a pleasant coastal path, but as you walk beside the bay, look out for oystercatcher, curlew and ringed and golden plover. You pass through Portgordon, once a fishing village of some importance and still boasting a pretty harbour, then beyond Portgordon you move a little away from the Moray Firth to join the course of an old railway – a taste of things to come later on. It's delightful walking within sight of the sea, and the excellent signposting leads you on to a beautiful woodland walk beside a golf course; emerging from the woods you go forward to Spey Bay village and Tugnet which stands at the mouth of the River Spey. This used to be the start of the Speyside Way. There are two features of interest at Tugnet, namely the old Ice House dating back to 1830, where ice was collected and used to preserve locally caught salmon, and the Moray Firth Wildlife Visitor Centre. From Spey Bay village you can enjoy splendid views towards Helmsdale and Wick across the Moray Firth, the wide expanse of water linking Inverness with the open sea, and you may see a variety of seabirds including the cormorant, fulmar and kittiwake. Pause to admire the meeting of the Spey with the Moray Firth, then swing southwards to head inland; almost immediately, however, you reach the Garmouth Viaduct, built in 1886, and you may wish to cross it in order to visit the twin villages of Garmouth and Kingston on the west side of the Spey. Garmouth, the site of the landing of Charles II in June 1650, is an olde-worlde village of narrow streets, while Kingston, on the seafront half a mile to the north, once housed important shipbuilders' yards using wood from the Strathspey pine forests.

Save for those occasions when the path meets the bank of the Spey, the five-mile walk from Spey Bay to Fochabers isn't the most beautiful or exciting part of the route. It follows a very winding track, initially beside fields and then through trees in a generally southerly direction, and it's important to follow the signposts. You do begin to wonder if you've strayed off course, but four miles or so from Spey Bay you reach a road and a reassuring signpost and then enjoy a very pretty riverside walk. You pass underneath the main Elgin-Fraserburgh road and after continuing briefly parallel with the Spey are signposted away from the river alongside a stream, now in the outskirts of the large village of Fochabers (10). Excellent signposting shows you where to leave the route to access the centre of the village, which has interesting origins. In 1776 the fourth Duke of Gordon decided to move the tumbledown village of Fochabers out of sight of his recently rebuilt home, Gordon Castle, and a new village for farmworkers and fishermen was built on a grid pattern a little way to the south; large-scale improvements were made by the Gordon family a century later, but many of the excellent Georgian buildings were retained including the late eighteenth-century parish church, with its pillared portico, by the market square. The village is the home of Baxter's food processing plant with its excellent visitor centre in which you may be tempted to enjoy samples of the soups and jams for which Baxter's is so well known. At the east end of the village is Milne's High School, opened in 1846 and built in Tudor Gothic style; it is named after Alexander Milne who worked at the castle in the eighteenth-century and was dismissed by the then Duke for refusing to cut off his pigtail which the Duke felt didn't fit the castle's image!

Fochabers to Craigellachie (13 miles) via Boat o'Brig and Arndilly

ENJOY: Earth Pillars, Boat o'Brig, Arndilly House, Craigellachie Bridge

Between Fochabers and Craigellachie there are no amenities whatsoever, so be prepared. You are signposted out of the village past new housing and then along a path which crosses a pretty burn and goes forward to a minor road which you will follow all the way to Boat o' Brig, a distance of some six miles. Whilst road walking doesn't sound hugely exciting, it is very pleasant walking indeed. Soon after joining the road you should leave it at the car park at Alltdearg signposted Earth Pillars; a path takes you through woods to a viewing platform from which there is a splendid view of the Spey and you can see down to one of these extraordinary geological phenomena, likened by Sandy Anton to 'strange giants surveying the scene.' Your road walking ends at Boat o'Brig, of interest not because of its houses or its amenities (there aren't any) but its two bridges over the Spey, one carrying the still extant railway between Inverness and Aberdeen, the other carrying a road. Bearing right at the T-junction just beyond the railway overbridge, don't go forward to the road bridge but bear left and climb steps to join a path leading you away from the valley southwards. Although maps suggest the path passes through the buildings of Bridgeton, there are in fact no buildings immediately beside the path as you swing left. After a few hundred yards taxi-ing, as it were, in an easterly direction you are then signposted south-westwards and begin a climb into woodland below the 1500 ft high Ben Aigan. The climb is quite steep at times, but at length you reach a T-junction with a forest track and, bearing right onto the track, you enjoy a quite superb high level walk with magnificent views northwards to the Spey valley extending to the Moray Firth. The bridges at Boat o'Brig look so insignificant suddenly! Watch the signposting carefully – there's a very important right turn off the track, and missing it would not enhance the enjoyment of your day — but all being well you'll descend to join a road which you follow for a couple of miles to reach Craigellachie. Through the trees to your right you can make out the pretty little town of Rothes, while closer at hand, also to the right, is Arndilly House, dating back to the mid eighteenth century and subsequently rebuilt; it is noteworthy for its splendid entrance porch, square keep and array of towers. At length you reach a T-junction with a busier road onto which you turn right, then bear shortly left into a park and arrive at a crossroads of paths. Close by here is the beautiful river Fiddich, a tributary of the Spey, and you'll notice that signposted to the left at the path crossroads is Dufftown, the home of Glenfiddich whisky. The path to Dufftown was formerly a spur route of the Speyside Way but because of landslip activity this spur has at the time of writing been stripped of its official Long Distance Path status. Some maps and guides still show this as part of the official route, but if you decided to leave it out, your conscience can remain squeaky clean — until Long Distance Path status is restored. Of course, you may wish to detour to Dufftown anyway, using the signed (former old railway) track, in order to visit the Glenfiddich distillery and enjoy the wide range of amenities that the town offers.

If you don't detour to Dufftown, you bear right at the path crossroads asterisked above and follow the Speyside Way signs for Craigellachie. Soon you'll find yourself on another section of old railway which you will follow for 12 miles! Almost immediately you'll find an excuse to leave it, though, in the form of the village of Craigellachie (23), a stone-built village with attractive cottages. In 1890 Craigellachie copied many of its neighbours by opening its own distillery, the White Horse, and nearby is the cooperage where wooden casks to store the whisky are made although this is some way from your route. The village's most notable feature is Craigellachie Bridge, built by Thomas Telford and consisting of a single arch of delicate ironwork with twin ornamental towers at each end; the bridge opened in 1815 and is still intact although a new bridge has replaced it as the chief crossing of the Spey. Look out for it to your right as you head away from the village.

Craigellachie to Cragganmore (12 miles) via Aberlour and Knockando

ENJOY: Aberlour, Carron Bridge, Knockando

Reassured that only a genius will get lost over the next dozen miles, you now head south-westwards to Aberlour, keeping the Spey just to your right and using the track of the old Speyside Railway. Old railway enthusiasts will enjoy the various pieces of railway paraphernalia including a tunnel and a huge retaining wall, and naturalists will love the variety of flowers lining the route. Aberlour (25) – full name Charlestown of Aberlour – is an attractive little town with a variety of amenities and eating places. It's the home of Walkers, the famous makers of delicious shortbread and fruitcake, and there is also a Speyside Way visitor centre in the old railway station buildings. The centre has everything a Speyside Way walker could wish for, including a DVD which in 20 minutes takes you from the start of the walk to its end. If the weather forecast – also available from the centre – is bad, you could be forgiven for just watching the DVD and saving the legwork.

From Aberlour you continue to keep the company of the old railway, with the Spey close by, all the way to Cragganmore ten miles away; it's good, easy walking, the Spey initially to your right but subsequently crossed by means of Carron Bridge. It then remains to your left as you continue to Knockando, heading initially north-westwards then south-westwards. Two features of interest en route to Knockando are the Dailulaine Distillery, still flourishing and producing not only whisky but a superior form of cattle feed known as dark grains, and Carron Bridge itself, dating back to 1863 and commanding lovely views. Around Knockando itself there are three distilleries, Knockandu (sic), Cardhu and Tamdhu, and in the village of Knockando, the centre of which is a little to the north of your route, there is a mid eighteenth-century church with three Pictish stones built into the churchyard wall. At Knockando the Way swings more decisively southwards, initially just east then just west of south, and stays on the old railway track, keeping the Spey to the left; a little way south of Knockando you reach Blacksboat, a quite beautifully kept old station building in lovely surroundings. Note the bridge crossing of the Spey, replacing a ferry that once operated here, but don't use it – yours is the next one! Just beyond Blacksboat you should look across the Spey to the church of Invera'an, superbly situated above the river. Two miles beyond Blacksboat you cross the Spey again by means of a splendid viaduct, and almost immediately after the river crossing, in the hamlet of Cragganmore (35), you reach the start/finish of the Tomintoul Spur. Unlike the Dufftown Spur, at the time of writing at any rate, this is still very much part of the Speyside Way, but it involves a 15-mile walk (one way) and 2200 ft of ascent and may require up to eight hours for the one-way trip. It will take a full day out of your itinerary and public transport back to the continuous route is negligible. But along the spur is not only Carn Diamh, the summit of the Speyside Way, but also the Glenlivet Distillery with guided tours, an excellent shop, a really good cafe and a lovely whisky aroma wafting from its complex. Has that tempted you onto the spur route? Yes, I thought it might.

TOMINTOUL SPUR: Cragganmore to Tomintoul (15 miles ONE WAY) via Glenlivet

ENJOY: Ballindalloch Castle, Hill of Deskie, Glenlivet, Carn Diamh, Tomintoul.

So, off up the Tomintoul Spur it is. It starts deceptively easily: you bear hard left past a picnic area and the houses of Cragganmore then walk along a road that takes you up to the busy A95 at Ballindalloch.

Turn left and follow alongside the A95 past a useful shop and over the River Avon, an impressive tributary of the Spey, then turn right off the A95 onto the B9008 signposted Tomintoul. A little further on up the A95 is a left turn to Ballindalloch Castle which dates back to 1540 and which with its towers, turrets and beautiful wooded backcloth is surely everyone's idea of what a Scottish Highland castle should be. Unfortunately it's completely invisible from the Speyside Way itself so if you want to see it you'll need to detour. You'll also need to avoid visiting on Saturdays… when it's shut.

Having followed the B9008 briefly, you bear left away from it along a road past Auldich Farm, beginning to climb. You pass a car park and Speyside Way information board, shortly beyond which the road becomes a rough track, rising all the time. Be very careful to fork right as signposted, but pause by the signpost as this fork is as close as you come to the summit of Ben Rinnes, which is to your left and isn't far short of a Munro at 2760 ft high. Now embarking on the right fork path, you continue to rise, but although the terrain is wild you shouldn't lose your way as the signposting is extremely reassuring! Your path goes over the left shoulder of Cairnacay, swinging south-east, then south-west to the summit of the Hill of Deskie; this is wild moorland walking that is quite reminiscent of the Pennine Way and seems a world away from the innocuous railway path walking of a few miles back. Veering southwards and enjoying magnificent views in to the adjacent glens, you descend steadily to the hamlet of Deskie, rejoining the B9008 briefly and then dropping down to the river Livet. You enjoy a brief and pretty walk beside the river, then cross it by way of a fine bridge, going forward to a road which you follow southwards to the distillery of Glenlivet (41), a name synonymous with fine whisky. There is a very welcome and useful coffee shop in the visitor centre which will be enjoyed by even the most ardent whisky haters.

You continue southwards along the road, then veer right to pass Blairfindy Lodge and as the road swings southwards a signpost takes you onto a path that strikes out south-westwards into the moors once again. This is superb walking, arguably the best so far on the Speyside Way; excellent signposting and a clearly defined path combine to ensure you will not get lost, and the views just keep getting better and better. Keep climbing, following the eastern fringe of forestry, and swing from south-westwards to southwards to pass to the west of Carn Liath, then keeping another large area of forestry on your right, and ignoring signs to Tomnavoulin to your right, you climb steeply to the cairned summit of Carn Diamh, at 1866 ft the highest point on the Speyside Way and commanding magnificent views. From the summit you now continue along an invitingly wide, clear path downhill. Having walked beside forests for much of the way since Glenlivet, the Speyside Way actually enters an area of woodland, skirting Carn Ellick and emerging to give another superb view southwards. The path, very clearly signposted, now proceeds south-westwards across very spongey ground, so much so that boards are provided in a number of places. You descend gradually then rise, once more keeping woodland to your right, passing through a gap in the trees and then skirting the right-hand edge of woodland before veering sharply right (westwards) and descending to a metalled road just south of the hamlet of Croughly. You bear left to follow the road, but as the road bends sharply left, you're signposted to the right and actually instructed to descend direct to the footbridge. It's one of very few instances of the Speyside Way being ill-defined on the ground, but unless conditions are very bad you will easily see the footbridge below and use it to cross Conglass Water, a very pretty burn indeed. Beyond the bridge the signposting directs you left (south-westwards) initially parallel with the burn along a field edge then along a clear track taking you to a junction with the A939. The information board here signifies the end of the Tomintoul Spur and what was originally actually the end of the Speyside Way. However you will certainly want to turn left here onto the road and follow it the short distance into Tomintoul (50).

Tomintoul

Standing at 1160 ft above sea level, Tomintoul was the creation of the fourth Duke of Gordon who in 1776 provided land for the village on either side of a military road built 22 years previously, but in fact three generations of stonemasons were responsible for its limestone houses and slate cottages. By 1794 37 families lived there and the parish minister wrote that the men, women and children lived to sell whisky – and drink it! It's now a touristy place, with museum, visitor centre, well-stocked general store and, at the time of writing, two cafes. But you're now 15 miles from Cragganmore so make sure you've sorted out some transport to get you back there. Your B & B host, if suddenly and without prior warning asked for a lift while he's in the middle of serving up your kippers and black pudding, will remind you of Queen Victoria when she visited Tomintoul in 1850 and arrived in the pouring rain – not amused.

Cragganmore to Grantown-on-Spey (13 miles) via Cromdale

ENJOY: Woods of Knockfrink, Cromdale Church, Grantown-on-Spey.

Certainly you would do well to be in Cragganmore in time to devote the whole day to the next section of the walk, the 13 miles to Grantown-on-Spey, as this is the toughest part of the Speyside Way. From the start/end of the spur at Cragganmore, things begin deceptively easily with another tranche of railway path walking in the shade of trees with the Spey to your right. It's all going very nicely. But barely a mile after starting, you're signposted uphill away from the old railway, first south-east and then south-west, along an attractive path with fine views especially to your right, to reach the A95 on the far side of Tormore Distillery. You cross the road and walk parallel with it awhile, then strike out left, south-eastwards, uphill into the forest. You bear right onto a forest track, continuing to rise, but barely have you got into your stride than you're directed off the track to the right, going downhill, and arrive in a pleasant valley. Now you must follow the signposting very carefully through the valley, taking care to keep a westerly course and not be tempted onto the hills to the south of you. Stepping stones assist you in the crossing of two strips of fairly fast-flowing water (wading is not recommended) and beyond the second you veer more to the north along what is a particularly muddy and rather poorly defined path. Watch for the signposts carefully as you bear half left and then left uphill to the eastern fringes of the Woods of Knockfrink, veering right (north) to follow the edge of the wood and enter it, joining a forest path with some relief.

A lovely walk follows along a broad forest track, the Way veering south-eastwards, uphill again, and once more you seem to be heading for the hilltops; the woodland relents to allow an absolutely glorious view of the Spey upstream on its way towards Grantown, with a majestic backcloth of woodland and heather-clad hills. But almost before you know it, you're being signposted back down towards the valley, the noise of the A95 very obvious, and there follows an extraordinary section of walking. OS maps at the time of writing suggest a straightish south-westerly course beneath an expanse of trees above the big complex of farm buildings called the Mains of Dalvey. You are, however, signposted along a succession of fields and field-edges, hemmed in by fences and getting from one field to another by means of metal squeeze-stiles of which there are a phenomenal number on this stretch. The ground is often slippery and muddy and it's very hard to get into your stride. It's a relief to cross a minor road just past the Mains of Dalvey and climb up onto a forest track which now proceeds clearly south-westwards, getting closer and closer to the A95, finally arriving by the side of the road. The forest walking is certainly far from claustrophobic or unpleasant, although views are limited. You cross back over the A95, going slightly back on yourself as you proceed parallel with the road, but then bear left and drop down by the buildings of Pollowick to rejoin the old railway line which seems especially welcome again after the exertions of the last few miles. It's now an easy, enjoyable railway path walk to Cromdale (60), with its exceptionally well maintained old station building and platform. A little way beyond you pass under a bridge and are signposted uphill to the right onto a road; you could access Cromdale and its limited amenities by turning right and following the road south-eastwards back to the A95, but to proceed along the Speyside Way bear left and follow the road to meet the Spey again. Just before the bridge crossing is Cromdale Church, which enjoys one of the prettiest settings of any church on a long-distance route but with sadly very limited opening times.

Cross the Spey using the fine bridge, perhaps pausing to enjoy the lovely views both upstream and downstream, then bear left to enjoy a pleasant valley walk along the left fringe of woodland. You are then signposted right, into the woods. By now you'll be quite tired after your walk from Cragganmore but you can't help but enjoy this beautiful woodland which you follow first south-westwards, then north-westwards, then south-westwards again to arrive at Grantown-on-Spey. As well as being part of the Speyside Way the pine and birch woodland is a very valuable community recreational facility, known for many sightings of the capercaillie bird, but vibrant with many other species of birds, plants and trees. Having skirted the golf course, you reach a T-junction with a road, where a right turn and a quarter of a mile's walk take you to Grantown-on-Spey (63), a tourist resort built predominantly on granite founded in 1776 and planned by Sir James Grant as centre for the Highland linen industry. A good example of a planned town, using a grid system, it boasts a spacious square, museum, bridge crossing built in 1754, and the imposing Grant Arms Hotel, where Queen Victoria once stayed incognito. She recalled 'when [the locals] heard who it was, they were ready to drop with astonishment and fright.'

Grantown-on-Spey to Aviemore (17 miles) via Nethy Bridge and Boat of Garten

ENJOY: Castle Roy, Loch Garten, Osprey Centre, Strathspey Railway

Having enjoyed a well-earned rest in Grantown-on-Spey, make your way back down to rejoin the Speyside Way and proceed straight on along the road downhill, bearing left at the next T-junction to follow a road round the hamlet of Speybridge and back over the Spey. Once more you need to cross the busy A95 – for the last time, you'll be glad to know – and almost immediately you're signposted back onto the old railway track which you now follow south-westwards for five miles as far as Nethy Bridge. It is quite delightful walking, being very easy, with no route-finding problems and lovely views and surroundings. Even the old railway paraphernalia, such as the overbridges and burn crossings, have real charm and interest. The meandering Spey is never far away to your right, and there's a nice mixture of woodland and open walking with good views to the distant hills. As you approach Nethy Bridge, six miles from Grantown, you may see the ruins of the Norman Castle Roy to your left, with the parish church of Nethy Bridge adjacent to it. You then continue forward into the village of Nethy Bridge (69).

Nethy Bridge

Nethy Bridge is a centre for skiing as well as fishing, climbing and of course walking; the village, with an attractive scattering of old stone cottages and conifer-clad slopes, straddles the river Nethy, a tributary of the Spey, with a bridge crossing that dates back to 1809 after the original one was washed away. In the eighteenth century it was the hub of a thriving timber trade and sawmills, brick kilns and a charcoal-fired ironworks were on a site in the north-east corner, the logs being bound into rafts which were floated down the Spey to the boatyards at Garmouth and Kingston.

At Nethy Bridge the old railway walking comes to an end, with no more to follow. You pass the old station platform and building and swing left to a T-junction with the B970. By turning left you will quickly access the village's amenities but the Speyside Way turns right, south-westwards, leaves the village and goes parallel with the B970 as far as the next left road turn. You bear left here and join a path going parallel with the road but are soon signposted to the right into Abernethy Forest and along a forest track heading initially north-westwards then swinging south-westwards and arriving at a long clearing with a line of pylons running through it. You swing sharply right, fractionally north of west, to follow a very well-defined path through the heather in the clearing, alongside the pylons, gaining height then beginning to lose it. As you start to descend, you're signposted left, into the woods, and arrive at a T-junction with a road. The Speyside Way turns right here, but by detouring left you'll reach Loch Garten and the very popular Osprey Centre. You're almost exactly halfway from Grantown-on-Spey to Aviemore at this point and the going from here to your destination is as easy as anything you'll have had to cope with thus far, so the two-mile round trip to the Centre is a detour you may well consider making. Just ensure there are likely to be some ospreys to look at when you get there. There aren't always!

Returning to the route, the Way continues north-westwards alongside the road coming up from Loch Garten, and once again the path planners have taken pity on those whose blistered feet have developed an aversion to tarmac-crunching by providing a good parallel path which even obligingly cuts a big corner where the road reaches a T-junction with the B970. You therefore arrive alongside this road a little way south-west of the junction, and proceed briefly beside it before being signposted off it to the right along a road heading fractionally north of west to Boat of Garten (74). There's a parallel path initially before a mercifully short tarmac crunch and a lovely crossing of the Spey. Make the most of this one as it's your last close encounter with the river which actually inspired the trail; the views, on a good day anyway, are as good as, if not better than, from any bridge crossing along the route. You go forward to pass under a railway bridge then go left at the T-junction to enter Boat of Garten. Almost immediately you meet Boat of Garten Station on the Strathspey Steam Railway linking Broomhill, further back downstream near Nethy Bridge, with Aviemore where you're heading, so there is in theory the possibility of letting the train take the strain for the last leg of the journey. Well, no-one need ever know…

Banishing such sacrilegious thoughts, you now set off on the last six miles to Aviemore. It has to be said that this is the gentlest conclusion to any of the official long-distance routes in Scotland and most of those in England and Wales. You bear sharp right by the station approach to reach the quiet main street of Boat of Garten – not exactly overladen with amenities but the village store provides hot drinks and a table outside for you to enjoy them – then shortly bear left along a road, heading resolutely in a south-westerly direction. The road becomes a very wide, very clear track which hugs the course of the steam railway, and with no route-finding problems you can enjoy a lovely walk through the heather dotted with trees and with a magnificent backcloth of the Cairngorm mountains to your left. The golf course which you pass as you close in on Aviemore must be one of the most pictuesquely sited courses in Britain. Unfortunately hideous anticlimax follows. Instead of emerging majestically from this beautiful countryside into Aviemore's main street, the Way chooses to veer north-westwards past modern housing to enter Aviemore effectively via the tradesman's entrance, arriving at a T-junction with the village street a good mile north of the village centre and then creeping diffidently southwards into Aviemore itself past a mixture of rather characterless houses and shops. The only indication that you've reached the end of the route is a multi-fingered signpost (80) with just the one finger bearing the words 'Speyside Way' pointing the way you've just come, and one of the ubiquitous Speyside Way information boards immediately adjacent. Aviemore was transformed in the 1960's by the building of a multi-million pound all-the-year-round holiday complex, catering principally for those who come to enjoy the skiing. The main street isn't quite as tawdry and touristy as some of the guides would suggest, and you'll probably welcome the many facilities it has, such as a railway station, a National Express coach stop, a big Tesco, and plenty of gift shops with ample supplies of Walkers produce which is as good a souvenir as any of the Speyside Way, having been made in a factory actually overlooking the long distance route. Which isn't to say you wouldn't be better off waiting till you get home and buying it a lot more cheaply at your local garden centre.

The Great
Glen Way

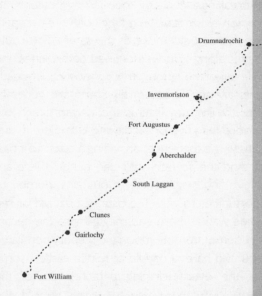

Inverness

Drumnadrochit

Invermoriston

Fort Augustus

Aberchalder

South Laggan

Clunes

Gairlochy

Fort William

Designation: Scottish National Long
Distance Route.
Length: 73 miles.
Start: Fort William, Highland.
Finish: Inverness, Highland.
Nature: A superbly waymarked walk
along the Great Glen in the Scottish
Highlands, mostly alongside lochs and the
Caledonian Canal.
Difficulty rating: easy.
Average time of completion: 5–6 days.

HIGHLIGHTS OF
THIS WALK:
- **Fort William**
- **Neptune Staircase**
- **Loch Oich**
- **Kytra Lock**
- **Fort Augustus**
- **Urquhart Castle**
- **Drumnadrochit**
- **Inverness**

The Great Glen Way is the answer to the prayer of every long-distance walker who has at some time or other trudged along indistinct or non-existent paths, been forced over stile after stile in depressingly close succession, squelched along muddy or rutted farm tracks under the watchful eye of inquisitive or aggressive cattle, been faced with back-breaking ascents or knee-jarring descents, or suffered ambiguous or non-existent waymarking, with the prospect of nothing but days or even weeks more of the same. The route of the Great Glen Way is along firm well-defined paths, lanes and tracks with not a single stile throughout, the signposting is mostly excellent, the gradients although occasionally sharp are generally not excessively lengthy, the journey itself is short, with even slow walkers requiring no more than five or six days to complete it, and the whole is a most satisfying experience, providing a coast-to-coast walk across Scotland. And the scenery isn't bad either: there are great views to Ben Nevis and neighbouring mountains, numerous forest walks with opportunities to view the osprey, buzzard or red squirrel, lovely waterside walks where you may glimpse the heron, cormorant, kestrel or guillemot, remote moorland scenery populated by the grouse and mountain hare, a couple of ruined castles, some spectacular waterfalls, the ever-fascinating paraphernalia of the Caledonian Canal (see below), and, if you are feeling very fit, the possibility of detours to climb one of the nearby mountains and get grandstand views of the whole of the Great Glen. Not forgetting, of course, the best line in Loch Ness Monster souvenirs.

The Great Glen Way is one of the newer of Britain's big walks, being opened in April 2002, and for much of its length it follows the Great Glen, a valley that forms a diagonal line between Fort William on the west coast and Inverness on the east; it is in fact the line of a geological fault which dates back 380 million years. Along the glen are three lochs, Lochy, Oich and Ness, and, filling the gaps between lochs and effectively linking the lochs with the west and east coastlines, is the man-made Caledonian Canal, the idea for which was put forward in 1773 and designed by William Jessop and Thomas Telford, and which was completed in 1822 at a cost of nearly a million pounds. Although it was built partially to boost local trade and industry, it enjoyed limited commercial use, but provided an important passage for naval vessels during the First World War and thereafter was to be used predominantly by leisure craft, as it is today; among the most attractive and interesting features of the canal are the beautifully kept *locks*, necessary to cope with the differences in level between the *lochs*.

Fort William to Gairlochy (10 miles) via Corpach and Banavie

ENJOY: Inverlochy Castle, Ben Nevis views, Caledonian Canal, Neptune's Staircase, Moy Bridge

Fort William, your starting point, gets its name from the stone garrison that was built there in 1690 by General Mackay who named it after the reigning monarch William of Orange; it enjoys an excellent range of amenities and is an ideal base for walking and climbing, but there is not much of great historic interest, and you will be anxious to get going, beginning by heading north-eastwards out of the town along pavement and clear footpath, soon crossing the River Nevis. To your left are the lovely waters of Loch Linnhe, but soon your route swings in a more easterly direction alongside the waters of the river Lochy to reach the impressive ruins of Inverlochy Castle, which you can wander around at any time at no cost. Inverlochy was in fact the old name for the town now known as Fort William; its castle was built by Sir John Comyn in 1260 but the site had been fortified a thousand years before.

Beyond the castle you cross the river Lochy then use suburban roads to return to the shores of Loch Linnhe, keeping the sprawling village of Caol to your right; swinging north-westwards, you then enjoy a pleasant lochside walk before your path veers slightly away from the loch and rises to meet the Caledonian Canal. Having reached this important point, you'll be tempted to get straight down to business, following the Way eastwards beside the canal towards Banavie and Gairlochy, but you really should make the short detour westwards to Corpach sea lock and pepper-pot lighthouse, and observe the official start (and finish) of the canal as it reaches Loch Linnhe. This will give you the opportunity to inspect what is one of many beautifully maintained locks on the canal, with its furnishings and attractive greenery, but also you will get a grandstand view of Fort William and Ben Nevis across the loch; on a clear day this will provide one of the most magical moments on the whole of the Great Glen Way, with barely three miles of it having been walked.

Now you can turn eastwards, your predominant direction of travel all the way to Inverness, and follow the canal towpath for seven miles to Gairlochy. After a mile you reach the A830 at Banavie, providing your last chance to stock up with supplies before an amenity-less stretch of 18 miles, then immediately beyond the road crossing – you also cross the scenic Fort William-Mallaig railway here – you reach another amazing landmark on the canal, Neptune's Staircase. This is a flight of eight locks in very close succession, bringing the Caledonian Canal up (or down) a total of 64 ft, and provides the starkest difference in height between any two sections of the canal; the meeting of the canal and Loch Oich, roughly 20 miles further east, is its highest point at just over 100 ft above the sea. It's worth stopping to watch if you're fortunate enough, as I was, to witness a loch cruise ship making its way 'downstairs', although, since it takes on average 90 minutes to complete, you could probably be forgiven for deciding not to stay for the whole performance.

From Neptune's Staircase the walk to Gairlochy is magical, for you have at last shed the slightly suburban feel which has persisted all the way from Fort William to Banavie, and are now truly seeing the Scottish Highlands at their best. This is true heaven for the walker, with a good firm surface, no danger of getting lost, and quite magnificent surroundings with impressive hills and tremendously varied woodland and plant life all around you; there are tremendous views to the right (south) to Ben Nevis and its companions Aonach Mor and Carn Mor Dearg, and to your left there is the less lofty but conspicuous peak of Meall Bhanabhie, still well over 1000 ft above the sea. Don't neglect to look back, either, at the numerous mountains standing guard over Loch Linnhe and its sister Loch Eil. Immediately to your right you will see the river Lochy which you crossed by Inverlochy Castle, and as you near Gairlochy you pass Moy Bridge, an old swing bridge with adjacent cottage, in a setting which, with the backcloth of the mountains, is astonishingly beautiful. Soon you find yourself approaching the houses of Gairlochy (10): you can't help feeling that there really ought to be a waterside pub complete with beer garden here. But as you trudge off eastwards towards Loch Lochy, whilst you may regret the absence of a pint or two to supplement your Morrisons pork pie and Walkers crisps, at least the canal bank remains lush, unspoilt and unsullied by the aroma of half-consumed pub meals and freshly deposited fag ash.

Gairlochy to Laggan (14 miles) via Clunes

ENJOY: Loch Lochy, Clan Cameron Museum, Cia-aig Waterfall

There's a bit of a change now. You cross the canal at Gairlochy (10) and briefly follow the B8005 north-eastwards before joining an undulating path on its west side, with, one infers, the sole purpose of avoiding a tedious road trudge, for shortly you return to the road and follow a clear path down to and alongside the water. Although in negotiating the private land around Gairlochy you won't have seen it happen, the Caledonian Canal has given way to Loch Lochy, and assuming your day's walk is ending at Laggan, some 12 miles away, Loch Lochy will be your companion for the rest of the day. And what a companion: within seconds of reaching the lochside there is the most wonderful view of Ben Nevis and company, and you will not get a better view of them after this. Your path proceeds close to the loch but soon arrives back at the road which you're then forced to follow all the way to Clunes, some two and a half miles further on; any danger of monotony is broken at Bunarkaig, a short distance along the road, where there's a chance of a detour of just under a mile to the Clan Cameron Museum at Achnacarry which contains not only a detailed history of this clan but also of the time during Second World War when it was used as a training centre for commandos.

At Clunes the Way leaves the B8005. However, you could detour to view the fine Cia-aig Waterfall along a section of this road known as the Mile Dorcha or Dark Mile because of the trees overshadowing it, even though the detour is actually a mile and a half each way. The extra three miles may not sound too onerous in the overall scheme of things, but could just prove decisive, particularly if the walker is aiming for Laggan that evening and started that morning from Fort William having travelled overnight on the coach.

Coach travel

The coach isn't traditionally regarded as the most stylish or salubrious way of getting around. Indeed, the thought of long-distance coach travel may bring back memories of your infamous coach journey to Greece at the height of the Cold War when your vehicle broke down just outside Innsbruck, was held by Yugoslav border guards for eight hours, and got to Athens two days late. Nowadays, domestic long-distance coach travel is reliable and remarkably good value for money. In travelling overnight by coach you save a day as well, and although levels of comfort tend to be less there is the consolation of the obligatory Refreshment Stop which is almost an institution in itself: the ominous announcement by the driver that 'if you're not back at 3.40 a.m. the coach will leave without you' (it's almost tempting to delay your return to the coach to 3.42 a.m. just to see if it did) and the rude shock of staggering from an overheated vehicle into the freezing night air and thence to a brightly-lit world of bleeping computer games consoles, Take That being piped into the refreshment area at 120 decibels, and bacon butties at a tenner apiece.

The Great Glen Way

At Clunes, having left the road, you now follow a clearly defined forest track north-eastwards, which will convey you all the way to the north-east head of Loch Lochy. Pause to enjoy one final great view of Ben Nevis, then head north-eastwards; having been almost exclusively on the flat for the first 14 miles of the Way, you now need to be prepared for some moderate up-and-down work. Although significant areas of the forest north of the loch have been felled, the opportunities for views to the loch through the gaps in the trees are limited, with some stretches entirely hemmed in by the conifers and few obvious landmarks to provide an indication of progress. To your left are two Munros (Scottish mountains over 3,000 ft high), Meall na Teanga followed closely by Sron a Choire-Ghairbh, and a little further on is the rather more easily pronounceable Ben Tee, just 34 ft shy of being a third Munro. The walking is straightforward and enjoyable, although it is remarkable how the traffic noise from the A82 can still be heard from the other side of the loch, and in that respect, this section is reminiscent of the walk beside Loch Lomond on the West Highland Way, albeit nowhere near as challenging.

Eventually you emerge from the forest and can for the first time clearly see the head of Loch Lochy and the houses forming the straggly community of Laggan. Before that, you walk through the little village of Kilfinnan, near to the site of the Battle of the Shirts in 1544, so called because the heat of the day forced the two warring clans to fight in their undershirts! At Kilfinnan, the forest track becomes a metalled road and it's an easy walk down to Laggan Locks where Loch Lochy ends and the Caledonian Canal resumes; it's lovely to be back by the canal, and a beautiful canalside walk of about a mile and a half ensues, with the same combination of lush surrounding vegetation and mountain backcloth you enjoyed between Banavie and Gairlochy. After three quarters of a mile or so the path comes close to the A82 and you can conveniently leave the route here to access accommodation opportunities in and around Laggan, but the route continues beside the canal to the crossing of the A82, the end of this section of canal and the start of Loch Oich. By detouring to the left here along the A82 you will soon reach the Laggan Swing Bridge (24); there was at the time of writing a nearby shop, and you could go on a little further to inspect the monument of the Well of the Seven Heads, which was built in 1812 and recalls a clan massacre in 1663, in which seven members of the MacDonnell clan were killed as an act of retribution for the killing of members of a rival clan. The severed heads were washed in the well and taken to nearby Invergarry Castle as proof that the deed had been done!

Laggan to Invermoriston (17 miles) via Fort Augustus

ENJOY: Loch Oich, Bridge of Oich, Kytra Lock, Fort Augustus, Loch Ness

Beyond the A82 you join a concrete drive taking you past the Great Glen Water Park where meals may be available, and go forward to join the course of an old railway line which you now follow along the eastern banks of Loch Oich. This is beautiful walking north-eastwards along an excellent path with fine views through the trees to the loch, although in order to get a classic view back to Laggan Swing Bridge with the Loch Lochy-side mountains as a dramatic backcloth, you may need to scramble right down to the water's edge. In due course you leave the old railway track, but the path remains clear and well defined, and there are great views to the ruins of Invergarry Castle where Bonnie Prince Charlie once stayed. You emerge from the trees – it's worth detouring from the path to enjoy the views across the loch – and go forward to cross the A82 at Aberchalder where there are two features of interest: the current swing bridge, from which the views are splendid, and the old Bridge of Oich with its double-cantilever design, which dates back to the mid nineteenth century and carried cars till 1932.

The Great Glen Way

Aberchalder marks the end of Loch Oich and the start of another section of the Caledonian Canal, and initially beyond the A82 you walk along the east side of the canal, but shortly at the attractive Cullochy Lock you switch to the west bank, and with the summit of Meall a Cholumain over to your right, continue along the towpath to the stunningly beautiful Kytra Lock. Given the right conditions, this is arguably the best moment of the whole Great Glen Way: the lock, like so many of the others on the canal, is splendidly kept, but its setting is really special, in the shade of mixed woodland with mountains forming a lovely background. Between here and Fort Augustus, you have the canal to your right and the river Oich immediately to your left, and you may feel as though you're on a wide causeway between the two strips of water. Two miles from Kytra Lock you reach Fort Augustus (33), the biggest settlement reached since you left Fort William; once a hub of a network of military roads, and a base for troops, it got its name from William Augustus, Duke of Cumberland, in 1729. It's an exciting moment to round the corner and to be faced with a smaller-scale Neptune's Staircase bringing the canal down to Loch Ness, which can clearly be seen behind. Either side of this 'staircase' are rows of houses, shops and eateries, offering all the amenities you need, and there is ample accommodation for those who wish to call it a day here; you may find it something of a surprise, and not a very pleasant one, to pass from the blissful solitude of Loch Lochy and Loch Oich to a major tourist centre, beloved of coach parties and motor trippers alike, where you are just one of many mouths to feed, and it's unlikely that your time here will rank among your fondest Great Glen Way experiences. Then again, perhaps I am prejudiced, having visited the town cafe after ten miles' non-stop walking and been advised that they were just out of the advertised apple crumble and custard.

Sadly you say farewell to the canal here and you will not see it again till you reach Inverness, another 40 miles away. Leaving Fort Augustus northwards initially along the A82, you bear left to climb steeply along a metalled road, then, having promptly lost some of the height gained, are directed to the left on to a path which goes uphill through thick woodland. Swinging to the right, you now follow a forest track which will take you north-eastwards almost all the way to Invermoriston, eight miles away; initially you feel rather hemmed in by the trees, but soon the woodland relents and you are able to enjoy your first of many grandstand views of Loch Ness. This first view is particularly special, as you can see not only the south-west corner of the loch but also the buildings of Fort Augustus and the hills you passed on your way down the canal from Aberchalder. Thereafter the going is straightforward but undulating, with several rises and falls, and a number of excellent views of the loch between the thicker patches of woodland; progress is difficult to monitor, but some six miles from Fort Augustus you may observe the buildings of Invermoriston far below you through the trees. However instead of taking a direct route downhill to the village, the track swings sharply north-westwards away from the village and the lochside, and it is only after a good mile and a half that a signpost (watch carefully for it!) leads you off to the right, down a steep narrow path to the valley floor, where you turn right to join a lane which takes you just south of east into Invermoriston (41). This village, with (at the time of writing) a shop, hotel/bar and several B & Bs, is a logical stopping place for the night, there being no amenities apart from the youth hostel at Alltsigh between here and Drumnadrochit 14 miles away; its finest feature is the old bridge, designed by Thomas Telford and commenced in 1805, across the lovely falls of the river Moriston. On the occasion of my visit, the place was extra busy as it was a checkpoint on a cycle race along much of the Great Glen Way, and indeed I met large numbers of cyclists as I walked. But at least the path was not shut to walkers. Few things are more infuriating to long-distance walkers than to be confronted with an official-looking notice, pinned to a gate or stile, that the next part of a route has been closed for some reason, especially if time is tight. The frustrated walker may feel there is no alternative but to cut losses and return another day: if that is not practicable, there is the grim prospect of having to find a potentially time-consuming and morale-sapping alternative route. Even more psychologically devastating is to emerge at the other side, bloodied but unbowed, only to be informed that the original route was perfectly passable and the council have simply been too busy to send someone out to remove the notice.

Invermoriston to Drumnadrochit (14 miles) via Alltsigh, Grotaig

ENJOY: Loch Ness, Meall Fuar-mhonaidh

The Way, having flirted with the A82 in the village, now leaves it by way of a road going steeply uphill, soon joining another forest track which resumes a north-eastward loch-side course, albeit some way above the loch and the main road. As on the walk from Fort Augustus, the trees can sometimes obscure the views, but it's fair to say that you get more vistas of Loch Ness for your money along this section than you did prior to your descent to Invermoriston. Landmarks are again few, the youth hostel at Alltsigh the only obvious one, but perhaps more noticeable is the stiffness of one or two of the climbs, and indeed in due course you find yourself embarking on a significant ascent which culminates in a quite magnificent panoramic view of the loch. You enter Ruskitch Wood and soon pass over a waterfall which, if it were more easily accessible, would surely be a major tourist attraction; the river which feeds it, in the cool shade of the surrounding woodland, is a wonderfully refreshing spot on a hot day (and yes, there are hot days in the Scottish Highlands!).

You continue along an excellent path, but gradually lose height, then swing away from the loch into a more pastoral landscape to reach the car park and houses at Grotaig from which there's the chance of a detour along a clearly marked path to climb the summit of Meall Fuar-mhonaidh, which is clearly visible to the west. It is a magnificent and on a clear day very inviting summit, and if you've got the time and the weather is kind it is well worth going for, with the summit providing views up and down the whole of the Great Glen. Unfortunately the five and a half miles of the Way itself from Grotaig to Drumnadrochit present a bit of an anticlimax after what you have enjoyed up to here; Loch Ness is now lost to sight and you follow a road through a moorland landscape punctuated by houses, in due course entering an area of forest. You bear left on to a path through the woods, briefly enjoying an excellent view ahead, but then swing right, downhill, into the Coiltie valley and the straggling settlements of Lewiston and Drumnadrochit which carpet much of the valley floor. A pleasant but unexciting path takes you to the banks of the Coiltie and it's then straightforward valley walking to the A82, where you turn left and follow the A82 into Drumnadrochit. You could, however, detour right and follow beside the A82 for a mile to reach Urquhart Castle, built around 1250 and the scene of many battles between then and 1692 when it was partially destroyed; many of the present buildings date back to the sixteenth and seventeenth century, with the five-storey Grant Tower, dating from the sixteenth century, being arguably the best preserved part of the castle. The views from the castle to the loch are excellent, and although you may resent paying a fair sum to visit (and perhaps may prefer not to bother to visit) the castle, you can at least enjoy being properly back by the Great Glen again having forsaken it at Grotaig. You can then simply follow the A82 back and along to Drumnadrochit (55), now back on the Way; it's the last settlement on the Way before Inverness, 18 miles away, to offer amenities including food and accommodation, and there is plenty of both in the village with pubs, cafes, supermarkets and even a takeaway at the time of writing. The obvious attraction in the village is the Loch Ness Monster exhibition.

Drumnadrochit to Inverness (18 miles) via Achpopuli

ENJOY: Abriachan Forest, Beauly Firth, Inverness, Clachnaharry Lock

Heading out of Drumnadrochit on the final leg towards Inverness, the going is initially easy, as you simply proceed eastwards along the A82 beside Urquhart Bay, effectively an inlet of Loch Ness, and then along a path running parallel with and to the left of the road. However, the path leaves the roadside and in the vicinity of the hamlet of Tychat it climbs away from it to enter a substantial area of forest. Pause before going through the forest gate, and enjoy one final look back across Urquhart Bay to the castle and the loch – you won't get a better view of the loch again – then follow a forest track which climbs steeply through thick woodland. Signposting was sparse when I walked this section, and although the way is clear and unambiguous it is a relief to reach a sharp bend and see a Great Glen Way marker pointing hard right, uphill, and in fact hereafter the track widens significantly and continues to climb north-eastwards, providing excellent views. You pass a cairn, the only one on the Way to my knowledge, but it doesn't actually mark a summit; you keep trudging upwards, going through a gate and entering an area of moorland, passing a remote moorland farm. The Way is well marked at junctions and very clear to follow, as you keep on climbing, swinging northwards through a moorland landscape to enter the Abriachan forestry area, with its profusion of forest trails, then veering slightly west of north, you pass a plinth indicating 'footpath highest point' and shortly descend slightly to reach a T-junction with another track at the hamlet of Achpopuli.

Here you turn right, north-eastwards, on to a path which is every walker's dream, being dead straight, wide, firm and sloping gently downhill; you pass two or three wooden posts giving mileages to various locations, and it's good to know that you've covered over a third of the distance to Inverness with the hard graft now completed. You cross a narrow minor road and carry on straight ahead, along a fine airy path through the heather, feeling on top of the world in more ways than one. In the midst of this remote scenery I was somewhat surprised to find a board advertising the availability of coffee, the answer being provided by the proximity of a popular campsite just off the route. You continue to a T-junction with another road where the Way turns left, but you may wish to turn right to inspect the hut circles at Caiplich, just over a quarter of a mile away; these circles, dating back 2000 years, mark the site of a prehistoric settlement and field system, but with ten miles still to do you may think at this late stage of the walk that wear and tear on boots, socks and blisters, and drainage on supplies of energy and morale, would be expended on better things than a few humps on a heathery hillside.

Having hit the road at the T-junction and turned left you now enjoy a very easy section indeed as you follow the quiet road north-eastwards for the best part of four miles across the Abriachan plateau. It is a moorland landscape, passing three hamlets, Ladycairn, Altourie and Blackfold, with no amenities available at any of them. The views are excellent, with many hills visible in the distance including those of Glen Affric, but tarmac tramping is never the most exhilarating sort of walking and it is good to bear left at Blackfold on to a path that enters another area of thick woodland. The initial section of this path, in the shade of the woods, is most refreshing after the stark moorland of the past few miles, and the going remains good as the obvious path – I again found the signposting sparse but the way is so clear – proceeds steadily north-eastwards downhill, keeping a wall and the forest to the right, and splendid views of Beauly Firth to the left. A short way beyond a gate, it's good to have the reassurance of a Great Glen Way signpost pointing you right, and suddenly the trees relent to give you a superb grandstand view of Inverness, your final destination. You pass through another gate and along the right hand edge of a small reservoir, looking down across an open hillside to

Craig Dunain, a very fine looking old building indeed which looks as though it might be a rather desirable country residence – in fact it once housed the local mental hospital.

You now begin to lose height rapidly, as you head in an easterly direction for the city. You pass quite close to Craig Dunain but after skirting an industrial area you continue on through open country, going forward to a suburban residential area, and proceeding through an underpass where there's a reminder of the proximity of a big city in the form of some unsightly graffiti. Suddenly it all seems a bit of an anticlimax. But then things take a turn for the better: having passed a golf course, you bear right to join the bank of the Caledonian canal, and after the lack-lustre walking of the last mile or so you will really feel as though you're being reunited with an old friend; after a pleasant stroll along the canal bank, you meet another old (or should it be auld?) acquaintance, the A82. You cross the A82 by Tomnahurich bridge, enjoying fine views up and down the canal, then immediately bear right alongside Bught Road, passing a leisure centre and (at the time of writing) a coffee shop in the Floral Hall. You cross the road and swing to the right (north-east), going forward to the bank of the river Ness, shortly crossing the river by means of an attractive bridge, then having passed along a path between two channels of the river, you cross again to gain the right (east) bank of the river. Now you really are on the home straight, enjoying a lovely riverside walk; in due course, with the twin towers of the nineteenth-century Inverness Cathedral clearly visible across the bank, you bear right to climb to the castle, which dates back to the early eighteenth century, and the stone monument which marks the start and finish of the Way (73).

That is the end of the official route, and there are ample refreshment opportunities nearby for you to celebrate, but if you want to finish the job properly you need to cross the river by the next bridge, turn right into Kenneth Street and in due course left into Telford Street as far as the canal, then turn right to enjoy a lovely towpath walk to Clachnaharry Lock via the railway crossing. Continue as far as you can to the lonely lock-side house, and gaze out to the beautiful Beauly Firth with its magnificent mountain backcloth; this is the true end of the Caledonian Canal and surely a much better end to the Way, despite the long trudge back to Inverness city centre, its amenities and its ample transport links. It is a significant imposition, yes, after 18 miles hard walking from Drumnadrochit, but well worth it. And there'll still be plenty of fish and chips waiting for you in Inverness.

THE
BIG WALKS
OF THE SOUTH

Including: The South Downs Way, The Cotswold Way,
Offa's Dyke Path, The South West Coast Path,
The Pembrokeshire Coast Path

DAVID BATHURST

THE BIG WALKS OF THE SOUTH

David Bathurst

ISBN: 978-1-84953-024-8   Paperback   £8.99

From the South Downs Way to the Pembrokeshire Coast Path, there is no better way to discover the spectacular diversity of southern Britain's landscape than on foot. Whether you enjoy exploring green and gently rolling valleys or tackling rugged cliff-top paths, there are walks here to keep you rambling all year round.

An indefatigable walker, David Bathurst has unlaced his boots to produce this invaluable and definitive companion to the ten best-loved long-distance footpaths in the south of Britain, with each split into manageable sections. Combining practical, detailed descriptions with an appreciation of the beauty and history of the British countryside, this in an indispensable guide for both experienced and novice walkers alike.

- Recommends historic and geographic areas of interest on or near the paths, from ancient burial mounds to flora and fauna.

- Routes range in difficulty from the gentle 85-mile Ridgeway Path to the massive 628-mile South West Coast Path.

WALKING THE
SOUTH COAST
OF ENGLAND

A Complete Guide to Walking the South-facing Coasts of Cornwall,
Devon, Dorset, Hampshire (including the Isle of Wight),
Sussex and Kent, from Land's End to South Foreland

DAVID BATHURST

WALKING THE SOUTH COAST
OF ENGLAND

David Bathurst

ISBN: 978-1-84024-654-4   Paperback   £8.99

For this detailed guide to some of the best walking in Britain, David Bathurst has walked over 700 miles of coast, taking in breathtaking natural landscapes and significant landmarks on the way. With rugged cliffs and ancient cathedral cities, historic ports and wonderful wildlife, there's something for everyone; whether you're a seasoned hiker ready to take on the entire walk, or a summertime stroller who wants to experience these rewarding rambles in smaller doses.

Includes:

• A complete guide with detailed descriptions of the route

• Useful information about the geography and history

• Practical advice regarding navigation and local amenities

• Recommendations for top ten weekend walks

This invaluable guidebook is a must-have for anyone going walking on England's south coast.

Have you enjoyed this book?
If so, why not write a review on your favourite website?

Thanks very much for buying this Summersdale book.

www.summersdale.com